THE SCHOOL UNIFORM MOVEMENT AND WHAT IT TELLS US ABOUT AMERICAN EDUCATION

A Symbolic Crusade

David L. Brunsma

ScarecrowEducation
Lanham, Maryland • Toronto • Oxford
2004

Published in the United States of America
by ScarecrowEducation
An imprint of The Rowman & Littlefield Publishing Group, Inc.
4501 Forbes Boulevard, Suite 200, Lanham, Maryland 20706
www.scaroweducation.com

PO Box 317
Oxford
OX2 9RU, UK

British Library Cataloguing in Publication Information Available

Library of Congress Cataloging-in-Publication Data

Brunsma, David L.
  The school uniform movement and what it tells us about American
education : a symbolic crusade / David L. Brunsma.
    p. cm.
  Includes bibliographical references and index.
   ISBN 1-57886-125-X (pbk. : alk. paper)
  1. Students—United States—Uniforms. 2. Dress codes—United States.
I. Title.
LB3024 .B78 2004
371.51—dc22

                                                    2003027647

∞™ The paper used in this publication meets the minimum requirements of
American National Standard for Information Sciences—Permanence of
Paper for Printed Library Materials, ANSI/NISO Z39.48-1992.
Manufactured in the United States of America.

For my angel, my support, my companion, Rachel
and
my inspiration, my icon, my grandfather, Wilbur Nachtigall

CONTENTS

LIST OF TABLES

ACKNOWLEDGMENTS

To acknowledge the incredibly diverse array of individuals who have helped me along the way is not viable—there are far too many. However, many individuals do indeed deserve recognition for their support and aid in helping me understand the issues, challenging my methodologies and explanations of findings, helping me gather information, helping me to comprehend the "on-the-ground" issues facing those who make decisions about implementing uniform policies and those resisting them, as well as those who have been there to support and provide validation to my work. In no particular order, I would like to thank the following people for providing me with the preparations needed to undertake research of this magnitude: Maureen Hallinan, Kathryn Schiller, Aaron Pallas, Richard Williams, Lyn Spillman, Vladimir Khmelkov, and Ann Marie Power. I would also like to tip my hat to the brave editors who have provided important outlets for research on this highly controversial topic and for their conscientious reading of manuscripts: Jeanne Bebo, Cindy Tursman, Sharon DeJohn, Andrew Yoder, and a whole host of anonymous reviewers of previous work. Inspiration for my work in the sociology of education and the ideology of schooling comes from a variety of those both here and on the other side: James Coleman, Paolo Friere, Anthony Bryk, Gregory Stone, Pierre Bourdieu, and Annette

Lareau—these individuals' work has greatly inspired my own.[1] My best friend and closest colleague, Kerry Ann Rockquemore, has always been there for me in so many innumerable ways; I want to thank her here for her undying support and her critical mind. For helping to amass endless pieces of data, research articles, website information, and other editorial grunt work, I must thank Shawn Taylor, Annie Harris, Lori Rounsvall, and Natasha Henderson for everything they have done to help me along the way. The staff of the Pennsylvania Department of Education, the Connecticut Department of Education, and the United States Department of Education's National Center for Education Statistics have been an indispensable asset in my work and the work of many other scholars of American schools—thank you. I would also like to express gratitude to Carmine and his family for their sacrifices, their insights, their support, and their unwavering dedication to exposing the issues contained within this movement. Along these lines, I must acknowledge the vast array of educators, parents, community members, and students with whom I have had long and involved conversations concerning the ins and outs of this issue of school uniforms; these include, but are certainly not limited to, a variety of ACLU lawyers, Todd DeMitchell, Margaret Davis, Stephen Ritz, Anthony Orton, Judy Hammond, and Jennifer Orton. Finally, the most important person I must thank is my wife, Rachel, who has provided everything I have needed to complete this project with sanity intact. I absolutely love and fully admire you and look forward to many more years of walking together.

NOTE

1. Concerning Coleman's work, see particularly his *High School Achievement* (1982, with Hoffer and Kilgore), *Foundations of Social Theory* (1990b), and *The Adolescent Society* (1961), as well as a collection of his influential essays (Coleman 1990a). Pierre Bourdieu's work is absolutely some of the best sociology available; he has passed away, but see *Distinction: A Social Critique of the Judgment of Taste* (1986) and *Outline of a Theory of Practice* (1977). Paulo Friere's work can be seen best in his classic *Pedagogy of the Oppressed* (2000 [1980]). For Annette Lareau's work see *Home Advantage* (2000).

INTRODUCTION

No good research goes unpunished.

—Peter Rossi (1969)

THE JOURNEY

It was 1996. It was windy, cloudy, and very cold in South Bend, Indiana. It was, if I recall, rather bleak outside, rather dark—the day I embarked on this project. It was late February. At the University of Notre Dame, inside O'Shaughnessy Hall, my friend and colleague Kerry and I were sipping mochas and lattes and preparing for our comprehensive examinations in the sociology of education. In between discussing theories and interpreting results from some of the most important educational researchers of the twentieth century, we would pause and peruse the headlines in the *New York Times* and the *South Bend Tribune*. Given the context of our meeting, one of these headlines stuck out and sparked further discussion. It read:

Clinton Will Advise Schools on Uniforms (Mitchell 1996)

Reading further, out loud and silently, we looked at each other. Having just polished off James S. Coleman and colleagues' extensive work on the differences between public and private schooling (Coleman, Hoffer, and Kilgore 1982) as well as Anthony Bryk and his colleagues' look at Catholic school structure and outcomes (Bryk, Lee, and Holland 1993), we began talking about the suggestion, highlighted by President Bill Clinton in his State of the Union Address, that public schools might look into the possibility that school uniforms could help to manage and possibly control the issues surrounding gangs, gang colors, and gang violence.

Our curiosity as sociologists of education had steeped. We were somewhat confused and also amused. Confused because all of the reading we had completed, all the conferences, all the sessions, all the discussions, all the lectures on public/Catholic/private school differences never *once* mentioned school uniforms as a basis or a fundamental distinction that allowed Catholic and/or private schools, throughout the 1980s, to surpass public schools academically and behaviorally (Coleman, Hoffer, and Kilgore 1982). There were solid structural and related cultural reasons why Catholic students, for instance, out-performed public school students (Bryk, Lee, and Holland 1993; Coleman, Hoffer, and Kilgore 1982)—but never was there any discourse about the issue of student dress.[1] Of course, in our minds, as in the minds of many American citizens and politicians, Catholic and private schooling was practically synonymous with the school uniform. Thus our confusion. Our sociological minds began to wander, to attempt to link school uniforms to the outcomes we had just been discussing over coffee and bagels. This produced more questions than answers.

We were actually flabbergasted at the overt simplicity and borderline commonsensical notion that school uniforms could reduce gang violence or produce some sense of unity. Of course! It made perfect sense. No wait . . . it makes no sense at all. Not at all. Sure. Sure it does. By creating uniformity in dress among a student body in a poor, urban, inner-city school, for instance, one would be able to tell the outsiders (e.g., gang members, individuals selling drugs on campus, vandals, etc.) from the insiders (the students).[2] We laughed at our common sense, but we also knew that Clinton was up for reelection in 1996, and it is just such commonsense notions, such superficial glossing over of complex social, demographic, cultural, material, and political issues, that can, at times, secure votes. Well, our amusement was at the beatific simplicity of the idea, the overt sidestepping of more important educational issues, and the fact that it had tapped into our own everyday *common* sense, our American *collective* myths, and, for us, sitting there in O'Shaughnessy Hall, our own scholarly desire to understand complicated issues—for education and the processes of schooling were extremely complicated and complex. Being "separated at birth," Kerry and I looked at each other, and we knew we had to investigate this nascent "reform effort." Little did we know where it would take us, or how much a fearful, deferent, and irrational nation would follow Clinton's anecdotal advice. The school shooting in Moses Lake, Washington, on February 2, 1996, had not yet taken place.

It would be a learning experience. A classic sociological clash between common sense and social scientific reasoning. An age-old battle between anecdote and evidence, between fear and reason, between business-as-usual and social change. If school uniforms were a cake—what were the layers? What were the multiple layers of meaning? But, alas, I am getting ahead of myself. Basic questions plagued our minds. How many public schools actually have uniforms? What do the advocates argue that such a policy might solve or alleviate? On what bases do these advocates root their claims? Has anyone empirically tested the relationship between school uniforms and violence? Achievement? Attendance? Gang colors? Unity and pride? We took our confusion and amusement and decided to investigate the literature and the possibilities of testing the advocates' claims using a rigorous data set.

I knew of a data set, collected by the United States Department of Education's National Center for Educational Statistics (NCES), that started with a nationally representative sample of eighth graders from all school sectors in 1988 and followed them every two years, through tenth grade, then twelfth grade, into the labor force or college, and so on. The highly regarded data set was called the National Educational Longitudinal Study of 1988 (NELS:88) and had its roots in the work of Coleman and his colleagues (see Coleman 1990a; Coleman, Hoffer, and Kilgore 1982) throughout the 1970s and 1980s. I had recently received training from NCES on the appropriate usage of NELS:88 and was comfortable with its structure and design. We would be able, if the appropriate variables were available, to test these claims by comparing students who wore uniforms with students who did not in a variety of sectors, from a variety of socioeconomic levels, minority statuses, parental backgrounds, schooling experiences, attitudes, and behaviors on an equally varied set of educational, behavioral, and social-psychological outcomes. After investigating the most recent available NELS:88 data at the time (the Second Follow-Up, when the students were in tenth grade), we were pleased to find the variable that coded schools that had uniform policies and those that did not. We decided to pursue the project further. Having the data, we looked at the extant literature to see what we would find.

What we found was a *mess*. Perhaps it is more appropriate to say that what we found was a completely chaotic chain of anecdotal meanderings on the effectiveness of school uniform policies in public schools. We found no solid empirical research of the qualitative or quantitative sort to hold onto. Our literature review was drawn largely from periodicals, newspapers, and online sources (as there were, at the time, no publications in refereed journals), and the claims they made concerning uniform policies and their possible effectiveness was sketchy at best. Lacking a proper and useful body of literature, we decided to use the advocates' claims *as the hypotheses* and simply test these. We sought to look for patterns in a nationally representative sample of tenth graders that would begin to guide our own thinking as well as the research and thought of the larger scholarly and journalistic community concerning this new movement toward uniforms. Interested readers can look into our original piece published in the *Journal of Educational Research* (Brunsma and Rockquemore 1998), for I do not desire to restate the entire article here, though I will summarize and refer to it often throughout this book; it was indeed one of the first attempts to rigorously and systematically investigate the patterns of effects in comparing uniformed students and nonuniformed students in high schools.[3]

To state the results of that study in a nutshell, we found that uniform policies did not distinguish between students who had attendance problems, behavioral problems, or substance use problems and those who did not. Furthermore, uniforms failed, in our empirical analyses, to increase academic preparedness, pro-school attitudes, or a peer structure that supported academics. Finally, to our surprise, we found a small, weak, yet statistically significant negative effect of uniform policies on academic achievement. In the end, this was what is typically referred to as a piece of "nonfindings" in scientific discourse; yet in this case the overwhelming pattern of *non*effectiveness of school uniforms (one way or the other) was of general interest to educators, scholars, and policymakers alike.[4] Eventually, after many rounds of reviews and helpful comments from those in the fields of education, sociology, and psychology, the piece appeared in *The Journal of Educational Research* in early 1998. It entered the discourse as a serious antidote to the plethora of anecdotal writings that were available.

Since its publication, that article has received a great deal of attention and has spawned other empirical research (e.g., Educational Testing Service 2000) much of which has remained, as of this writing, in the form of unpublished dissertations.[5] Despite the findings of that article and a handful of other work (Educational Testing Service 2000; Volokh and Snell 1998), school boards and administrators across the United States have continued to implement mandatory uniform policies at all levels of schooling, though the actual label of the policy has varied widely (e.g., "school uniform," "dress code," "standardized dress," etc.)—primarily to disrupt potential litigation and other problematic relations between schools and their various constituents. Despite our earlier call for even more empirical research, very little has been forthcoming, yet uniform policies continue to be adopted with *no evidence of their effectiveness* and no imminent plans to conduct the much-needed research at local, district, state, and national levels.

My first academic position was as an assistant professor of sociology at the University of Alabama in Huntsville in the fall of 1998. Quickly the drama began to unfold, as what was rapidly becoming a school uniform *movement* and its correlate anti-uniform movements[6] were well under way. Much to my surprise, early in my career as a sociologist interested in education and culture, I was becoming deeply involved in this project—a project that began over coffee two years earlier. Between 1998 and the present, I have given *countless* newspaper interviews from all corners of the United States as well as Canada, Britain, and Israel. This early exposure to the media and the manner in which they "represent" the issues in general, and the ways in which they consistently *misrepresent* lengthy phone conversations and interviews in small, rhetorical, decontextualized sound bites, was (and remains to be) exceedingly frustrating. Sure, our research and results were in demand, people were interested, but for what purposes, and to what ends? The uses and mis-uses of interview quotations, the misinterpretations of journalists' read-ing of my own work, and the interpretations of that body of work by oth-ers (primarily via the Internet) almost caused me to deny and redirect interview requests because what I had read to that point regarding the journalists' utilization of interview material and research findings of a complex issue like school uniforms, and the ways in which they simpli-fied and/or reified results and concepts, was incongruent with my sensi-bilities and ethics as a social scientist.

My experiences with the media were not limited to the printed press. I have sat on radio talk shows as a member of a panel representing the "expert" and been a "talking head" on CNN and a variety of other broad-cast news networks across the country. I must say that the CNN experi-ence was the most intelligent and responsible treatment of the subject; however, even then the key (and untested) elements of the wider dis-course on school uniform policies (which I shall summarize and discuss at length later in the book) were prominent there too (CNN 2001). In the end, regardless of my newfound ability to place my findings and re-sults in media sound bites so as to preempt any attempts to decontextu-alize them, regardless of raising my voice (via concerns over accuracy of representing the research) to those who interviewed me concerning the work, despite many attempts to correct the unacceptabilities inherent in the world of media "representation"—anecdote ruled the day.

Anecdote continued to rule the day in court as well. I have memories of several depositions, discussions with lawyers, reading endless reams of pages of testimony, cross-examinations, complaints, briefs, summary judgments, etc. In the end, it has become frustrating and equally inter-esting to me to view the role of "evidence" in U.S. courts. One memory that clearly exemplifies this process was taking the stand and presenting my research on the Waterbury, Connecticut, school system in *Byars v. City of Waterbury.* After finishing a PowerPoint presentation of my re-search on the Waterbury uniform policy and its effectiveness, where I found no evidence of positive influence of the policy in those middle schools, the next witness was a past superintendent of the Waterbury school district, Dr. Roger Damerow. The lawyer promptly asked Mr. Damerow what he felt about the uniform policy's effectiveness in Waterbury Middle Schools, to which he said something to the effect of, "I have seen benefits. I think it is a good policy." To which the lawyer replied, "No further questions." I am exaggerating here, but I do so to make a general point. We do not appear to trust science (Chesler et al. 1988). The role of hard evidence in court is, in my experience, typically disregarded, while common parlance, common notions, ideological positioning, and pure anecdote ("N of 1 thinking") wins out. This state of affairs has frustrated me, not because I am fighting on one side; no, on the contrary, my research has been quite middle-of-the-road in its findings regarding uniform policies and their effectiveness in our schools.

In the spring of 2001, I was asked to complete several studies representing cutting-edge research to inform the national school uniform debate in general and to provide a series of critical analyses and context for a specific case in the Mount Carmel (Pennsylvania) Area School District (MCASD). In a series of reports, I utilized every available option for empirical investigation at my disposal. I was able, through court orders and procedures of discovery in preparation for the trial(s), to demand data from MCASD concerning Mount Carmel Elementary (MCE) School's organizational structure, characteristics of their student body, demographic statistics from the surrounding community, test scores, attendance rates, etc. The data I received were quite appalling, full of holes, incomplete, and, in some cases, nonexistent when compared to the list of requests I had given MCASD. Nevertheless, I had a set of data to utilize, data that would allow me to understand the impetuses behind MCASD's desire to implement a school uniform policy in the fall of 2000.

It was necessary to supplement these data with additional information garnered from the Pennsylvania Department of Education (PDE) through various means of electronic communication: phone, fax, the Internet, and e-mail. The staff at PDE was extremely knowledgeable and helpful—I am indebted to them for their assistance. Indebted, because the PDE data allowed me to compare MCE with other comparable schools in the state of Pennsylvania. These proved to be crucial data for several reasons. First, the data allowed me more methodological movement and widened the scope of possible analyses I could perform—given that I had only *one* school. Second, the PDE data introduced me to a phenomenon heretofore unknown to me as an educational researcher accustomed to working with large, nationally representative data sets collected by the Department of Education's National Center for Education Statistics, which has decades of experience with collecting extremely useful and comprehensive sets of educational data on U.S. schools. The phenomenon I am referring to is the extremely regrettable and odious fact that, in certain educational contexts across this country, *school-provided data and state-collected data (usually reported to the state by the school/district itself) often do not match.* This realization led me to be wary of the MCASD data and to primarily utilize the PDE data because the variation across Pennsylvania schools should work itself out in the analyses. Yet all the while, knowing fully well that it was highly likely that, for whatever reason, the data reported by MCASD (and MCE) to PDE would be skewed—most likely in their favor—and given the context of a recent uniform policy implementation, I was even more wary, since those involved in the administration of the school and the district were standing by their policy no matter what.

What I found was that education and internal processes at MCE were comparable, and in many cases well above the average, to analogous schools according to the categories designed by the Pennsylvania Department of Education (PDE) well *before* the implementation of the school uniform policy. Despite the fact that there existed at that time, and still exists, no empirical research linking uniform policies to positive student- and school-level changes, there appeared to be no substantiated rationale for MCASD's decision to implement a school uniform policy, aside from administrative assertion of control and power.

These reports also delved much more deeply and widely into the available data sets from NCES and elsewhere that allowed researchers to analyze the empirical antecedents of policy formation as well as the patterns of effectiveness (or ineffectiveness) of uniform policies and dress codes. I also expanded the questions asked of the data during the writing of these reports for MCASD and wrote a critical review of the extant empirical literature on school uniform policies (Brunsma 2002). Much of the work I completed for the MCASD reports provided the grounding and foundation for this book.

My training is as a sociologist. My passion is to understand things human. I seek to understand, through empirical evidence, the world in which we live. Particularly, one realm of social life I have found extremely intriguing is the institution of education and the processes and role of schooling in American society. For readers who might be unfamiliar with sociology and the sociological method, some explanation is in order to prevent confusion regarding the findings in this book. Sociologists are primarily interested in two issues: variation/diversity and patterns/relationships. Given the immense degree of diversity in our public schools (e.g., racial, linguistic, ethnic, class, religious, ability, socioeconomic status, etc.) and the monolithic assumption of social mobility and education serving as the "great equalizer" of this heterogeneity, sociologists who study education are interested in understanding the patterns of achievement, learning, and opportunities (to name a few) that exist within this diverse group of K–12 students. We do so to investigate the classic social stratification (inequality) question: Who gets What and Why? Furthermore, the patterns that we do identity through a variety of methodological approaches (though sociology of education is highly quantitative in orientation—for obvious reasons) are just that: patterns. The effects of various social structures and educational policies, for instance, that we do uncover are *on average* effects—the strength a statistical significance of which is often, but not always, indicative of their substantive significance in schooling processes and the power of their effectiveness in maintaining or lessening inequalities in the educational process.

In particular, my training is as a sociologist of education. Sociology of education approaches the study of education from several vantage points. First is institutionally, investigating the set of ideas that comprise the way a given society "does education." An institutional focus looks at the meaning of education, role of education, and set of ideologies that provide the societal starting point from which sprout the varieties of political, economic, social, cultural, philosophical, and material conditionings upon which the daily processes of "doing education" occur and the implications that flow from these practices. Second, we are interested in understanding how these sets of ideas that constitute the institution of public education, for instance, become formalized into organizations devoted to the goals set out by the institution of education: organizations we call "schools." In this approach resides the classical sociological tradition of studying social structures, networks of relationships, hierarchies of interlaced roles and positions, and how these structures influence the lives and opportunities of those within them. In terms of schools, we study the influence of the educational structures on a variety of outcomes of interest: academic achievement; behavior; psychological well-being; aspirations; and gender, class, and racial identities. The list can be endless, and the list of the outcomes of interest is determined largely by the contemporary terrain of the institutional contours of education in America. Finally, we look at microlevel interactions between various actors in a context like a public school and how these influence both individuals and the very organizations and institutions within which they are embedded.

In addition to doctoral training in the sociology of education, I also focused my graduate training in the sociology of culture. Most people equate the term "culture" with the anthropological sense of "an entire way of life of a people"; however, cultural sociology concerns itself primarily with structures of meaning-making and how individuals utilize symbols and ideologies for a variety of purposes, including, but not limited to, political rhetoric, socioeconomic status, boundary formation between and within groups, and material mobility. Thus, my approach in this book also incorporates the study of uniforms and the concomitant policy formation, implementation, and rhetoric surrounding this symbol. In this book we will be involved in discussions of symbolic boundaries, meaning, images, institutions, and semiotics—in short, culture. These two foci of my doctoral training and my subsequent research agendas carve out a space in which I approach a reform effort, a movement, like school uniforms.

Despite much discussion and debate in this country about school uniforms and standardized dress codes, very little empirical research has been devoted to studying this movement. Surprisingly, no one has taken it upon himself as either scholar, journalist, educator, or concerned parent to put together what we now know and critically assess as this "reform" movement that has been literally sweeping the nation since the early 1990s. In deciding whether I needed to be the one to complete this arduous task, I realized that now was the time for a book such as this. My experience in conducting empirical research on the subject; numerous discussions with parents, educators, journalists, and academics regarding this important debate; and contributions to legal battles over school uniform policies have put me in a unique position to speak as a social scientist on these issues. I intend the book to raise awareness, to ask difficult questions, to map out the terrain of this movement, to articulate, as fully as possible, the current strands of the discourse for and against uniforms in public schools. I aim to provide readers with the most comprehensive set of analyses on the crucial questions and assumptions that flow throughout the current debate and to rely as little on anecdote as possible, to steer us away from hearsay and rumor regarding the protocol, promises, and pitfalls of adopting school uniform policies in American public schools. In the end, I hope this book will guide the discussion and discourse in more fruitful directions and fulfill the ever-present need to more fully understand the processes at work in our school systems and the future ramifications of the current debate.

AN OVERVIEW OF THE BOOK

The first chapter, "Dress Codes and School Uniforms: Past, Present, and Future," sets up the trajectory of the book in several ways. First, I explore the history of the idea of uniforming students and its link with particular social, material, religious, political, and cultural forces. Second, since there is no definitive work on the history of school uniforms, I begin that work here and attempt to explicate the history of uniform (and dress code) policies in the United States. As the history of such policies in the United States is traced, we will inevitably be involved in a discourse concerning the reigning "theories" and justifications of why such policies are needed in different contexts—theories of effectiveness. Here I discuss Catholic/private/religious schools versus public schools and their use of uniforms, theories about appearances and labeling, symbolic interactionist theories, and pure justifications based on assertions of administrative authority and control. Finally, from the Long Beach case, to Clinton's famous address concerning uniforms, to the Department of Education's *Manual on School Uniforms*, to the present, I trace how this type of school-level policy became a nationwide "reform effort."

Chapter 2, "A Review of the Literature: From Anecdotes to Research and Back Again" provides an updated literature review of the empirical work on the effectiveness of school uniform policies in the United

States. In this exposition, the state of empirical research on school uniform and dress code policies is described. It is not true that there has been *no* empirical research conducted to assess the effectiveness of school uniforms on student behavior and educational outcomes, but much of this research has not yet been published, and there is much to be done. The extant research is wide-ranging in terms of samples, methodologies, definitions of key concepts, theoretical grounding, and implications for those who wish to inform themselves in the midst of strong public debate. For some time now, there has been a need for a comprehensive and critical literature review concerning the growing interest in school uniform and other standardized dress code policies being considered to remedy what many see as a failing public education system.

Despite some efforts at summarization, there has yet to be a comprehensive, critical look at the state of empirical research designed to speak to the increasing numbers of concerned and intrigued. In this chapter I thoroughly review some 100 articles, ranging from the most superficial piece of anecdotal journalism to the most rigorous of quantitative empirical studies on the topic of school uniforms and/or dress code policies. The literature on school uniforms can be organized into four types: 1) legal (see chapter 3), 2) anecdotal, 3) empirical, and 4) theoretical. To critically review the literature, I first summarize the anecdotal literature, for it is the bedrock upon which the debate (and, unfortunately, much of the "research") stands, and it is important to understand its assertions for and cautions against uniform policies. Second, I critically review the empirical literature, its findings and suggestions, along with its strengths and limitations, validity and generalizability. The empirical research can be categorized as follows: perception studies, small-scale effectiveness studies, and large-scale effectiveness studies.

In the third chapter, "The Law and Student Clothing," Todd A. DeMitchell outlines the legal contours of the school uniform movement. DeMitchell tracks the historical precedents concerning free speech and litigation surrounding student grooming and appearance in the educational sphere. This chapter focuses primarily on the legal proceedings and results of litigation over school uniforms and dress codes in Arizona, Louisiana, Texas, and Connecticut. I wanted Dr. DeMitchell to write this chapter because of its importance to the debate at hand and his expertise on the law and school reform issues, as well as the fact that this part of the issue of school uniforms is solidly outside my realm of expertise and scholarly inquiry.

Chapter 4, "To Uniform or Not to Uniform? Empirical Antecedents to Policy Formation and Adoption," provides, for the first time, an empirical analysis of the correlates to uniform policy adoption. First, I delve into the reasons that administrators and educators give for pursuing school uniform policies for their educational jurisdictions. Second, for the first time, I give an empirical glimpse at three levels of schooling (elementary, middle, and high), at the empirical antecedents and correlates to schools that have adopted uniform policies and those that have not. There is a great deal of conjecture in the anecdotal literature about to the "type of school" or "type of community" that looks into and eventually adopts a uniform policy; however, no empirical evidence exists to verify these claims. This important analysis and discussion will provide unique insight into the growing phenomenon of school uniform policies. The various factors implicated in this analysis are demographic variation, socioeconomic variation, the political climate, the types of schools, student body characteristics, etc. Third, this chapter looks closely at the different methods of implementation adhered to by the various adoptees as well as the legal, educational, communal, and student-level pitfalls and promises experienced throughout the implementation. Finally, recently several districts and individual schools have repealed their uniform policies. This chapter also looks into the reasons behind the downfall of these policies and their social, political, and cultural correlates.

The fifth chapter, "The Effects of School Uniforms and Dress Codes on Educational Processes and Outcomes," starts where the original Brunsma and Rockquemore (1998) report ended, taking a much closer and more detailed look at the quantitative relationship between school uniform policies and academic achievement. It is desirable to go back to that analysis and conduct additional tests using specific achievement outcomes (e.g., mathematics, reading, science, history, etc.) and to test these at both the individual student level and the school level. These analyses will allow us to more fully conclude whether, even after controlling for other variables known to be associated with academic achievement, uniform policies undermine the academic achievement of students (i.e., students who must wear uniforms achieve at statistically

significant lower levels than those who do not wear uniforms). Furthermore, new data from the National Center for Education Statistics
(ECLS-K) allows us to look at the relationship between school uniform
policies and academic achievement (as well as other measures of
achievement and educational aptitude) for elementary school students.
Also, one of the enduring problems plaguing research on school uniforms is the lack of longitudinal data—data that would measure the outcomes of interest *before* the implementation of the policy as well as several points in time *after* uniforms are in place. The problem is
exacerbated when the outcomes of interest (e.g., self-esteem, school climate, student behavior, student substance use, etc.) are typically *not*
measured *at all* (reliably) by schools, districts, or, by extension, state departments of education. A methodological proxy that partially solves
these competing dilemmas is presented in this chapter. This analysis allows us to look for the effects of switching from a nonuniformed school
to a uniformed school in comparison to all other types of moves, to see
if the outcomes of interest vary as a result of such a change. Such analyses have also not been presented or conducted in the previous literature.

Chapter 6, "The Effects of School Uniforms and Dress Codes on Behavioral and Social Psychological Processes and Outcomes," empirically
tests the prominent assumptions of school uniform advocates that such
policies increase student self-esteem levels and other social-psychological
measures. In the literature, through some unnamed mechanism, school
uniforms are assumed to make students feel better about themselves,
make them more internally motivated to succeed in school, and, in general,
affect their psychological makeup positively—all this leading, supposedly,
to success in school. In addition to these individual social-psychological
characteristics, the anecdotal literature also presupposes that school uniform policies will create a sense of school pride and school unity, and, in
general, have an overall positive impact on school climate, both the safety
climate of the school and its educational climate. Given these conjectures,
this chapter conducts empirical analyses at both the student and the school
level, using data from elementary, middle, and high school students and
their respective schools. The results are the first to begin to rigorously examine the assumptions so often cited in the literature.

In the final chapter, "A Symbolic Crusade: The School Uniform
Movement and What It Tells Us about American Education," the main

thesis of the book is explored. The results from previous work and the new analyses published in this book are interpreted in a more critical light, with attention paid to the discourse and rhetoric surrounding school uniforms in the United States, to attempt to assess where we are in our understanding of the antecedents, processes, and effectiveness of school uniform and dress code policies in the United States. The main goal of this chapter is to address the very important question, What is the school uniform issue really about? Given what we now know, as well as what we have yet to learn, what does the uniform debate really tell us about American education, about school reform, about the role of courts in school reform, about the role of research in policy formation and implementation, about parental and child rights, about the purposes of education and schooling in the new millennium? These and other questions are addressed critically, with the ultimate goal to get people discussing more than a select few issues in this debate. Second, I consider the school uniform phenomenon as a social movement and what that means for its future and its results. Are school uniforms a serious reform or a Band-Aid approach to a complex structure of schooling in America?

THE DATA AND METHODOLOGY

This section briefly outlines the data, methodologies, and procedures used in the analyses reported in the pages that follow. They are outlined here in basic form, and readers will be aided throughout the analyses and interpretations of how statistics and models like the ones utilized in this series of reports are to be approached and understood according to conventions. Because of the sheer number of analyses run for this project, the methodologies that were applied to each one of these are described in this section.

To empirically investigate questions regarding the effectiveness of school uniform policies and to overcome the extant problems and concerns with the existing empirical literature on this subject requires large, longitudinal, nationally representative data sets; multivariate modeling techniques (e.g., regression); and a wide variety of indicators and measures of the important processes. The first requirement overcomes the problems of non-generalizability of the more local and parochial studies that have been published. This is crucial for the utility of the results for any number of schools with any number of characteristics and challenges facing them. The second requirement, multivariate modeling techniques, is necessary to overcome the methodological flaw of previous research: the lack of control variables. Though schools vary in the types of dress policies they employ, they vary on many more critical dimensions than dress policies alone.[7] Therefore, the assumptions of previous literature—if you find a correlation or a relationship between uniforms and an outcome, then there must be a significant impact of the policy—can be directly addressed within the analyses themselves. Thus, more than adequate control variables are employed in these analyses. Finally, the third requirement is fulfilled by the nature of the data sets themselves. NCES data sets are widely known for their comprehensiveness. This comprehensiveness exists because NCES has been collecting data of these sorts for more than three decades, all in tight collaboration with top researchers and scientists engaged in the educational literature and policy.

Data

Two primary sources of data were used in the following analyses. For the analyses of middle school and high school effects of uniform and dress code policies on academic and social-psychological outcomes, the public release version of the NELS:88 was acquired. This data set began with a nationally representative sample of eighth graders and their schools and followed them into tenth grade in 1990, twelfth grade in 1992, and the labor force and secondary education in later years. We are primarily concerned with the eighth-grade sample of students and schools, the tenth-grade sample of students and their schools, as well as the longitudinal panel of students for whom data are available for both waves. Data are available from parents, teachers, students, and principals—all linked together in a fantastic set. For the analyses here, I utilize the student and school (principal) files for most of the analyses. Though these data provide(d) one of the first useful data sets to investigate the effectiveness of uniform policies in American schools, because of their age (i.e., 1988 and 1990, several years before the steady increase in uniform policies implemented in public schools), they are useful only in assessing empirical patterns in the effectiveness of *uniform policies across all school sectors*. Thus, readers should understand that the analyses using the NELS:88 base year and first follow-up data are *not* used to look at the impact of uniform policies in *public* middle and high schools, but rather provide a look into the effectiveness of uniform policies before the movement in all American middle and high schools, controlling for school sector. This is emphasized throughout the discussion of results from these data sets.

The most important data I utilize to assess the impact of school uniform policies in *public* schools are from the Early Childhood Longitudinal Study (ECLS). Not only are these data more recent (1998–2000) and thus more in line with the chronology of the uniform movement (i.e., there were enough public schools adopting these policies by the late 1990s), but they also reflect a more appropriate schooling level to analyze the impact of such policies of standardized dress—elementary school. NCES's public release version of the ECLS was used to assess the impact of uniforms on elementary students (kindergartners) and these same students as they complete their first grade as well. This is an exceptional new data set. Both waves of ECLS data contain data from students, parents, teachers, and principals on a *wide* variety of educational, social, cultural, and psychological phenomena at the elementary school level. For the analyses in this book, I rely primarily on the student and principal data that are uniquely linked together to provide individual-level and school-level (contextual) analyses. In addition, with the ECLS data, we now have K–1 longitudinal data that make possible rigorous testing of uniform policy effectiveness at an educational moment of early intervention. The data were downloaded using SPSS v11.0 for Windows from the NCES-provided CD-ROMs. For the NELS:88 data, I desired to have a sample of all students with completed survey instruments, those who were in-school for the year, and those for whom all standardized achievement scores were available. After this process, I had two data sets, an eighth-grade data set with 23,392 students coming from 1,017 schools, and a tenth-grade data set with 25,474 students coming from 1,289 high schools. Third and fourth data sets were constructed in which I aggregated all of the student-level data to the school level. Thus, I have an eighth-grade school-level data set and one for tenth grade as well, with the same number of cases as stated above (1,017 and 1,289 respectively). A final NELS:88 data set was constructed for these analyses—the paneled eighth- to tenth-grade data. After linking the two data sets through what NCES calls "flags," one ends up with a student-level data set containing students whom NCES followed from eighth through tenth grades, who have complete data, and who have achievement data. This paneled data set contains 14,852 students.

The process for obtaining workable data files from ECLS was similar to that for NELS:88. Retaining all kindergartners and first graders who had complete files, with all of the assessment data, provided a data set (the largest to date) of 12,340 kindergartners/first graders—representative of the entire kindergarten population of the United States in 1998 and the cohort of first graders in 1999. These children attended some 820 schools.

Measures

There were so many variables utilized for these analyses that it would be impossible and extremely impractical to describe each one in detail in this methodology section. Instead, appendix A gives the variable, the data set it is from, and a description of its metric and coding scheme (i.e., do high values indicate positive educational climate or negative?), as well as some descriptive statistics: means, standard deviations, and ranges—the building blocks for the analyses to come. I have tried whenever possible to give the scales I have created easily understandable names and to use these throughout the reports. I also attempt to clearly discuss the results of each table as thoroughly as needed to engage the reader so as to create an understanding of my approach to modeling as well as my coding methodology. Appendix A contains all of the pertinent information needed to reproduce the analyses in this book. This appendix is also useful for readers who wish to witness the sheer variation in schooling processes at all levels. It is this variation in outcomes and processes that we wish to take into account when analyzing the effects of uniforms on a wide variety of outcomes.

Statistical Procedures

To replicate the complexity of schooling processes and the effects of policies on student achievement and behavior, I use multiple regression techniques (Ordinary Least Squares method). This technique allows for the simultaneous evaluation of multiple variables' effects on a single outcome. It is a predictive modeling procedure that seeks to explain the variation in an outcome (e.g., student achievement) from a variety of sources (e.g., socioeconomic status of the student's family, gender, peer group influences, and policies such as school uniforms). To overcome the problem of correlation not implying causation, regression techniques process the unique influence of particular variables, taking out the influence of other variables that are also correlated with the variables of interest. In other words, if the variable for whether or not a school has a uniform policy has a positive impact on school climate in a bivariate sense (i.e., the correlation between uniforms and school climate), it is entirely possible (as was evident in the Long Beach studies; see chapter 2) that schools that have uniforms covary significantly with other factors that *also* have an impact on school climate; thus, regression takes into account the explanations of school climate coming from those other variables to provide more "pure" evidence of the effects of school uniforms. I thoroughly explain the methods and procedures as I go through each analysis in detail.

During the data collection of NELS:88 (as well as ECLS-K) certain students and schools representing key subpopulations were given higher selection probabilities—that is, NCES (for both of these data sets) over-sampled key social groupings of students due to these populations' uniqueness in order to have more data than usually obtained on these special populations. Because of the oversampling of certain groups of students, weighting procedures are necessary to take into account differential sampling probabilities. Weighting survey data compensates for these unequal probabilities of selection and also adjusts for the effects of nonresponse. However, since the designs of both NELS:88 and ECLS-K involve stratified sampling techniques, oversampling of certain subgroups, *and* clustered probability sampling of the student members, statistical variability is much higher than expected from a simple random sample of similar size. A new weighting variable must be constructed using design effects provided by NCES that take into account these departures from expectation due to sampling strategies. The accepted practice in using weights in NELS:88 is to create a new weight by using the following equation:

$$weight = (NCES\ weight/mean\ of\ NCES\ weight)(1/design\ effect)$$

Using this new weight, calculated statistics will reflect the reduction in sample size (these reduced or *effective sample sizes for statistical calculations* are called "effective N" in the tables throughout this report) in the calculation of standard errors and degrees of freedom.[8] Such techniques only approximately capture the effect of the sample design on sample statistics. However, this procedure is a much better approach than conducting an analysis that assumes the data were collected from a simple random sample. For more detailed information about NELS:88 weights, design effects, sampling probabilities, and their relationship to using national longitudinal data sets, see the pertinent NCES publications.

Case Studies

At various points throughout the book, I supplement the results of the empirical, quantitative analyses with more in-depth discussions of individual case studies of schools and districts that I have investigated more closely in their journey through uniform policy implementation. The cases I refer to primarily are the Mount Carmel, Pennsylvania, and the Waterbury, Connecticut, cases. These instances help to illustrate what the larger analyses mask—the processes occurring during the formation, implementation, and daily experiences with uniform policies at the school buildings. I am a big fan of mixed methodologies and see them as paramount in our search for understanding complicated social issues such as school reform and specific policies.

This book, *The School Uniform Movement and What It Tells Us about American Education*, represents the most thorough exposition on our present understanding of the impetuses, debates, legalities, and effectiveness of school uniform policies that have rapidly entered the discourse about school reform in the United States. The book provides an antidote to the ungrounded, anecdotal components that define the contemporary conversation regarding policies of standardized dress in American K–12 districts and schools. Drawing upon my years of experience and research directed at objectively and empirically understanding the issue of school uniform policies, this book provides, for the first time, a comprehensive collection of history, critical evaluation of the extant literature, reviews of several case studies, and results of nationally representative empirical research. All of this is of the utmost importance for those who wish to be informed and insightful participants in the contemporary debate on school uniform policies. Educators, parents, concerned community members, and others have approached me and asked when such a compilation of present understandings of the crucial empirical, sociological, cultural, political, and legal dimensions of the school uniform debate would be available—the time has come for such a book. This book will appeal to a wide and diverse audience of educators, administrators, parents, policymakers, and all who are involved and interested in the issue of school uniforms as a reform effort. It will also appeal to scholars and laypersons alike who are interested in the politics and critical realities behind the school uniform movement underway in the United States. In the end, the school uniform movement reveals a great deal about the politics, social realities, and highly contested terrain of educational reform and the process of schooling in the United States.

1

DRESS CODES AND
SCHOOL UNIFORMS:
PAST, PRESENT, AND FUTURE

A hippie is someone who walks like Tarzan, looks like Jane, and smells like Cheetah.

—Ronald Reagan

Come on man, I doubt if you'd recognize a hippie. I'm a capitalist, baby. I work for my living, not suck off somebody else.

—Kelly MacNamara (from the movie *Valley of the Dolls*)

It was January 23, 1996. It went something like this:

Our second challenge is to provide Americans with the educational opportunities we will all need for this new century. In our schools, every classroom in America must be connected to the information superhighway, with computers and good software, and well-trained teachers. . . . Every diploma ought to mean something. I challenge every community, every school and every state to adopt national standards of excellence; to measure whether schools are meeting those standards; to cut bureaucratic red tape so that schools and teachers have more flexibility for grass-roots reform; and to hold them accountable for results. That's what our Goals 2000 initiative is all about. I challenge every state to give all parents the right to choose which public school their children will attend; and to let

1

teachers form new schools with a charter they can keep only if they do a good job. *I challenge all our schools to teach character education, to teach good values and good citizenship. And if it means that teenagers will stop killing each other over designer jackets, then our public schools should be able to require their students to wear school uniforms.* (State of the Union 1996 emphasis added)

Thus, the "official" start of a movement toward uniforming students in American public schools.

This chapter sets up the trajectory of the book in several ways. First I explore the history of the idea of uniforming students and its link with particular social, material, religious, political, and cultural forces. While the idea of mandating a uniform policy for public school students in a country like the United States is novel, the idea of uniforming students in a variety of educational settings is not new. Understanding the historical, cultural, religious, and class-based roots of the educational uniform in other times and places provides an important foundation for understanding its current rationales and motivations as a reform movement in American public education. Much of this discussion will require us to look at the history of uniforms in England. Second, the current movement toward school uniforms in public schools is, in several ways, ironic and somewhat puzzling, given the student movements that occurred in this country in the 1960s and 1970s. Thus, I also look into the discussions of student dress during these key moments of our history and how it is that we have, to some extent, reinstated restrictions on student clothing. As the history of such policies in the United States is traced, we will inevitably be involved in a discourse concerning the reigning "theories" and justifications of why such policies are needed in different contexts—theories of effectiveness. Here I discuss Catholic/private/religious schools versus public schools and their use of uniforms, theories about appearances and labeling, symbolic interactionist theories, and pure justifications based on assertions of administrative authority and control. Finally, from the Long Beach case, to Clinton's famous address concerning uniforms, to the Department of Education's *Manual on School Uniforms*, to the present, I trace how this type of school-level policy became a nationwide "reform effort."

A BRIEF HISTORY OF SCHOOL UNIFORMS AND DRESS CODES[1]

To my knowledge, there exists no definitive history of the school uniform. However, it is clear that the practice has existed in varied forms, for various reasons, in an equal myriad of contexts, for an impressive length of time. The school uniform has always been a conservative policy, rooted in conservative ideologies, yet the school uniform has morphed and altered its existence based on the ebb and flow of societal and cultural changes (Davidson and Rae 1990). Given this lack of *direct* scholarly attention to the history of school clothing, I will provide an overview of some key points and issues that speak to the current situation in the United States.[2] Readers may be disappointed in the pre-nineteenth—century history that follows, yet in order not to reconstruct, in an unruly way, a history from only glimpses of its sketches, I will stick with the sketches themselves to provide a base. We know much more about the use of school uniforms starting in the nineteenth century; before that time there is relatively little to go on.

We do know that Hellenic school children wore *no* uniforms (Davidson and Rae 1990). School uniforms, as we see in contemporary public schools, have their roots in the confluence of secular and religious influences that contextualized the earliest universities in Germany, France, and England. The *cappa clausa* represents perhaps the earliest recorded, institutionalized use of standardized academic dress, originating in 1222, when Stephen Langton, then Archbishop of Canterbury, ordered the wearing of *cappa clausa*, which, from our vantage point almost 800 years later, looks akin to the stereotypical monastic form of dress—sleeveless, roomy, and covering the feet (Hargreaves-Mawdsley 1963).

ENGLAND: CLASS, SCHOOLING, AND SCHOOL UNIFORMS

No attempt at mapping out the historical terrain of the school uniform would be complete (or even worth reading) without a discussion of the institution of school uniforms in England. The tree of our collective memory in the United States regarding school clothing has its roots planted deeply in British soil. Though the systems of education are fundamentally different in structure (Turner 1960), the common symbol of the uniformed school lad or lass is firmly etched in our minds as one of the English school system, structured as it is by much more rigidly defined ideologies about class and position. The school uniform in England has a long tradition in both the university and the primary and secondary schools the population are compelled to attend. It is a tradition steeped in symbolic imagery of class and social status, as a piece of material culture acting as a marker of symbolic boundaries that had (and continue to have) real socioeconomic consequences in England.

Rigid regulations on clothing, grooming, and other such socially and culturally rooted behavior hails, in England, from its earliest universities. In the sixteenth century, administrators at Cambridge, an institution that had been enforcing various forms of standardized dress in its hallowed halls for some three or four centuries by that point, wanted to keep the flamboyancy of fashion in the society outside the ivory tower at bay. University students at this point in time strongly desired to dress in silks and lace and to express themselves through a vibrant array of colors (Davidson and Rae 1990). This was in stark contrast to the required dress for undergraduates: long scholastic robes and a skullcap (a modified version of the *cappa clausa* mentioned previously). Cambridge graduate students could wear a different type of cap, but they were strongly counseled against ruffles and linen shirts. The administration at the time published the following edict:

> No scholler shall weare any Barilled Hosen, any great Ruffs, any clocks with wings." Or fabrics like "silke or any other stuffle of the like chardge, nor secondly of Galligaskan or Venetian or such like unseemly fashion, and no Slopp but the playne small Slopp without any cut, welt, pincke, or such like, nor thirdly of any color but blacke or sad-colour neere unto blacke, excepte white Hose for boys. (Wichelns 1968, 30)

The dress codes at Cambridge became more and more specific over time, attempting to control and define what was acceptable and what was not. Students, however, continuously resisted and challenged the rules and definitions of acceptable school attire throughout the sixteenth century, and, by and large, they typically wore what they wanted to. According to Wichelns, "even while the Spanish were ready to invade England in 1588, the Lord High Treasurer of England worried about hatts" (1968, 30).

The most outstanding history of the school uniform in England is Davidson and Rae's *Blazers, Badges and Boaters: A Pictorial History of the School Uniform*. Providing a myriad of visual recollections of the use of school uniforms and a wealth of well-documented history, this book is likely the most important attempt to chronicle the history of the school uniform in primary and secondary schools in England. I rely heavily on this book to relay this phase of the history.

According to Davidson and Rae (1990), what would become the model for school uniforms among schoolchildren in England and, therefore, for private and parochial schools in the United States, had its foundation in the clothing worn by children at Christ's Church Hospital in the sixteenth century. These were "cassock-like cloaks" and, contrary to common assumptions regarding the links with class and uniforms that would characterize much of the modern era of British school uniforms, these early uniforms at Christ's Hospital were designed to emphasize the *lower status* of the children who wore them—the charity children. Some 100 years later, breeches were added to the Christ's model. This interesting historical fact, that uniforms were actually used to distinguish the lower classes from everyone else in British society, is important for our understanding of the contemporary reality of school uniform discourse in American society.

This social stigma attached to the school uniform is not completely foreign given the original reasons for European uniforms in the academies more generally, and uniforms in English schools early on more specifically: to encourage docility and obedience toward "rightful authority" (Myers 1963). In the United States and Britain, however, the school uniform eventually would become solidly fixed as a status symbol for those who could afford private and elite parochial schools. So uniforms, as a mode of educational clothing, were used in Britain as a marker of social status—first for the lowest classes (orphaned children from poor families) and later as a symbol of elite tradition of excellence in education (i.e., as a badge worn to signify future opportunities in the class structure).

Another use for the school uniform in England was as an instrument for indoctrinating the masses and inculcating the herd instinct. That most of England was working class required a powerfully rigid system of education as a trajectory into the hierarchy of the occupational world but also a powerful tonic against individuality and individual expression. The unstated message was: "You are a mass, you are the same, you will take your rightful place among the working mass in the industrial machine." Rarely discussed in the literature on school uniforms, then and now, is that wearing jeans or a belly-shirt with a piercing is also a "uniform" in many respects, not one dictated by an educational authority but rather by an even more powerful authority: society.[3]

As can be seen in the history of the school uniform, such requirements of standardized dress also include a symbolic rhetoric of legitimate authority, a reservoir of institutional and organizational values of the school, and a method of social and cultural control over cohorts of students moving through the system. Those without a school uniform would feel left out. As Davidson and Rae put it, in England the uniform may indeed represent an "unseen, insidious, mode of social control" (1990, 25). Divergence from the uniform was akin to divergence from the values held by the institution and therefore punishable by a variety of sanctioning procedures.

The iconography inherent in the additional wearing of badges on the uniform represented a further basis of distinction (Synott and Symes 1995)—a distinction between schools. *Within schools*, the idea, of course, was that a common uniform would eliminate status distinctions between students within the same school; however, in England the basic fact of having badges for each school, as well as, in some cases, separate uniform colors, etc., for each school, made the distinction *among schools* clear.

The tradition of uniforming students in English schools, much like the situation in earlier times, was not without student resistance. Far from it. For instance, while salesmen in the 1930s were marketing shoes for the school uniform that would make boys look taller, rebellion against the uniform tradition was extremely widespread throughout England. Over the history of the use of school uniforms in England, there have been many protests.

As evidence of Americans' memorial fetish with English school uniforms as well as Americans' unrelenting mockery of Britain's *overt* class structure,[4] the *New York Times*, in 1972, saw fit to run an article describing the imminent demise of the old tradition of school uniforms in one of England's most illustrious schools, Eton. For over 100 years, boys at Eton were required to wear their characteristic black top hats and tails *both on and off campus*. On November 13, 1972, it was declared that students at Eton would no longer have to wear their hats and tails off campus—that they could wear "regular clothes." As one student stated, after the decision, which was prompted by the disciplining of eighteen students who went into town "in hippie attire" to attend a rock concert, as quoted by the *New York Times*, "No longer will we look so conspicuously idiotic" (Etonians 1972, A12). Today, students at Eton wear mostly whatever they wish.

School uniforms in England have largely stood the test of time. There have been changes to the regulations over time, particularly in the twentieth century, for material, political, cultural, and social reasons. For instance, during and after World War II, school uniforms in England were placed on the symbolic back burner for a period of time due to the cost and scarcity of fabric. Social movements akin to the Free Speech Movement in the United States have also occurred in many other countries, including England, resulting in changes in regulations, definitions, and overall policy strategy concerning student dress and grooming. Despite the fact that British parents seem to like uniforms for their durability and cost-effectiveness, their tradition and symbolic capital, in England schools have increasingly abolished, and more still have relaxed, their uniform requirements. Many public schools, such as Ampleforth and Wellington, now demand little uniform beyond smart casual wear, and neither academic nor social standards seem to suffer as a result (Davidson and Rae 1990).

THE RISE OF PUBLIC SCHOOLING AND STUDENT DRESS

Along with the advent of the Industrial Revolution, the movement of populations from rural to urban areas, and the important shift of the locus of work (from the home to outside of the home), public schooling in the United States dates back to the middle of the nineteenth century. The growth of public schooling in the United States since the 1850s has been extraordinary when compared to other industrialized nations (Walters 2000). Public schooling arose in the United States primarily as a means of preparing and socializing the young for their adult roles: as citizens and workers.[5] Thus, the beginnings of American public education corresponded closely with the needs of industry. The curriculum was, at that point, largely focused on the "three R's" but also linked heavily to the religious and moral climate of the period. Of course, public schooling was, contradictorily, not available to everyone. The elite continued to support and send their children to preparatory schools, while the poor and minorities were denied public schooling (Coleman 1990a; Walters 2000).

Eventually, schools were available for poor and minority American children and were considered equal despite the obvious and glaring inequalities of educational opportunities and subsequent occupational trajectories. There were early links between class, race, gender, and region and the quality of schooling received by American students. Yet unlike the system of schooling in Britain, where the structure was clearly understood by the English population as blatantly class-based, U.S. citizens understood public schooling to mean that everyone had an equal chance and that such a school system was designed to be a "great equalizer." Student dress in these separate but equal schools was largely determined by material and cultural precedents for the students and maintained a significant gendered quality that would be sustained for almost a century, until the student challenges to the gendered, racialized, and classist order of the United States in the 1960s (Cohen and Zelnik 2002).

Though the rhetoric of public schooling was one of separate but equal, it was clear that black schools, for instance, were indeed inferior. This fact was recognized in the famous *Brown v. Board of Education* (1954) case. This case, as is well known, determined the notion of "separate but equal" (from *Plessy v. Ferguson* 1896) to be blatantly false, and eventually we came to define and redefine "equality of educational opportunity" in several different ways (Coleman 1990). Such definitional challenges linked and interlaced with reform experiments laid at the schools' feet and influenced the overall climate of education in this country as well as the experience of schooling in American schools. Student dress during this period continued to be primarily anchored within the extant gender and material structure of students' and their families' lives.

A bit about private and Catholic schools: The uniform (designating what must be worn) has strong roots in the private/parochial sector—primarily as a symbolic marker of class status and really for no other reason save perhaps a deep and strong tradition stemming back to England. By the early 1960s, 50 percent of Catholic schools had uniform policies, which had been unquestioned for much of the first half of the twentieth century. However, by the early 1960s and perhaps as early as the late 1950s, there were some protests and concerns among the Catholic laity regarding the requirement for school uniforms. The protests focused on such issues as 1) uniforms as an invasion of parental rights and duties—that parents should be encouraged to fulfill their obligations and not defer to the long-standing in loco parentis dictated by private and parochial schools, as well as universities, and the uniform was indicative of waning parental rights; 2) the inherent statement that uniforms make of conformity and similarity—that these should be the goals of an educational organization was being questioned; 3) the school uniforms were actually not cheaper, at that time, for poorer families—a group that the Catholic Church was trying to serve; and 4) children will eventually find out social class boundaries, racial boundaries, gender boundaries, etc., upon entering the "real world" (Myers 1963). In fact, the concern was so great that the laity demanded it be brought up at the national convention of Catholic educators. This change also came at a time when Vatican II significantly altered the mission of the Catholic Church and the mission of Catholic education (Bryk, Lee, and Holland 1993). This is significant partially as a precedent for the imminent Civil Rights Movement and student movements.

Aside from the regular discussion (and almost unquestioned assumption) of school clothing among parochial schools in the private and Catholic sectors, the first 100 years of literature concerning educational dress in American schools is sparse. This paucity of literature on the debates concerning "appropriate" school clothing or even the issues of whether clothing impedes or encourages unity and academic success is indeed curious. However, the 1960s clarified what was *not* apparent in the previous popular and scholarly work from earlier educational history: that clothing in American public schools mirrored, to a large extent, material, social, and cultural contextual realities. In material terms, the clothes that children wore to school were predicated upon their economic situation—their class.

Affluent children who *did* attend public schools wore clothing that was marketed to mainstream Americans through various media. Theirs was a fashion that bespoke their parents' positions and the ideology of individualism so prevalent even during the early decades of the twentieth century. Working class children primarily wore clothes designated for their station in society. Poor children and minority children, who were overrepresented in the poorest rural areas of the United States, wore whatever clothing they had or hand-me-downs from older siblings.

Culturally, the first 100 years of student clothing in American public schools was, at the center, wrapped up with early traditions of religious and symbolic class and gender distinctions derived from Protestantism and British roots. However, there is more to the story. Though early American schools did not mirror the actual diversity of cultural and ethnic backgrounds that existed in the United States, one can think back to early photographic records of Native American children dressed in "school clothes" and the degree of passing that took place among free slaves and mulattos in the late nineteenth century. What of the cultural influences in dress from the tribe or Africa? Seeing these children dressed in school clothes is not indicative of a set standard of acceptable clothing for school during this period; rather, I think, these visions show us the process of eradicating otherness and difference through clothing. In other words, culturally, in separate schools, the clothing reflected the typical clothing of nineteenth- and early twentieth-century Native Americans and African Americans, which primarily reflected, as mentioned above, their station in the socioeconomic structure. But when there was contact with whites (primarily through contact with white teachers and administrators), these minority children (who were largely poor) were being dressed to appear more white, more "American," to give the illusion of educational opportunity, while denying them full participation in American society. What was given was a double message: "You are different from us/you'll never succeed like us" and "this is how we do it/we don't know why." I'll revisit this in the last chapter.

During this period of time, in which there was little mention of school clothing, there was quite a lot of mention of the role of dress in public life, in the occupational world, in the American dream. Starting with Dale Carnegie's *How to Win Friends and Influence People* (1990 [1936]), it is clear that the role of dress is important for the "equation" of success in the United States (Rubenstein 1995). If our concern for appearances has its roots in nineteenth-century Europe and America, the role of dress and identity, dress and success, dress and social mobility, has only become stronger, but with many, many variants—variants outside the scope of this book.

To pick up the history at a very important moment, it was during the 1950s and 1960s that the Baby Boom generation (then in the preteens and twenties, respectively) became a target market for Madison Avenue. With this group, as large as it was, and having disposable income as it did, the role of fashion, music, and other forms of expression became tightly linked with identity—what it meant to be American was changing. Identities in flux, new influences. This was a far cry from the notion that schools would create citizens of a certain type, workers of a certain type, sexualities of a certain type. From this cohort, student dress would be challenged in very short order. Not only student dress, but also traditional notions of gender expectations (e.g., "the cult of womanhood") of dress, class notions of dress, etc., would be questioned. These cultural boundaries still exerted pressures but were being seriously challenged by the 1960s. There is no doubt that the battles fought in the 1960s and early 1970s concerning student rights and freedom of expression were largely influenced by the sheer size of the Baby Boom generation and the increasing diversity of student bodies at various schools, at various levels of schooling.

BABY BOOMERS, THE STUDENT MOVEMENT, FREE SPEECH, AND DRESS

To "dress like a hippie" is culturally and semiotically analogous to ideologically clothing oneself against the status quo conceptions of sex, dress, music, and politics. Yes, these were the people their parents warned them against. This phrase, "dress like a hippie," is used even today to describe the "slovenly" dress of youth and a correlate indictment of the corresponding inner reality of youth culture, as it manifests itself in a wide variety of clothing styles expressing dissent and disillusionment with the conservatism, capitalism, standardization, and overall McDonaldization of society (Ritzer 2000, 2004). As we have seen, the stereotype of the slovenly student (Speer 1998) certainly hails from several centuries hence, but it was the 1960s, the Baby Boom generation, and the student movements from prominent American universities that challenged this and revealed it. Not only were ideological structures cracked and beginning to be dismantled, but it was in the sixties and seventies that high school students successfully fought mandatory dress codes. By the end of the run, one could say that the emperor had fewer clothes than before the decade began.

The primary issue in the battles for freedom of speech and expression on the educational dress front was whether dress caused a disruption to the educational process. From sandals being banned at a Bloomfield, New Jersey, high school in 1963, to disagreements over Beatles-style haircuts (or lack of haircuts, as many would argue), to the issue of whether girls in Boston could wear slacks to school in 1969—the constitution of constitutional rights concerning appearance and dress was being raised. In 1969, the United States Supreme Court interpreted dress as a protected form of expression and pronounced that students do not shed their constitutional rights at the schoolhouse gate (*Tinker v. Des Moines Independent School District* 1969).

Several authors who published in the area of student dress agreed, during this period, that there is only one justifiable reason for schools to adopt dress codes—when manner of dress interferes with the learning process. But does the student's dress affect his values and attitudes? No, they say. It is the reverse: Attitudes and values affect mode of dress. Distractions, if any, are brief and passing. Those manners of dress that were hazards to health should be regulated, but these were rare and, most argued, should be handled individually. Policies can have reverse effects: more rebellion, more policing, more arbitrariness (Scriven and Harrison 1971).

In the trenches, the debates were over where the line between decency and indecency was located. John Stinespring, the chair of the Social Studies Department at Elkhart High School in Elkhart, Indiana, stated in the *NEA Journal* in 1968 that the line was impossible to define: "Teachers want precise rules so that they need not make any judgments, but rules have a tendency to become more and more detailed and less and less useful" (Stinespring 1968, 58). This representative recognition from some thirty-five years ago mirrors contemporary policies of standardized dress; the problem of this cultural, political, and ideological line of decency/indecency; the teacher-recognized problem of becoming "fashion police"; and how these all take up more time than one has in the classroom. Bottom line for this educator: Relationships in school are the key to success—not appearance. Evidence of these feelings appeared in a 1969 NEA poll of public school teachers in which 86.8 percent agreed that their schools should have authority to regulate the wearing of apparel and the personal grooming of students; however, the vast majority (90 percent) stated that appearance, clothing, and grooming did not create distractions or serious problems in their schools (Teacher Opinion Poll 1969). The consensus from the educational and administrative literature of this period seems to be that we get in trouble when we overreact to a problem before one really exists.

What was occurring during the 1960s and early 1970s was the age-old conflict between the needs and rights of individuals and the prescriptions and expectations dictated by the larger society (Weinberger 1970). The sixties exhibited classic sociological symptoms of anomie, a condition of normlessness when expectations are no longer regulated, everything is in flux, changing—but to what? The concept of in loco parentis so long held by educational organizations was now being considered problematic and seriously challenged—certainly this was one of the primary arguments of the Sproul Hall demonstrations and the issues surrounding student rights at Berkeley in 1964. Post-Vatican II, and realizing that one could not separate the school from the outside world, during this time even private and parochial schools, which subscribed almost wholeheartedly to the ideology of in loco parentis, were "liberalizing their dress codes" (Savage 1973)—akin to the reforms in student clothing stipulations at Eton in England. By 1978, Joseph Califano Jr., President Jimmy Carter's Health, Education, and Welfare secretary, proposed taking the U.S. government out of the business of long hair and jeans in schools "once and for all" (Peterson 1979). Yet after Ronald Reagan's election in November 1979, Califano's successor, Patricia Roberts Harris, reversed his proposal. Big government was beginning to reverse the results of the student movements of the 1960s with regard to freedoms of expression as manifested through clothing and appearance.

THE TIDE IS TURNED: FROM D.C. TO LONG BEACH

The student movements of the 1960s and 1970s and the manifestations of these efforts that rippled throughout the institutions of American society once again came under attack as the seventies came to a close and the eighties began.[6] The 1980s brought a powerful conservatism and a Mc-Donaldization of society not before seen in the United States. We were rapidly becoming a nation focused on consumption, success, and national policies bordering on imperialism while inequalities, discrimination, and "newly discovered social problems" (e.g., AIDS, homelessness, teenage mothers, etc.) were rearing their ugly heads. Though not unlike the majority of the history of the primary institutions of American society, we were concerned about the "decay" of public education, the family, civic participation, and adolescence. The mass media were ever-growing and increasingly interlinked to create the culture industry influencing every corner of the United States. That these changes would result in renewed attention to issues of student dress and appearance is not surprising given the powerful culture of superficiality in the 1980s.[7]

After the free speech movement and the important Supreme Court decisions (see chapter 3) regarding rights of expression in realms of appearance, grooming, and dress, and up until the early eighties, states had been wary of enforcing dress codes because they feared losing federal funds. Federal regulations up until the Reagan administration prevented aid recipients from discriminating against any person in the application of any rules of appearance (Carro 1982). In 1981, Education Secretary Terrel H. Bell proposed canceling such federal regulations on public school dress codes (Feinberg 1981), and ultimately the Reagan administration did not enforce these stipulations.

The first documented discussions regarding school uniforms as an option for public schools came from the Barry administration in the nation's capital. Late in 1980, Washington, D.C., Mayor Marion Barry began discussing with his administration the possibility of proposing a standardized dress code for D.C.'s public schools (Richburg and Cooke 1980). Prompted by recent incidents of violence in or near D.C. public schools (one was a fatal shooting), which were blamed on individuals who were not students of the schools, Barry figured that uniforms would help to remedy such situations. Not using the term "uniform," because it "sounded too militaristic," he speculated that such standardized dress would foster school spirit, save parents money, and deter the infiltration of outsiders into public school campuses. Reaction to this idea during this time was disbelief, sarcastic criticism, and even, for some, cautious approval.

There is some evidence that dress regulations indeed made a come-back in the conservative 1980s. In 1982, a Burbank, California, junior high school sent a formal statement to parents detailing appropriate dress. Forbidden were tube and bikini tops, the "no-bra look," and short skirts. (Madonna would release her first album two years later.) Publicity about this statement generated requests from parents and schools across the nation for copies of it. Yet this is an example of increasing attention to dress code regulations in public schools—not standardized mandated student clothing. Again, dress codes stipulate what may not be worn; uniform policies stipulate what must be worn. It wouldn't be until 1987 that the first heavily publicized public school uniform policy was implemented.[7]

The context of American education and the public's perception of it radically changed with the publication of *A Nation at Risk* in 1983. Written by an eighteen-member commission assembled by President Reagan, this report, in its most famous line (which would be cited hundreds of time in the ensuing press coverage as well as from the bully pulpit of the presidency) stated that, "the educational foundations of our society are presently being eroded by a rising tide of mediocrity that threatens our very future as a Nation and a people" (*A Nation at Risk* 1983). The 1970s and early 1980s were characterized by a host of social and economic problems, including high inflation and unemployment and the rise of homelessness. However, the most important context in which this document was produced was within the Cold War. America, competitively, was not doing so well—and schools were to blame, or at least, schools were the institution to be utilized to gain America's prominence and its ability to win that war. Twenty years after that extremely influential publication, many critics point out that we were not in an educational crisis (Berliner and Biddle 1996) but an economic one. Schools have improved over time, but because they do not exist in social vacuums, they have been unable to respond to the vast social and economic changes over the last twenty years. *A Nation at Risk* provided the context of irrational and misguided fear about our schools that turned back the tide of student rights and freedoms and paved the road for ideas about how to "fix" the system—not the economic system, not the corporations' performances and behaviors, not the political system—the educational system.

The first public school to heavily publicize its uniform policy was Cherry Hill Elementary School in Baltimore, Maryland. The policy took effect in the fall of 1987. Cherry Hill, a predominantly black elementary school of students from lower- to middle-income families, implemented its policy based on the original impetus of cutting clothing costs and reducing social pressures on children (Baltimore School Rule 1987). A *New York Times* article about this policy began as follows: "In their distinctive school uniforms, the boys and girls traversing the streets of Baltimore's Cherry Hill neighborhood are indistinguishable from the millions of students in private and parochial schools throughout the country" (Daniels 1987). But this certainly wasn't the beginning of a movement such as we are witnessing currently; Chicago, Denver, and Seattle had absolutely no plans to adopt pilot programs in specific schools, let alone districtwide policies. There are conflicting reports, but by the end of the 1987–1988 school year, some five public schools in the Baltimore area (including Cherry Hill) and three schools in Washington, D.C. (Patapsco, Pimilco, and Burrville) had adopted the policy. Baltimore dubbed its initiative the "School Uniform Project."

Baltimore's policy is linked to a shooting that occurred in the spring of 1986, when a Baltimore suburban public school student was shot and wounded in a fight over a $95 pair of sunglasses. From there Baltimore decided to launch a program they had "discussed for years" (Baker and Michael 1987). Prophetically previewing the protocol of discussing uniform policies, articles appeared as early as December 1987, in various newspapers and periodicals, with statements like the following: "a sense of togetherness and orderliness that has *already* sharply reduced discipline problems at the school . . . it is more than just wearing a uniform, it's building their drive to make something of themselves, to become part of the system" (Daniel 1987, emphasis added). In their article on Cherry Hill, Baker and Michael (1987), revealed that officials in Baltimore hoped that uniforms would lead to higher grades, better behavior, increased self-esteem, school pride, and a sense of belonging (for minority children)—all would become classic assumptions and central facets of the discourse. There is some evidence that other schools in the mid-1980s attempted to initiate uniform policies (Bass 1988), but parents were against them and, thus, at least for the moment, that was enough to prevent implementation.

By the fall of 1988, fifteen more Baltimore schools and seven more in Washington, D.C., planned to make the change to uniforms (Baker and Michael 1987). In actuality, by that fall thirty-nine elementary schools (a third of the system) and two junior high schools in Washington, D.C., required uniforms. The movement was beginning to spread beyond the nation's capital (Lewis 1988b). Helene Grant Elementary School, a predominantly poor and minority school in New Haven, Connecticut, initiated its policy on October 3, 1988, as part of an effort to build self-esteem and to end competition stemming from clothes. Camden, New Jersey, also signed on board that fall (Camden School District 1988). Similar policies were adopted in PS no. 5 in Perth Amboy, New Jersey, which, by October 1988, was already hailing success in self-esteem and a host of other factors (Curry 1988). By 1988, fifty public schools had adopted uniforms (many called them "dress codes") (New Haven School 1988), and many more were inquiring into the process. At this point the vast majority of these were largely urban schools serving a predominantly minority and poor population. Enter New York.

On October 6, 1988, New York City Mayor Ed Koch voiced support for a pilot school uniform program in the Big Apple, with support from Richard Green, then school chancellor of New York City. Koch and Green gave a powerful voice to the school uniform movement; as Green stated, "In other parts of the country, the use of uniforms has been one of the variety of models that seem to work in improving attendance and discipline" (Lewis 1988a). Koch, who told the press that he liked the idea of public school uniform policies because they reminded him of private and parochial schools and because they foster a sense of "common respect and improve the learning environment" (Woodard 1989), was mustering public support and donations from clothing manufacturers to begin a pilot program in New York City. Schools were being called to participate. Most of these schools were very poor and predominantly minority. The pilot program was launched in the spring of 1989. Several influential educational leaders and organizations chimed into the discussion in 1989. Thomas Shannon, then executive director of the National School Board Association, added his voice, while Mary Hatwood Futrell, executive director of the National Education Association, said anecdotally of school uniforms that they can "provide an element of safety" (Woodard 1989).

By 1990, school uniform programs had also been implemented in Chicago, Detroit, Los Angeles, Miami, Philadelphia, and San Fernando (to name a few). All of these programs were a mix of voluntary policies, some very close to districtwide, others isolated in individual schools; most of them were at the elementary school level; and the vast majority were directed at poor and minority urban students.

Before entering the 1990s' era of school uniform policies, I wish to briefly discuss the concerns that were raised during the first three to four years of implementing uniform policies in public schools. During this period some dissent was published within the discourse. The concerns can be broken into two basic issues: constitutional and educational.

In 1988, William Olds of the Connecticut Civil Liberties Union went on record stating that uniforms in public schools were "blatantly unconstitutional" (New Haven School 1988). Olds quoted a 1985 Connecticut Department of Education publication, *Student Rights and Responsibilities in Connecticut's Public Schools*, to *New York Times* reporter Sharon Bass: "The way a student looks and dresses is a fundamental form of personal expression and should be protected by Constitutional guarantees of privacy and freedom of expression" In response, superintendent John Dow Jr. replied, again prophetically for the contemporary situation: "I don't even give that credence . . . urban education has failed and failed miserably—the parents want this. Uniforms have been a great model of private schools, and private education has been hailed as the great savior of this nation" (Bass 1988). Others noted that the right for women to wear pants was hard fought and hard won and that, in terms of civil rights and civil freedoms, uniform policies would represent a step backwards (What's Wrong with Public School Uniforms 1988). Others pointed out that such policies appear to skirt the real pressing issues of American public education, such as the lack of parental involvement (Comer 1988); the outmoded and unequal process of funding schools through local property taxes; and the fact that schools, especially in the areas where uniforms were emerging, needed basic items like books and supplies. Some educational psychologists were disturbed, remarking that such a policy is akin to a totalitarian concept, as a punitive, militaristic way to make kids behave. For others, such a policy represents yet another evasion of educators' responsibility to come up with workable solutions (Baker and Michael 1987).

Then it happened: An entire school district was implementing a mandatory school uniform policy in all K–8 schools. This was unprecedented. The year was 1994, the district was the Long Beach Unified School District (LBUSD) in California. The policy was unanimously adopted by the school board in January and followed a five-year experiment involving eleven Long Beach public schools (Melvin 1994) in which compliance ranged from 30 to 90 percent (California District 1994). Realizing the sheer guts it took to adopt such a policy, LBUSD set aside $175,000 to defend itself against legal challenges (Melvin 1994). The primary reasons given for LBUSD's policy were 1) to combat gang wear/colors, 2) to quell the competition and fury among students over designer clothing, 3) to level economic disparities, and 4) to help students focus on learning.

By the fall of 1994, Governor Pete Wilson had signed a bill stating that public schools can require students to wear uniforms and that the children of parents who oppose the bill would be ensured "the appropriate education" (California Goes Beyond Dress Codes 1994). There were three stipulations in the new law: 1) It required a school district to consult with parents, teachers, and principals before adopting a uniform code; 2) it demanded that parents be given six months' notice; and 3) it gave parents the opportunity to opt out by demonstrating to the board a "good reason." Initial anecdotal reports from principals were of better grades, better behavior, and less absenteeism (School Uniforms Growing 1994). Other districts were following LBUSD's lead; Los Angeles, San Diego, New York City, Miami, El Paso, Yonkers, Tacoma, and Seattle were among them. So, while private schools were loosening their dress requirements, public schools were dramatically increasing theirs (Do Clothes Make the Student? 1995). By the end of 1995, an Arizona state court judge had rejected arguments of several parents who contended that the public school district's uniform requirement was unconstitutional, the first time a judge had upheld the right of a school district to require uniforms without providing parents the right to say no (Jacobs 1995), and Philadelphia Mayor Edward Rendell was calling for public school uniforms as a "contribution to discipline."

In almost ten years, the idea of uniforming public school students had gone from a few isolated schools to a wide variety of schools in a wide variety of locations across the United States. One district had been bold enough to plunge into mandatory, districtwide uniform policies. The

movement was in seminal form, the issues were raised, the early anecdotal "findings" were out and entering solidly into the discourse—but
the spark that would truly light the fire was just around the corner.

THE MAKING OF A NATIONAL "REFORM" EFFORT

At the beginning of this chapter I quoted a selection from Clinton's
State of the Union Address (the full version is in appendix B). As Maureen Dowd said, "with one strike, Clinton became a cultural conservative" (Dowd 1996). That was on January 23, 1996. It was an election
year. On February 24, Clinton instructed the Department of Education
to distribute manuals to the nation's 16,000 school districts advising
them how they could legally enforce a school uniform policy. Similar
speeches would soon follow in Washington, D.C., California, and other
states crucial for Clinton's reelection (Mitchell 1996). In speeches given
throughout the spring of 1996, Clinton advised Americans on school
uniforms, playing off the "rash" of school shootings early in that year
(Moses Lake, Washington, and St. Louis, Missouri), and, for the first
time, citing the then-unpublished "effects" of the Long Beach Unified
School District's foray into a districtwide uniform policy some two years
earlier. By the end of that crucial year, the word was out, and a movement was solidly underway in the United States. On May 16, 1996, New
Jersey Governor Todd Whitman signed a uniform bill, and Connecticut
announced that forty of its public schools had uniform policies.

By the end of the 1996–1997 school year, the media had quoted individuals stating that half of the urban school districts in the United States
had adopted and implemented school uniform policies. More than 60
percent of Miami public schools, 66 percent of Cleveland's public
schools, 80 percent of the schools in the Chicago area, 50 percent in the
Boston, Massachusetts, area, and between 10 and 25 percent of the public schools in New York City, the largest district in the nation, claimed to
have adopted policies of standardized dress (Lewin 1997). That it was
largely an urban phenomenon seemed unmistakable, yet in 1996–1997
schools in places like Zion, Illinois, and Greenville, Mississippi, had such
policies as well. The majority of these policies were in elementary
schools, followed by middle and high schools. The year of 1997 was

capped off with the creation of the Land's End school uniform division, designed to capitalize on the movement.

Eyes were on New York City to see what it would do regarding school uniforms, for it had been relatively out of the picture—that would change early in 1998. William C. Thompson, then president of the New York City Board of Education, made a statement/proposal on February 9 that all 550,000 elementary school students in the New York City public school system should be wearing uniforms by the fall of 1999. Two days later, Mayor Rudolph Giuliani gave his support. Editorials fumed about and praised the idea throughout the month of February. A closer look at those editorials underlines the basic argument that those who were for uniforms gave their support from a position of fear of violence, gangs, and minorities, while those who opposed the measure made arguments along the lines of uniforms representing a political and administrative diversion away from issues of inadequate funding and class sizes to something that was free and politically effective—school uniforms. By March 18, 1998, the New York City Board of Education had voted and passed a resolution to require all K–6 public school students in the system to wear school uniforms.

While Denton, Texas, was debating what exactly "saggy" is and what exactly constitutes "baggy," Clinton was taking the message on the road again. At the annual convention of the American Federation of Teachers during the summer of 1998, Clinton continued to praise uniforms and suggest widening the scope of their adoption in public schools. He mentioned the school shooting in Springfield, Oregon, earlier that year, and made what some consider to be an extremely paradoxical statement that school uniforms would help children in public schools "feel free" (Bennet 1998). By the end of calendar year 1998, there were two new developments in the discourse surrounding school uniforms: 1) Some schools were having to abandon the policy for reasons of compliance, parental support, "fashion policing," etc. (Saslow 1998); and 2) the Educational Testing Service released its report on the effectiveness of various violence prevention efforts—including school uniforms—which concluded that it was impossible to draw any conclusions regarding the effectiveness of school uniforms on behavioral outcomes. The first studies were being cited in the press (Educational Testing Service 2000; Stanley 1996, see chapter 2 for a review of these studies).

On April 20, 1999, fourteen students and one teacher were killed and twenty-three others were wounded in Littleton, Colorado. Columbine provided even more fuel to the fire of the school uniform movement. The level of fear was raised a serious notch by this particular incident— primarily because it was so often linked to clothing (i.e., "The Trench-coat Mafia"). This unfortunate event played into the school uniform dis-course in several ways, politically, legally, and culturally.

By this time in the history of the school uniform movement, several court cases were well under way as parents, with the aid of the Ameri-can Civil Liberties Union, fought various school boards and school dis-tricts on the basis of the constitutionality of such policies of standardized dress. (See chapter 3 for summaries of these cases and interpretation.) A judge in Waterbury, Connecticut, released a preliminary ruling, pend-ing trial, that children attending public schools did not have a constitu-tional right to wear whatever they want (School Dress Code 1999). In New York City, opening day of school saw some 24 percent of the pub-lic elementary schools in that system agreeing to participate in New York City's program. By the end of 2000, thirty-five of the fifty states had schools with uniform policies, with the Philadelphia system joining that group in the fall (Sterngold 2000). In New York City, there was a may-oral race, and Bloomberg stated that he would, if elected, require *every* student to wear a uniform (Goodnough 2001). According to a 2000 school safety study, the CDC found that uniforms were required in about 20 percent of public and Roman Catholic elementary and middle schools and 10 percent of high schools (Zernike 2002). The events of September 11, 2001, also changed Americans' perceptions of American institutions. These reactions are outside the scope of this book; however, 9/11 seemed to do three things relevant to our discussions here: 1) It continued the path of limited freedoms and privacy rights; 2) it both in-creased suspicions as well as bolstered Americans' faith in government; and 3) it exponentially elevated the already irrational culture of fear in the United States to unprecedented heights.

The last two years have seen increasing numbers of uniformed public school students, more lawsuits, more rhetoric, terminological confusion between dress codes and uniforms, as well as talk of a trend *away* from school uniforms. By spring of 2002, the Memphis city school district had voted to require all of its public school students at all levels to wear uniforms. President George W. Bush, when governor of Texas, allowed a tax break for school uniforms (Sack 1998). Schools with these policies have had problems with compliance; some schools, after implementation of the policy, saw 100 percent of their students' families opting out. Mirroring the white-flight of the 1970s, Los Angeles schools have argued that instead of eliminating racial tensions, the uniform policies have actually exacerbated them as white parents are opting out—some argue that uniforms have indeed represented a stigma for the poor and minorities (Zernike 2002). Even in New York City, Mayor Michael Bloomberg actually scrapped the idea of public school uniforms after the system had reached 75 percent participation among elementary schools because, he said, "the policy had not reaped benefits in other cities . . . because of the cost and constitutional issues—the idea is not worth pursuing" (Steinhauer 2003). Still, many have not heard that message.

THE CONTOURS OF ANTI-UNIFORM
AND PRO-UNIFORM DISCOURSE

One of the aims of this book is to understand the symbolic and rhetorical discursive structure of the school uniform movement in the United States. Indeed, the empirical analyses (chapters 4, 5, and 6) reported in this book draw from the discourse the very assumptions and conjectures made by educators and parents about the effects of school uniform policies in public schooling—and I utilize these as hypotheses. The pro-uniform discourse of the school uniform movement is highlighted primarily in chapter 4. However, I briefly describe the contours of the anti-uniform discourse in this section to highlight the counterarguments and concerns of those activists and parents who are involved in argumentation and rhetoric to underscore what they say is the primary problem with the idea of school uniforms in public schools as a reform effort.

The following is a parody of the process of moving from the idea to the practice of uniforming public school students in DeKalb County, Georgia. I use it here to illustrate the primary concerns of anti-uniform coalitions and parent groups, because I think it summarizes (in satirical fashion) the main objectives of such an idea in the public education arena:

Once upon a time, a school system in DeKalb County decided to improve education by imposing mandatory apples.

The administration knew that apples are healthful and that healthy children generally do better in school. They used their common sense to postulate that children who ate an apple a day would have less absenteeism and be more attentive and thus the county's test scores would rise. So they formulated their Eat For Success initiative to require each child in the county to bring an apple to school each day and charged the teachers with ensuring that those apples were eaten.

Someone pointed out that requiring families to supply an apple each day could be construed as a fee for public education and the county would therefore have to provide apples at no charge for underprivileged families. The administration, in all its wisdom, said "OK, we won't require an apple. We will require an apple, a pear, OR a peach. Each school may choose two of these fruits and each student shall bring one if its Official School Fruits. That way, we're offering a choice so we do not need to supply free fruit."

And it was so.

Some families liked the mandatory fruit. They were families who ate apples (or pears or peaches) anyway and who bought into the administration's claim that requiring this on a county-wide basis would improve test scores. Other families were unhappy for a variety of reasons and requested to opt-out of the policy. One girl had braces and could not eat apples, pears, or peaches, but the administration would not let her eat bananas. One boy had digestive problems and was subject to diarrhea when he ate fruit, but the administration refused to consider vitamin supplements. One family owned a vineyard and so could get grapes free, but the administration would not allow the substitution. Some children just plain did not like the Official School Fruits, and those children were scorned as trouble-making deviants. One by one concerns and objections were expressed, but the administration refused to back down, saying that the program would not be successful unless ALL children ate an apple, a pear, or a peach every school day.

It was suggested that the school system could achieve its objectives better by teaching the children nutrition, but the administration thought that would put too much burden on the teachers.

A nutritionist stepped forward to state that, from a nutritional point of view, there was no evidence to support the theory that a mandatory fruit policy would improve test scores, but the administration preferred to rely on anecdote and personal opinions.

A concerned citizens' group pointed out that it is not the role of the school board to dictate nutritional policy—that was a parental right and responsibility. The administration blew a raspberry in response.

Meanwhile, the families who supported mandatory apples were getting upset because they didn't realize that they were allowed to provide their children with the Official School Fruit even without the Eat For Success policy. Somehow they got the impression that if any students were permitted to forego the approved mandatory fruit, their own ability to get their own children to eat apples would be compromised. So they said, "Hey, if it's good enough for me, it's good enough for you! Get over it and eat an apple!" And they tried to argue their point:

"It's easier to throw an apple in the kids' lunch boxes than to have to decide what to feed them each morning!"

"Apples are cheaper than the 'Lunchables' my kids make me buy, so I save money!"

"If you require your kids to eat apples, then they will be too full to eat Jello and other food that is obscenely jiggly."

The citizens against mandatory apples shook their heads sadly and despaired for their school system and their fellow parents who had good intentions but who couldn't see the forest for the apple trees. (Beale n.d., used by permission)

As this parody illustrates, those who oppose mandatory school uniform policies use several arguments to make their points. First, they are concerned that schools and school boards should not have the right to dictate what children should wear—that, they argue, is a parental right and responsibility. Second, parents (and educators) in the anti-uniform movement also have concerns that this not only crosses into parental rights but also squelches and undermines students' rights of free speech and freedom of expression. Third, there is quite often an undercurrent in this camp of concern that administrators simply cannot "see the forest for the trees," that they are not looking at the bigger picture, the larger issues facing public education in the twenty-first century, that they rely on their common sense and utilize anecdote and personal opinion to make the claim that uniform policies, in their school/district, will raise test scores, create a positive educational/safety climate, etc. Fourth, there has been much parental concern over the widening gulf between the written policies of "opt-outs" and the on-the-ground, practical ways in which administrators apply the policies regarding exemptions and opt-outs. Fifth, these anti-uniformists argue that teachers have enough to do without policing dress code violations, and that teachers should be allowed to simply teach and forge relationships with students, parents, and the community. Finally, though this is by no means an exhaustive list (see chapter 7), these groups and individuals argue that, in the end, mandating a school uniform policy is akin to charging a fee for public education, and that, they argue, is against everything that American public education stands for.

2

A REVIEW OF THE LITERATURE: FROM ANECDOTES TO RESEARCH AND BACK AGAIN[1]

If you have an anecdote from one source, you file it away. If you hear it again, it may be true. Then the more times you hear it, the less likely it is to be true.

—Anthony Holden (1979)

In this exposition, the state of empirical research on school uniform and dress code polices is described. It is not true that there has been no empirical research conducted to assess the effectiveness of school uniforms on student behavior and educational outcomes, yet there is much to be done. The extant research is wide-ranging in terms of samples, methodologies, definitions of key concepts, theoretical grounding, and implications for those who wish to inform themselves in the midst of strong public debate. For some time now there has been a need for a comprehensive and critical literature review concerning the growing interest in school uniform and other standardized dress code policies being considered to remedy what many see as a failing public education system. Despite some efforts at summarization, there has yet to be a comprehensive, critical look at the state of empirical research designed to speak to the increasing numbers of concerned and intrigued. For this chapter I draw on some 100 articles, ranging from the most superficial piece of anecdotal journalism to the most rigorous of quantitative empirical studies on the topic of school uniforms and/or dress code policies. I thoroughly review a quarter of these (the empirical studies). The literature on school uniforms can be organized into four types: legal, anecdotal, empirical, and theoretical. I first summarize the anecdotal literature, for it is the bedrock upon which the debate (and, unfortunately, much of the "research") stands, and it is important to understand its assertions for and cautions against uniform policies. Second, I critically review the empirical literature, its findings and suggestions, along with its strengths and limitations, validity and generalizability. The empirical research can be categorized as follows: perception studies, small-scale effectiveness studies, and large-scale effectiveness studies.

INTRODUCTION

President Clinton, in his 1996 State of the Union Address and several subsequent speeches and addresses (Presidential Radio Address 1996; Presidential Radio Address 1998; Remarks Prior to a Roundtable Discussion, 1996; see also appendix B), announced that all 16,000 U.S. public school districts should "consider the issue of mandatory school uniforms" (Bedard 1996; Ryan and Ryan 1998). The reason given for implementing such policies was primarily to reduce gang-related incidents and violence occurring on school grounds. Almost on cue, the U.S. Department of Education published its *Manual on School Uniforms* and distributed the manual to all school districts. In what would set the tone for the coming school uniform debate and current movement, as "evidence" Clinton said that he "speaks from experience on the advantages of student uniforms" (Bedard 1996). This approach signifies the impetus behind school uniform policies, in that the debate surrounding their effectiveness as well as discussions concerning when and how to implement such policies are rooted in *anecdote*.

Many cite the advantages and disadvantages of school uniforms from the perceptions of parents, the observations of administrators, the feelings of students, and other interested parties. The debate rarely moves beyond this anecdotal flavor and, in fact, the nature of this reform effort, grounded in anecdote, serves to keep the debate on an emotional level, one void of discussions of empirical evidence, theoretical insight, or solid science. Meanwhile, administrators and parents across the country are currently struggling to decide whether to implement a uniform policy. Because of the assumed lack of empirical research, these groups get swept up in the tide of anecdote and perception, limiting their ability to make informed, prudent decisions. There is, therefore, a great need for a systematic look at what the research says, what it means, and what yet needs to be assessed. In this chapter I wish to describe the state of empirical research on school uniform and dress code polices.[2] It is *not* true that no empirical research has been conducted to assess the effectiveness of school uniforms on student behavior and educational outcomes, indeed, several attempts to summarize what has been written come to mind (Black 1998; Gregory 1998; King 1998; West et al. 1999; White 2000). However, these fail to distinguish between empirical and speculative literatures; thus, *much is* yet to be done.

Despite earlier efforts at summarization, there has yet to be a comprehensive, critical look at the state of empirical *research* designed to speak to the increasing numbers of concerned and intrigued. I reviewed some 100 articles, ranging from the most superficial piece of anecdotal journalism to the most rigorous of quantitative empirical studies on the topic of school uniforms and/or dress code policies.[3] Research and writing concerning school uniform policies really began in earnest around 1994, the year that Long Beach Unified School District became the first in the country to expect all elementary and middle school students to wear uniforms, though there were some serious considerations of the topic as early as 1991. The literature on school uniforms can be organized into four types: legal, anecdotal, empirical, and theoretical.[4] I first summarize the anecdotal literature, for it is the bedrock upon which the debate (and, unfortunately, much of the "research") stands, and it is important to understand its assertions for and cautions against uniform policies. Second, I critically review the empirical literature, its findings and suggestions, along with its strengths and limitations, validity, and generalizability. The empirical research can be categorized as follows: perception studies, small-scale effectiveness studies, and large-scale effectiveness studies.

ANECDOTES ARE NOT ANTIDOTES: THE PROS AND CONS OF SCHOOL UNIFORMS

Sifting through the literature on school uniforms, one is struck by the overwhelming reliance on anecdote, perception, personal experience, and hearsay presented as evidence for the successes and/or failures of school uniforms. The lack of critical insights and empirical evidence within these articles is not surprising during times when little scholarly research specifically devoted to investigating such issues existed (i.e., before 1998). The often-cited Long Beach data (discussed more completely below) were the primary piece of empirical evidence; however, this study suffered many limitations. Limitations or not, empirical evidence or not, much of the writing on the impact of uniform policies on student outcomes *still* ignores the available research and continues to surround itself with anecdote, politics, fear, and drama. The observation that the literature is ignoring research and reiterating the same themes again and again is not new (Behling 1994; Black 1998; Hinchion-Mancini 1997; Thompson 1999; King 1998; Paliokas, Futrell, and Rist 1996; Posner 1996; White 2000; Wilkins 1999). These authors recognize the need for more rigorous empirical research, yet in the face of pressures to publish, in the desire to enter an opinion into the debate and movement, individuals continue to write "pro and con" articles based on little or no evidence and instead "press forward" on the basis of previously published anecdotes.

The "pro and con" format had its time and its utility when there was virtually no empirical research being conducted on school uniforms. In fact, the musings and arguments offered for or against such policies provided the catalyst for many scholars to consider whether the assumptions from the anecdotal debate could be upheld in statistical analyses. Even more important, the anecdotal meanderings, some conclude (see Black 1998; Buckley 1996; Chaika 1999; Murphy 1998; Portner 1998; Volokh and Snell 1998; Wilkins 1999; Williams-Davidson 1996), say more about the issues of fundamental concern to educators, parents, students, and community members than they ever can about whether uniforms will provide a respite from the ills of public education, real or perceived. Only empirical evidence derived from rigorous, well-controlled, methodologically sophisticated, theoretically grounded research can answer that question. I studied these anecdotal articles (see reference list) to understand two facets of this prevalent format: 1) What are the salient issues of importance that individuals assume will be helped or harmed by school uniform policies? and 2) Which educational actors are most concerned with which factors?

First, which issues are assumed to be linked to school uniforms? Or, which educational process factors do individuals and groups assume will be enhanced or alleviated by school uniforms? Though Clinton originally was concerned solely with school violence and gang-related behavior, the list has grown to include virtually every aspect of public education and a number of social problems. The most prevalent arguments raised in these anecdotal articles are that uniforms will prevent gang-related activity, decrease distinctions between students (in particular, socioeconomic distinctions), produce a student body that is more focused on schooling, reduce violence (of all kinds), instill an orderly school climate, inculcate discipline, and increase student achievement. Secondary assertions, though not necessarily less important to those espousing uniforms, are that they will lessen clothing hassles, reduce crime and theft on campus, produce school unity and pride, create a safe environment at the school, increase attendance (or reduce truancy), make it easier to recognize intruders, and increase self-esteem among students. There are numerous others; these are the prime assumptions derived from the anecdotal literature.

Concerning the arguments against school uniforms (again derived from conjecture and not evidence), the most prevalent reasons for *not* having a uniform policy are that uniforms infringe upon students' First Amendment rights of free speech and expression, will *not* decrease distinctions between students (i.e., how can one eradicate racial distinctions? gender distinctions?), really represent a tool of administrative power, may produce economic hardship for a segment of the public student population, and will *not* reduce violence. Secondary arguments against uniforms are that they will *not* reduce gang-related activity; are simply another "quick fix" reform effort that fails to face the complex social, economic, and cultural realities;

are based on conformity and therefore will deplete creativity; are becoming tightly coupled with corporate interests; will *not* instill discipline and order, and give a false sense of security that "everything is alright." Again, numerous other arguments against uniforms are based on speculation.

When one examines the assumptions made by administrators, they appear mostly concerned with order, discipline, and safety, as indicated by a belief that uniforms will prevent gang activity, reduce crime, create an orderly climate, and, thereby, construct a student body that is more focused on school than on other diversions. This concern with order replicates the concerns of parents, community members, and students, according to the anecdotal literature. It is clear that this list of assumed effects of school uniforms does tap into the concerns, hopes, and fears of those involved in public education; although it is important to understand these fears, this is not what the anecdotal uniform literature does. Instead, it amplifies them, reifies them, and, with no supportive evidence, somehow still drives home the point that we need school uniforms regardless of what the research says. A more sensible approach is to conduct scientific research to determine whether there is a statistically significant link between school uniforms and the host of factors they are assumed to combat or strengthen. What does the *research* say about these links? What is the match between the anecdotal literature and the growing body of empirical literature? It is to these questions that I now turn.

THE RESEARCH: PIECES OF THE PUZZLE

The rest of this chapter summarizes the state of the empirical literature on school uniforms as it addresses the effectiveness of these policies on the most salient issues of concern—those most often described by the anecdotal literature. A great deal of research has been published, but there is also a great deal more to conduct. The available research can be categorized into three main areas. First are *perception studies*, which represent a step up from anecdotal discussions. Their data are typically questionnaire responses about what educators, parents, and students *think* about uniforms. Second are *small-scale effectiveness studies*, which typically look at an in-depth case study of one school that has forged the pathway and implementation of a mandatory school uniform policy or collect data on several schools and/or students within schools to assess the impact (if any) of the policy on outcomes of interest. Finally, there are *large-scale effectiveness studies*, which typically use nationally representative samples of schools and students within schools to compare, usually cross-sectionally, uniformed schools/students with nonuniformed schools/students on a variety of dimensions of concern using either a theoretical model or the quasi-theoretical musings of the anecdotal literature.

The dependent variables of interest in these empirical studies are wide-ranging. The perception studies usually focus on the opinions, level of support, attitudes, and perceptions toward school uniform policies of parents, educators, students, etc. These types of studies are more concerned with giving educators tools (albeit weak, unsubstantiated ones) to embark on the quest to convince parents and students of the need for school uniform policies, rather than testing their efficacy. The effectiveness studies link more tightly with the anecdotal "hypotheses" and reigning theories to test whether uniforms do indeed have an impact on the issues of concern: academic achievement, behavioral problems, school climate, violence, discipline, attendance, safety, self-esteem, delinquency, substance use, etc. I present the studies in each type of category in chronological order, summarizing their methodologies and findings and discussing their limitations and implications.

Perception Studies

I review eight perception studies here (Stevenson and Chun 1991; Woods and Ogletree 1992; Behling 1994; Gullatt 1999; Kim 1999; West et al. 1999; DeMitchell, Fossey, and Cobb 2000; NAESP 2000). It is important to note, before reviewing these studies, what the reasoning behind them is, what they can do and cannot do. Such research can offer us a glimpse into the opinions, feelings, gut reactions, and observations of a number of relevant educational actors. They can give us insight into the tone of the movement and who is speaking for what side. What they cannot do is test effectiveness of such policies. Though many have assumed that perception is enough, to *believe* that an effect of school uniforms exists is not to *cause* it to happen.

In the District of Columbia, at the end of the 1980s, forty-six schools had voluntary uniform policies. The superintendent commissioned a study to assess the attitudes toward and impact of these uniform policies in the District of Columbia Public School District. The result was one of the first perception studies, by Stevenson and Chun (1991). Their surveys, intended to document the perceived impact of the policies on financial stress on families, attendance rates, "educational attainment" (i.e., academic achievement), and school climate, were given to 301 principals and teachers as well as 268 parents. The schools in the study served primarily African American students from low socioeconomic backgrounds. Both elementary and secondary schools were included in their sample.

Descriptive statistics of the perceptions of this nonrandom sample of educators and parents as well as correlational analyses were presented. The descriptive data served to represent the perceptions as to why uniforms were thought to be needed at these schools; the focal reasons were as follows: an interest in teaching students that clothes are not what is important, to save parents money by not having to purchase name-brand clothing, and to answer parents' fears that children may engage in deviant activities to acquire the desirable fashions. Both principals and teachers believed that wearing uniforms cut down on fights and improved overall student behavior, while parents perceived that uniforms allowed them to save money on clothing expenses and *did* teach their children that clothing is not what is most important; about a third (30 percent) believed that uniforms increased their children's focus on schooling. Both groups believed that school uniforms had a positive impact on the school climate. Correlational analyses attempted to "test" these perceived benefits by looking at compliance rates (as determined by the principal), academic achievement, and attendance rates. There were no statistically significant correlations linking the uniform policy compliance rates with increases in either academic performance or attendance.

A year later, Woods and Ogletree (1992) conducted a similar, but smaller-scale, study, inspecting data from thirty parents (fifteen African American, fifteen Hispanic) whose children attended a Chicago-area elementary public school. The survey tapped into attitudes toward designer clothing, peer pressures surrounding fashion, uniforms as a way for parents to save money, the perceived impact of uniform policies on student self-esteem, and academic achievement, among several other issues. A majority of this small, nonrandom sample of parents agreed that peer pressure concerning clothing was a problem and that uniforms could eliminate teasing and competition among peers. Almost two-thirds (60 percent) did not think that uniforms would alter negative interactions among students at school. This study, as well as the study conducted by Stevenson and Chun (1991), showed that parent support was absolutely necessary for the implementation of a uniform policy. From a critical research standpoint, however, if *no* evidence exists beyond perception that uniforms affect the very processes of concern, then what difference does parental support make, if the support they give is based on anecdotal perceptions and empirically questionable assumptions?

In 1994, Dorothy Behling published a paper that would become widely cited across the literature. Her study took the ideas behind the uniform movement (then in its infancy) and applied the idea of "person perception." She was interested in investigating whether style of clothing (controlling for gender and school type) influenced how high school students and teachers *perceived* the wearer's academic abilities, behavior, and potential. The assumption, theoretically developed in previous social psychology and a favorite within popular culture, is that clothing communicates something about the wearer. What it communicates, among other things, is the wearer's degree of sociability, his leadership abilities, her intelligence, his potential; supposedly people think they can clearly identify a person's grade point average simply by looking at her clothing.[5] The study used a nonrandom sample of 270 sophomores and 20 high school teachers from a single-sex, religious private school and a coeducational public high school in a middle-class, medium-sized city in Ohio.

Behling showed photographs of a college-aged male and female, each wearing one of four styles of clothing: 1) a "dressy" uniform; 2) a "casual" uniform; 3) a casual nonuniform, typical style of clothing; and 4) a jeans, sweatshirt, and jean jacket combination to represent the less than casual. Respondents were then asked to answer items that eventually formed three scales indicating perceptions of the person's behavior, achievement (GPA), and "academic potential." Without going into detail here, Behling indeed found evidence that clothing produces what she dubbed a "halo effect." The jean and jacket combination was the combination carrying the most negative connotations. Gender differences were noted in that males who were dressed in casual clothing were seen as more likely to have behavioral problems than females in the same style. On the other hand, uniforms made boys look more "angelic" than females in the eyes of the respondents.[6] Those models who wore a uniform were rated with higher academic ability (current and potential) by teachers and students than those wearing the jean/jacket combination. Behling adequately notes the limitations of her study: The sample was not random, respondents were not given flexible options, and more rigorous methodologies are needed. Other authors have commented on this halo effect, saying that this indicates that the "benefits of uniforms are more perceptual than real" (Hinchion-Mancini 1997, 63) and that "uniforms seem to be a way of circumventing, rather than solving the problem of teacher prejudice" (Kohn, cited in Posner 1996, 2), and this certainly begs the question: Why would we want to produce this halo effect in our public schools? Perhaps, the micro question Behling is asking about this halo effect is precisely what is being produced through the overutilization of anecdotal evidence and perception studies.

Gullatt's (1999) research represents yet a different kind of perception study. He was interested in gauging the level of support from and the reasons for considering implementing uniforms given by school-level and state-level superintendents. He surveyed all sixty-six Louisiana public school superintendents as well as all fifty state superintendents. The survey attempted to assess the superintendents' perceptions in their jurisdictions regarding who holds the authority to mandate dress codes or uniforms, the grade levels implicated in such policies, the procedures applied in the selection of a uniform, respondents' perceptions of the effectiveness of uniforms on a variety of outcomes (school harmony, gang violence, discipline problems, school climate), and whether there is discussion about faculty uniforms.[7] What of the perceived links between school uniforms and other outcomes? Roughly a third of all state superintendents felt uniforms would improve discipline (34 percent), lessen gang activity (30 percent), increase school harmony (32 percent), and positively affect the learning environment (32 percent), while roughly two-thirds of district superintendents felt that way (64 percent, 62 percent, 64 percent, and 62 percent respectively). Perception research like

Gullatt's is misleading in that while only a third, or two-thirds, perceive a link between uniforms, no tools are given for readers to answer the following questions: What about the other two-thirds or third who did not see a link? What is the match between perception and reality? Although authors of these studies seem uninterested in these questions, those who use their findings assume that one-third *perception* equals 100 percent effectiveness. This is dangerous, and, as we shall see, not the case.

Yunhee Kim published a dissertation in 1999, at the University of Minnesota, regarding school uniforms and student self-image. Kim focused on teachers, parents, and students from three high schools in the St. Paul/Minneapolis area. The sample ultimately consisted of 352 teachers, students, and parents from the three high schools: one with a restrictive school uniform policy/dress code, one with a flexible school uniform policy/dress code, and one with no policy.

Kim's (1999) descriptions point clearly to the conceptual confusion at times between uniform policies and dress codes. This flaw in and of itself is enough to call Kim's research into serious question. The goal of the dissertation was to assess whether 1) teachers, parents, and students differ in their opinions about wearing uniforms; 2) there were school differences in perceptions of uniforms; and 3) school uniforms affected these high school students' self-images. The findings indicate that parents and teachers agree with proponents' arguments regarding the effectiveness of school uniforms (that they eliminate competition over clothing, improve school climate, improve behavior, increase self-esteem, increase school pride, etc.) much more than the students do. Schools varied on teacher perceptions regarding the effectiveness of student uniforms along the dimensions of improving attendance and homework completion; however, Kim does not control for objective measures of attendance and/or homework completion at either of these schools. Using Offer's (see Offer et al. 1981) Self-Image Questionnaire, Kim finds that there is no effect of school uniforms on all aspects of student self-image. This last set of analyses moves away from the perception approach in Kim's study; however, the methodology, sampling schema, and analysis procedures are extremely weak, lacking in control and valid measurement.

Another perception study (West et al. 1999) looks at the attitudes of the parents of fourth-grade students toward the use of school uniforms.

All parents of fourth graders in schools in Lafayette County, Mississippi, were sent surveys ($n = 426$), and 33.8 percent returned completed questionnaires.[8] The researchers chose fourth graders because they argue that ages ten to eleven represent a developmentally important stage for children when clothing and appearance become more salient than before. Fifty-six percent of these children's parents "strongly favored" or "favored" the use of school uniforms in public schools. A majority of parents agreed that uniforms eliminate clothing as a means of cultural expression, eliminate visible differences in family economic and social background, cost less than other types of clothing, do not violate a child's rights under the law, and do not limit a child's creativity or individuality. The authors also looked for social correlates to these perceptions and found only one set of significant correlations: that family income influences perceptions of the cost of uniforms versus other types of clothing. Research such as this adds little to our understanding of school uniforms; however, educators and parents are swayed by such perceptions.

DeMitchell, Fossey, and Cobb's (2000) research looked into the perceptions of a randomly selected sample of principals from elementary, middle, and secondary schools across the nation. They were interested in several perception issues: uniforms' impact on student behavior, students' constitutional rights, uniforms' utility in preparing students for the adult world, the worth of enforcing uniforms versus the perceived benefits, uniforms' impact in reducing sexual harassment of students by students, and the level of support for mandatory school uniforms. Though interested in all of these issues, the researchers only really focus on the latter. Results indicated that middle school principals favor mandatory uniforms more than elementary school principals and even more than high school principals. The authors do not push much further in their empirical analysis, only to say that more research is needed.

Finally, what may be the clearest link between the corporate world[9] and the debate on school uniform effectiveness is the collaboration between Land's End (a clothier and uniform supplier) and NAESP (2000) to conduct a nationwide telephone survey of 755 principals. Though the methodological approach to this study is difficult to uncover, this study is receiving quite a lot of attention. The report states that more than two-thirds of the principals surveyed have observed that uniforms appear to improve the school's image in the community (84 percent), improve classroom discipline (79 percent), decrease peer pressure (76 percent), increase school spirit (72 percent), allow students to concentrate on schoolwork (67 percent), and improve students' safety at school (62 percent). In what is likely the most interesting aspect of the report from the perspective of educational and social scientific research, gauging the effects of a school uniform policy was based on observations by the principal and staff (88 percent), comments by parents (78 percent), comments by teachers or school staff (76 percent), comments by students (62 percent), discipline logs (57 percent), and attendance records (47 percent). Noticeably absent from this list is *scientific evidence!*

Conducting perception studies is one of several research strategies noted by King (1998) for assessing the effectiveness of school uniforms, particularly in preventing violence. He does not indicate why he believes this research methodology is necessary, and, given the inherent flaws of perception studies in evaluating policy *effectiveness* noted in these summaries, it is better to understand the nature of these studies as they exist now, work at improving them, and understand what they can and cannot add to our understanding of school uniforms as a reform strategy. The NAESP (2000) study points to the overwhelming flaw inherent in perception studies: They attempt to prove effectiveness through the use of quantifying anecdotes and opinions. This is not possible without stringent controls, random samples, and valid measures. Many of the perception studies outlined previously are weak not only methodologically and statistically but substantively as well. This state of affairs begs the question: What is the point? The criticisms of the halo effect are clear. Interestingly enough, the bulk of perception studies, and the use of their "findings" by others as "evidence" of uniform policy benefits, actually creates a macrolevel halo effect. Schools with uniform policies are "seen" and "perceived" as effective schools; however, this masks the real problems and issues underlying the concerns and inequalities of public schooling. What perception studies *do* provide for those interested in the movement is a description of the ideology of the movement and the level of support for uniforms.

Small-Scale Effectiveness Studies

Apart from looking into the perceptions of parents, teachers, administrators, and students regarding uniforms as a violence prevention strategy,

King (1998) and Paliokas et al. (1996) suggest a number of other research strategies that need to be employed if we are to come to an empirical understanding of the effectiveness of school uniform policies:

- Use trend analysis within the school or district to determine whether changes are true changes or predictable changes.
- Compare uniformed students (experimental group) and nonuniformed students (control group) on a variety of outcomes.
- Adequately measure and control intervening variables and processes for statistical analysis to determine cause and effect relationships.

Several studies have been conducted to test the effectiveness of school uniform policies that utilize small samples and experimental and control groups, as well as attempting to control for other factors associated with the outcomes of interest. I review six such studies here (Tanioka and Glaser 1991; Murray 1997; Williams-Davidson 1997; Gregory 1998; Murphy 1998; Stevenson 1999). These studies go beyond perception studies to begin to quantitatively and qualitatively test whether uniforms influence the issues of concern to educators and parents.

An earlier study in the effectiveness of school uniforms comes to us from Japan. Tanioka and Glaser's (1991) empirical test of three important theoretical models of delinquency brought them unknowingly into the debate on school uniforms. This study looked at delinquency among over 1,000 Japanese youth in Osaka private and public schools. For our purposes, their main finding regarding the effectiveness of uniforms on delinquent behavior (vandalism, theft, burglary, and "joyriding") is that "the uniform, by creating identifiability as a student and a juvenile, seems to inhibit delinquency, but those most motivated to offend carry a change of clothing in a bag or find other ways to be free of their uniforms before reaching home" (Tanioka and Glaser 1991, 62). They found that uniforms inhibit delinquency *if students remain in uniform* (they were looking at off-campus, out-of-school offenses). Their conclusions give a clear word of warning concerning their findings for those who may wish to utilize their results as evidence that uniform policies would function similarly in U.S. public schools:

> This finding on identifiability of potential offenders as preventing delinquency in Japan merits testing in other nations where uniforms are worn, such as some private schools in the U.S.; however, its facilitation of informal control of students may not be so effective in countries lacking Japan's widespread volunteer family, school, and police informants that are capable guardians of crime and intimate handlers of juveniles. (Tanioka and Glaser, 1991, 70)

The implication is an important one: The United States could not support such a correlation because its mechanisms of informal control are not as strong as those in Japanese society.

One of the key anecdotal assumptions of uniform proponents is that school uniforms will create a more positive school climate that, in turn, will positively affect virtually every aspect of schooling. Richard Murray, a high school principal in South Carolina, set out to test this assumption in 1997. Using NASSP's Comprehensive Assessment of School Environments School Climate Survey, Murray surveyed 306 sixth-, seventh-, and eighth-grade students: 153 randomly sampled from an urban middle school with a school uniform policy and 153 from an urban middle school without a uniform policy. He states that controlling for racial or socioeconomic factors in his study is unnecessary because these schools are "almost identical" along those dimensions—though he says nothing about the type of uniform policy the one middle school has. He "tested" several dimensions of school climate for comparison between the uniformed and nonuniformed schools. However, several issues make the results of this study unacceptable and uninterpretable:

1. Murray neither describes the metric with which these variables are measured, nor
2. describes what his school climate dimensions mean;
3. his table of results is unintelligible and suffers from typographical errors; and
4. though he conducts his analysis at the individual level (aggregations of the 153 students from each school), he provides no statistical tests to determine whether the differences he reports are *real* differences or simply due to sampling error and chance.

All in all, Murray (1997) provides absolutely no evidence that uniforms affect school climate.

The importance of sampling procedures, sample size, and valid/reliable measurement in assessing the effectiveness of school uniform policies on student outcomes cannot be overstated. However, case studies, in which a researcher looks in-depth at one school, can often illuminate more clearly the fundamental processes at work in any social phenomenon. Often qualitative research helps build theory and indicates important directions for large-scale quantitative studies to pursue in statistical analyses. One such study exists, a 1996 dissertation by Carolyn Williams-Davidson from Arizona State University. She looked at the processes, pitfalls, trials, tribulations, and critical elements surrounding the mandatory enforcement of a voluntary student uniform policy in an urban elementary school.

Using qualitative data as well as fifteen months of participant observation, she found that how one frames the situation varied greatly between those who are converted proponents of school uniforms and those who are opposed. She poignantly discusses how uniform movements and other social reform movements have always been linked with fears and assumptions in the public sphere.[10] Furthermore, Williams-Davidson argues that such policies highlight larger issues of the struggle between adults and students over change, control, and the meaning of education. Though she found no effects of uniforms that could not be traced to other procedural, curricular, policy, or other changes occurring at the school, her dissertation clearly assesses the reality behind the push for standardized dress in our public schools: micropolitics; irrational fears; normlessness associated with social, cultural, and educational changes; and the meaning of public education.

In the following year at the University of Washington, another fascinating dissertation was completed reminiscent of, albeit not as meticulous as, Williams-Davidson's (1996) work. Murphy's (1997) dissertation again followed an elementary school that had implemented a uniform policy, using a mixed methodology of an in-depth case study and basic descriptive pre-uniform and post-uniform statistics, looking at discipline referrals; academic achievement on standardized tests; and student, parent, and staff perception surveys. Murphy found that standardized test scores did indeed increase after the implementation of the policy; however, she links this basic increase to students being in "a consistent academic program for a second year and good test preparation practices" (Murphy 1997, 67), thus arguing that the increase was not caused by the school uniform policy. Behavioral referrals decreased after the establishment of a school uniform policy, yet Murphy argues that, from her understanding of the case and the other programs implemented at the same time, that the decline in behavioral referrals was more likely due to the fact that the elementary school also began a schoolwide "problem-solving curriculum." She concludes that it is important for a uniform policy to be a part of a larger comprehensive plan using all human, material, and social resources to focus on the academic success of all children by providing:

1. A strong curriculum that meets the needs of all students
2. A looping model, where students spend two years with the same teacher providing more efficient use of time for academic instruction
3. Effective instruction delivered by a staff that works together to maintain high academic and behavioral standards for all children
4. Staff development which provides opportunity for continued education and professional growth
5. A counseling program which coordinates community resources and social services to assist children and families in need
6. An efficient, well-managed, secure facility with rules and procedures that provide the best environment for learning
7. Instructional support which coordinates parent and community involvement
8. A building decision making process which facilitates communication and incorporates input and decision making from those who are impacted by the results of the decision. (Murphy 1997, 101–102)

Her research on this one elementary school, again, though not generalizable to much outside of itself, does provide thick descriptions of the processes involved and the way that researchers need to be thinking about developing models that mirror the complexity of schooling (i.e., including all the relevant control factors).

Yet another small-scale effectiveness study comes in the form of a doctoral dissertation. Gregory (1998), in her "casual comparative study," looked into the effects of school uniform policies on student self-esteem, academic achievement, and attendance utilizing a sample size of two "demographically similar" inner-city schools enrolling 165 and 170 students respectively, one with a uniform policy, one without. Using the Cooper-smith Self-Esteem Inventory for self-esteem (which included four dimensions of self-esteem), Gregory (1998) found that students who attended the school with the uniform policy had higher school-academic esteem than students who attended the school without a uniform policy. No effects were found for the other three dimensions of self-esteem. This effect, however, is extremely weak in magnitude and in correlational analysis (0.15 out of 1.00). Gregory also finds a relationship between uniforms and decreased absences. The effect is quite strong; however, asking students to report their own absences is not a valid indicator of truancy. She also finds significant differences for achievement in math and language arts: uniformed students achieving higher than nonuniformed. The methodology Gregory uses in her dissertation is appropriate for the sample size and the number of measures she is utilizing; however, educators should be extremely cautious of results such as these (ANOVAs). Only multivariate analysis (i.e., regression models) can adequately control for other factors that also contribute to self-esteem, achievement, and attendance. Gregory's research cannot even be used to generalize to the very schools she uses when the necessary controls are not in place. Once one places adequate controls in place, the effect of uniforms may disappear. This problem becomes even clearer in the case of the Long Beach study, as follows.

Stevenson, as reported in his 1999 Texas Southern University dissertation, tested the effectiveness of school uniform policies in twenty-one public middle and seven public high schools in Texas. He looked at the impact of uniform policies on discipline incidents, student attendance, fights, weapons possession incidents, assault/battery incidents, vandalism, number of suspensions, expulsion rates, and school crimes. The population attending these schools was mixed but largely minority (10.6 percent white). No other descriptive statistics were given (nor were any controlled for in the study). Using basic t-tests with no controls to determine whether there were any statistically significant differences, Stevenson found

1. no decrease in school discipline incidents (actually incidents went *up* by about 12 percent and, by conventions with samples this size, that *is* a statistically significant *increase*),
2. no significant decrease in fights,

3. no significant decrease in weapons possession incidents,
4. no differences in assault/battery before and after the uniform policy,
5. no effect of uniforms on decreasing vandalism,
6. no significant decrease in the number of suspensions, and
7. the number of school crimes did not differ significantly between a time when the schools had no uniforms and after uniforms were established.

Two findings were statistically significant, but not substantively and methodologically significant. First, attendance was significantly different after the implementation of uniforms, but the increase was weak: an average of less than a percentage point (0.63). Second, the average number of expulsions went down by almost 2 (1.93, from 8.64 before uniforms, to 6.71 after uniforms), a significant decrease in statistical terms. These two "findings" are seriously questionable for a variety of reasons. First, Stevenson assumed that school characteristics did not change (i.e., he did not control for school characteristics) and that the methods of recording student behavior among sample schools remained constant from time one to time two. Such assumptions cannot be made in effectiveness research; they must be accounted for. Second, the sample was not random, and no other policies or changes taking place within these schools over the period of the study were controlled for. Therefore, the "effects" found on attendance and expulsions are most likely *not* due to the uniform policy.

As a whole, these small-scale effectiveness studies have indeed pushed forward the research as well as our understanding of the processes involved in uniform policy effects. However, overall their results suffer from an endemic lack of rigorous statistical controls and a general oversight of methodological assumptions. These factors, and many described in the review of these studies above, in the end make many of these studies unreliable as empirical indicators of evidence that uniforms are effective as a reform effort. Furthermore, these small-scale effectiveness studies are quite parochial and not useful as generalizable evidence that can be used by other schools struggling with the decision to implement a uniform policy. These studies (especially the case studies) do offer unique insight into the processes and political conflicts touched by uniform policies.

Large-Scale Effectiveness Studies

Attempting to remedy many of the methodological, statistical, and logical flaws in both perception studies and the small-scale effectiveness studies, several researchers (Stanley 1996; Brunsma and Rockquemore 1998; Educational Testing Service 2000) have conducted analyses on the effects of uniforms with much larger samples, more control variables, and greater statistical sophistication. These large-scale effectiveness studies represent the cutting edge of valid empirical research to date; however, these studies also suffer from problems that will need to be remedied in the very near future.

When reviewing the literature on school uniforms, the most often touted study is the data prepared by the Long Beach Unified School District (LBUSD), the first district in the United States to mandate the wearing of school uniforms for *all* of its elementary and middle school students within its jurisdiction. The data have been espoused by many (particularly by Cohn, LBUSD's superintendent, in Cohn 1996 and Cohn and Siegal 1996; see also Caruso 1996), and indeed for some time these were the only "data" available testing the effectiveness of a school uniform policy on many of the educational issues of concern. Though the results had been circulating on the Web for quite some time, Sue Stanley published them in *Education and Urban Society* in 1996.

When my colleague and I began our research on the effectiveness of uniform policies in 1996, we were aware of the LBUSD data and investigated it as well. Stanley's (1996) study was on a combination of perception data as well as district-provided[11] data in several behavioral and disciplinary outcomes (e.g., class disruptions, dress code violations, violence on the playground, suspensions, etc.). Looking across a two-year span (1993–1994 through 1994–1995), the now-classic findings are as follows. Suspensions in elementary schools declined by 28 percent, and middle schools' suspension rates went down an average of 36 percent. Kindergarten through eighth grade *reported* crime rates also showed signs of decrease: Assault and battery decreased by 34 percent, assault with a deadly weapon went down 50 percent, fighting decreased 51 percent, sex offenses were cut by 74 percent, vandalism went down 18 percent, and so on. At the time (and currently) these data were held in high esteem by proponents of school uniform policies.

Advocates used Stanley (1996) to support their anecdotal musings; however, many did not read the study carefully enough. First, Stanley herself clearly states that "it is not clear that these results are entirely attributable to the uniform policy" (1996, 431) and "caution should be used in interpreting such data" (1996, 433). Stanley is absolutely correct in her assertions that in the absence of adequate controls (i.e., other changes occurring in the schools at the same time, added security measures, socioeconomic factors, school climate issues, etc.) such correlational data *do not* support a causal argument. Stanley (1996) does not offer a statistical analysis beyond correlational data; we do not know whether these decreases resulted from the uniform policy, chance, or other changes. Furthermore, many wished to use these findings to generalize to their specific school districts, or worse, their particular schools. In this sense, the LBUSD data and results were not as generalizable as subsequent large-scale effectiveness studies would be. The "Long Beach Study" has been thoroughly criticized elsewhere (Black 1998; Brunsma and Rockquemore 1998; Portner 1998; Posner 1996; White 2000); however, in terms of large-scale effectiveness studies, finally we had over time data points to compare and correlate. Stanley's (1996) research pushed the boundaries of what had previously been done, raised new questions, and forced researchers to focus their energies away from correlational analyses and into more rigorous multivariate predictive models to assess the effectiveness of school uniform policies.

In an attempt to remedy the situation presented by the anecdotal debate on school uniforms as well as to increase the methodological rigor in the study of school uniforms' effectiveness, Brunsma and Rockquemore (1998) used a nationally representative sample of tenth graders to test the claims of advocates, using multivariate regression models. At the time, the National Educational Longitudinal Study of 1988 (NELS:88) was the only nationally representative secondary data set that collected information on school policies, school structure, and climate, as well as student achievement, behavior, and attendance. The proponents' claims formed our hypotheses, and we set out to empirically test whether students who wear uniforms have statistically different achievement, behavior, drug use, and school attendance than students who do not wear uniforms. We also looked into whether uniforms affect the very student climate processes that *do* affect the dependent variables of interest. These processes were their peer group's attitudes toward school, their own personal academic preparedness, and their own pro-school attitudes. In what still is considered the most rigorous empirical study of school uniform effects—nationally representative and therefore much more generalizable, controlling for a variety of personal, social, economic, and educational processes that are known to affect the outcomes of interest—Brunsma and Rockquemore (1998) found *no effects* of uniforms on absenteeism, behavioral problems (fights, suspensions, etc.), or substance use on campus. We also found no effects of uniform policies on the intervening processes of pro-school attitudes, academic preparedness, and peer attitudes toward school. In addition, we found a significant, albeit weak, *negative* effect of uniforms on academic achievement. In a much-cited line from our study, which also mirrors Stanley's (1996) concerns with her data suffering from the "Hawthorne Effect," we stated that, "Instituting a uniform policy can be viewed as analogous to cleaning and brightly painting a deteriorating building in that on the one hand it grabs our immediate attention: on the other hand, it is only a coat of paint" (Brunsma and Rockquemore 1998, 60). We concluded by pushing for more serious looks at not only school reform efforts but also *social* and *cultural* reform efforts whose subjects involve the very foundations of the problems school officials, parents, and teachers are concerned about.

In 2000, the Educational Testing Service published a study on the Web that looked at the numerous proposals, strategies, and policies aimed at dealing with the problems of disorder and violence in our public schools. Using the same data that Brunsma and Rockquemore used (NELS:88, although ETS used the entire longitudinal panel from eighth through twelfth grade), the Educational Testing Service (2000) analyzed the effectiveness of several approaches to dealing with disorder, including zero-tolerance policies, smaller schools, heightened security at the school, violence prevention programs, and school uniform policies. Their espoused research question was "to measure the relationships among school disciplinary policies, student delinquency, and academic achievement" (2000, 3). They state the limitations of the data (i.e., that other prevention measures are not available in NELS:88), the fact that dropouts between eighth and twelfth grades are not included in the analysis, and that more appropriate multilevel regression techniques are necessary to precisely quantify the effects. The main finding of concern here is that schools that required school uniforms did not differ significantly on any of their dependent measures of delinquency (drug use, nonserious infractions, and serious infractions) than schools that did not require uniforms. These results replicated Brunsma and Rockquemore's (1998) findings. In regard to the assertion that school order affects academic achievement, uniform policies had no impact on academic achievement. Instead, two factors reduce school violence: 1) enforcement of severe punishments for violations, and 2) limiting student movements during the school day through a set of security procedures.

These two studies (Brunsma and Rockquemore 1998; Educational Testing Service 2000) have taken research on school uniforms to new heights. The introduction of multivariate statistical analyses, the strength of statistical controls, the longitudinal approach to change, and the complexity of modeling complex processes with more representative, random data foreshadow the kind of work that will need to be done to increase our understanding of school uniform policies and their effects on educational outcomes. These studies have found *no* evidence that uniforms affect student achievement, behavioral incidents, violent offenses, attendance, or substance use. It will be the work of the next generation of researchers to see if these results can be replicated with even more rigorous methods.

WHERE DO WE GO FROM HERE?

This review of anecdotal writings, perception studies, and small- and large-scale effectiveness studies lays out the pieces of the complex puzzle of school uniform policies and their impact on schooling. Putting these pieces together reveals that the puzzle is *far* from complete. What has emerged from this review of the literature is a picture far different from that presented to countless school boards, educators, parents, students, and community members in the anecdotal literature. Even if one discounts the serious validity problems of perception studies and the inadequate (or nonexistent) controls and ungeneralizability of the small-scale effectiveness studies, *School uniforms do not appear to have any effect on the variables of concern established by the anecdotally based school uniform movement*. However, it is also clear from this review that there is a great deal more research to be conducted to uphold this statement or alter it. I want to close by discussing a variety of issues that the next wave of research must take into consideration as well as methodological and statistical strategies to be considered by those conducting the studies.

First, the methodological and statistical advice given by King (1998) and Paliokas, Futrell, and Rist (1996) must be heeded. To reiterate the most important aspects of their suggestions and add some new ones, future research *must*

1. collect random samples that have a longer longitudinal span of data;
2. look carefully and rigorously at trend lines to assess whether changes are real or predictable;
3. include crucial student-level, school-level, and community-level controls for factors that are also associated with the outcomes of interest, to more effectively evaluate and isolate an effect of school uniform policies (if any);
4. use valid and reliable measures of the variables of interest and ensure that data have not been tampered with, altered, or groomed by those holding an interest in the outcomes; and
5. begin using more sophisticated statistical procedures, ones that offer statistical control and can model multiple levels of data, such as the Hierarchical Linear Modeling or LISREL, to allow researchers to make causal statements regarding how uniform policies (a school-level factor) affect student-level educational and behavioral processes.

This book addresses many of these methodological concerns.

3

THE LAW AND STUDENT CLOTHING

*Todd A. DeMitchell, Professor of Education, Law and Policy,
University of New Hampshire*

How small, of all that human hearts endure, that part which laws and kings can cure.

—Oliver Goldsmith, *The Traveller*

Deciding what to wear to school would seem like an innocuous, rather benign question with which to start the day. But for some school children that decision is often serious and linked to their nascent development of self and place. For many others, the question revolves around what clean clothes are handy. "When left to decide what clothes to wear to school, students do not always make choices that adult agree with" (Lumsden and Miller 2002, 1). The issue of what to wear often goes beyond the clothes closet to the courts. As schools struggle with problems of discipline and security, many have turned to the formulation of dress codes and most recently to mandatory school uniforms as a possible solution. For some, dress codes "have been justified as a means of creating a more disciplined learning environment" (Killen 2000, 461). However, when questioned about enforcing a school uniform policy, an elementary school principal responded, "My job is not to dress the public" (Goldstein 2003, 6).

What students wear has become a significant issue in the nation's public schools.[1] Former President Clinton and former Secretary of Education

Richard Riley supported the role of uniforms in reducing violence and se-
curing an environment for students and adults.[2] In some quarters, school
uniforms are viewed as the reform du jour.

In a time of concern for civility in society, respect for legitimate authority, and security for schoolchildren, the debate about dress codes
and uniforms has been sharp. Do we as a society value the rights of students to wear clothes of their choice to school even if they are considered vulgar and offensive and filled with sexual innuendo, or are issues
of clothing and appearance at school too trivial to lay claim to the limited resources of the courts? In other words, do students possess a constitutional right of freedom of expression to wear clothes of their choice
to school? A corollary question is what constitutes expression. The
morning question of what to wear to school has moved from being
merely vexing and benign to being draped in constitutional considerations. This chapter explores the intersection of free speech and restrictions on student choice of what to wear to school.

FREEDOM OF SPEECH

Freedom of speech in our society is arguably the touchstone of our con-
ception of individual liberty. Justice Cardozo characterized free speech
as "the matrix, the indispensable condition of nearly every other form of
freedom" (*Palko v. Connecticut* 1937, 327). The right to free speech is
extensive and robust. Supporting this view, Justice Holmes, in a dissenting opinion, observed that, "it is . . . not free thought for those who agree
with us, but freedom for the thought that we hate" (*United States v.
Schwimmer* 1929, 654–655). Another example of the breadth and depth
of the First Amendment right to free speech is found in a Supreme
Court case involving race-baiting speech. The High Court wrote that,
"[a] function of free speech under our system of government is to invite
dispute. It may indeed best serve its high purpose when it induces a
condition of unrest, creates dissatisfaction with conditions as they are, or
even stirs people to anger" (*Terminello v. Chicago* 1940, 4).

Free speech is indeed a right that is vigorously protected in our society. It is often used as the example of what it means to be an American
and to be free. But is the right to free speech robust in all places and as

vigorously defended by the courts for all groups of individuals? Clearly there are restrictions on speech; the right is not absolute. One place where the right to free speech is not full-bodied is in the public school. Even though students do not shed their constitutional rights at the schoolhouse gate, they do not receive the same measure of protection for their free speech inside the school as adults do outside the schoolhouse gate.

The School As a Special Place

The various courts have carved out a special niche in our society for the public schools. Actions that a student may take outside the schoolhouse gate often may not be taken inside that gate. "Free expression rights [of students] may be limited by policies that are reasonably designed to take into account the special circumstances of the educational environment" (McCarthy, Cambron-McCabe, and Thomas 1998, 114–115). The public school setting demands a special approach to free speech issues. The courts have curtailed student First Amendment rights by giving deference to school administrators' judgment as to what speech is appropriate in the context of the public school (*Denno v. School Board of Volusia County* 1997). Historically, the courts have been loath to intervene in the decisions of school boards unless it can be shown that the board acted in an arbitrary, capricious, or unreasonable manner.

Although students are considered "persons" and are therefore entitled to constitutional protections, their protected rights of speech and expression are limited. Chief Justice Burger asserted "that the constitutional rights of students in public school are not automatically coextensive with the rights of adults in other settings" (*Bethel School District No. 403 v. Fraser* 1986, 3164). Forms of expression allowed by adults may be prohibited to children in a public school. Public school children enjoy some measure of freedom of speech within the schoolhouse gate, but that freedom "is balanced against the need to foster an educational atmosphere free from undue disruptions to appropriate discipline" (*Bivens v. Albuquerque Public Schools* 1995, 559).

Student constitutional rights to free speech are not unfettered. "The very nature of public education requires limitations on one's personal liberty in order for learning process to proceed" (*Richards v. Thurston* 1970, 1285). The right to free speech must be balanced against the need of the state to provide an efficient system of public education. Public schools inculcate fundamental values necessary to the maintenance of a democratic society. These fundamental values include "habits and manners of civility." Although toleration of divergent and unpopular views is important to civility, sensibility to others, including fellow students, is also important. The freedom to advocate unpopular and controversial views in schools and classrooms, according to Chief Justice Burger:

> must be balanced against the society's countervailing interest in teaching students the boundaries of socially appropriate behavior. Even the most heated political discourse in a democratic society requires consideration for the personal sensibilities of the other participants and audiences. (*Bethel School District N. 403 v. Fraser* 1986, 3164)

Students have the right to freedom of expression at school, but that right is balanced by a compelling interest to have public schools run in an efficient manner while teaching and preserving fundamental values.[3] "Students retain the protections of the First Amendment, but the shape of these rights in the public school setting may not always mirror the contours of constitutional protections afforded in other contexts" (*Sypniewski v. Warren Hills Regional Board of Education* 2002, 253). The public school is a special place.

Student Speech and the Supreme Court

It is noteworthy that no student dress code case has been argued before the United States Supreme Court. However, the Court has provided some guidance with respect to the parameters of student freedom of expression at school. Discussions of dress codes and free expression typically begin with one if not all three of the Supreme Court cases discussed in the following paragraphs.

It has been almost forty years since the Supreme Court extended the protection of the Constitution to students inside the schoolhouse gate. In 1965, the Tinkers were suspended by Des Moines School officials for wearing black armbands to school in protest of the Vietnam War. They brought suit in federal court arguing that the First Amendment gave them the right to express themselves in this quiet and dignified way.

The Supreme Court, in *Tinker v. Des Moines Independent School District*, established that students do not "shed their constitutional rights to freedom of speech or expression at the schoolhouse gate," . . . although school officials possess "the comprehensive authority . . . to prescribe and control conduct in the schools" (1969, 736). The Court found that school authorities could not justify prohibition of student expression unless the conduct would "materially and substantially interfere with the requirements of appropriate discipline in the operation of the school" or "collid[e] with the rights of others"(740). Using this line of reasoning, a restriction on student clothing that arguably had some expression must be supported by a showing, or reasonable forecast, of a material substantial disruption.

However, *Tinker* may reveal less support for an expansive view of a student's right to wear any clothing of his or her choice. First, the Supreme Court acknowledged the requirements of appropriate discipline in the operation of schools. Furthermore, and more important for this discussion, the Court wrote:

> The problem posed by the present case does not relate to regulation of the length of skirts or the type of clothing to hairstyle or deportment. [Internal citations omitted] It does not concern aggressive, disruptive action or even group demonstrations. Our problem involves direct, primary First Amendment rights akin to "pure speech." (1969, 737)

Arguably, *Tinker*'s material and substantial disruption standard does not apply to dress codes. In fact, the Court may have viewed a student's choice of clothing for school as being devoid of constitutional protection. The High Court differentiated dress from primary First Amendment rights.

There is a second argument that may limit the impact of *Tinker* on dress codes. The second prong of the *Tinker* Test is collision with the rights of others. If a student's clothing is intimidating, threatening, or harassing, does it collide with the rights of other students to be free from such conduct? If students have the right to attend school in a safe environment conducive to learning and free from harassment, can T-shirts with sexual innuendo on them create an environment that collides with that student's right to a hostility-free environment in which to learn?[4] The second prong of *Tinker* may add support to a dress code that seeks to protect the school environment from unwelcome, unwanted, and uncivil expression.[5]

The Supreme Court carefully chose the wording of the second prong. It is not found in typical nonschool First Amendment rights, which characterize the freedom of speech as the touchstone of individual liberty. The Supreme Court, while acknowledging that students possess constitutional rights, did not imbue them with the robustness found outside the schoolhouse gate. The Court views the public school as a special place. The role of the state as educator is different from the role of the state as sovereign. A second student rights case underscores this point.

The Supreme Court, seventeen years after *Tinker*, decided a case that would dramatically affect students' rights of expression at school. In *Bethel School District No. 403 v. Fraser* (1986), the Court ruled that school officials could sanction a high school student for using lewd, vulgar, or offensive sexual metaphors during a political speech at a school assembly. The Supreme Court found that public education "inculcate[s] the habits and manners of civility" (3164). This fundamental value of civility must take into account the "sensibilities of others" (3164). "This statement, coupled with *Tinker*'s collision with the rights of others, tends to support dress codes aimed at supporting a civil school environment" (DeMitchell 2001, 7). Arguing that our nation's leaders in the legislative halls have rules against offensive expression in a venue that often requires vigorous political debate, could the Supreme Court expect no less degree of civility in our schools? "Can it be that what is proscribed in the halls of Congress is beyond the reach of school officials to regulate?" (*Bethel* 1986, 3164). The Court held that "[t]he determination of what manner of speech in the classroom or in a school assembly is inappropriate properly rests with the school board" (3165). Further, the Court affirmed that the constitutional rights of students in public schools are not automatically coextensive with the rights of adults in other settings. Although adults have wide freedom in matters of public discourse, it does not follow that "the same latitude must be permitted to children in public school" (*New Jersey v. T.L.O.* 1985, 742). As cogently expressed by Judge Newman, "the First Amendment gives a high school student the classroom right to wear Tinker's armband, but not Cohen's jacket."[6]

A third important Supreme Court decision is *Hazelwood School District v. Kuhlmeier* (1988). This case has implications for mandatory school uniform policies. *Hazelwood* was a case involving student constitutional rights. In this case, student contributors to a school newspaper published as part of a journalism class contested the principal's deletion of material from the newspaper prior to its publication. The Supreme Court started with a free speech forum analysis. If the general public had not opened the school for indiscriminate use, then the school was not considered a public forum. If the school is not a public forum then "school officials may impose reasonable restrictions on the speech of students, teachers, and other members of the school community" (1988, 267). After determining that the student newspaper was not a public forum, the Court focused on whether the students' expression was school sponsored. The *Hazelwood* court found that the school had authority over such school-sponsored publications as theatrical productions and "other expressive activities that students, parents, and other members of the public might reasonably perceive to bear the imprimatur of the school" (271). The Supreme Court held that educators do not offend the Constitution by exercising editorial control over school-sponsored expression "so long as their actions are reasonably related to legitimate pedagogical concerns" (273).

Deference to school authorities was given full weight when the Court reasoned, "We thus recognized that the determination of what manner of speech in the classroom or in school assembly is appropriate properly rests with the school board rather than the federal courts" (1988, 267). Nevertheless, the Court has never retreated from the core principle that public school students enjoy some First Amendment rights to engage in free speech while at school. The standard that is used to assess whether the student's speech is protected varies according to the facts of the situation. Typically, *Tinker* reviews speech that is lewd, vulgar, or offensive using; *Bethel*, school-sponsored speech; and *Hazelwood* all other speech.[7] Students have the right to freedom of speech in school, but that right must be balanced and is not absolute, nor is it expansive.

LITIGATION OVER DRESS CODES

Students have sued over the constitutional right to wear distinctive clothing, clothing which, in the students' view, conveys some constitutionally protected expression. For example, only a year after *Tinker*, a New Hampshire sixth grader persuaded a federal court that he had a liberty interest in wearing blue jeans to school even though they violated the school's dress code (*Bannister v. Paradis* 1970). Although the judge admitted that the constitutional interest was minor, he ruled that the school district had not justified its infringement on a child's right to choose his own pants to wear to school. In a contrary decision, a federal district court in North Carolina upheld a principal's prohibition against wearing blue jeans to a graduation ceremony, finding no violation of the student's constitutional rights (*Fowler v. Williamson* 1978).

In 1987, students sued an Ohio school district for refusing to allow them to attend a prom dressed as a person of the opposite sex. A federal court found no First Amendment violation (*Harper v. Edgewood Board of Education* 1987). In the court's view, schools have the authority to enforce dress regulations that teach community values and promote school discipline. Using the community standards argument, a state appellate court upheld a school policy banning the wearing of earrings by elementary school boys. The court held that the policy was reasonably related to the desire of the community to have its schools reflect its values and instill discipline (*Hines v. Caston School Corporation* 1995).

Also in 1987, an Illinois student challenged a school rule, invoked to curtail gang activity, against males wearing earrings (*Olesen v. Board of Education of School District No. 228*, 1987). Like the Ohio crossdressers, the plaintiff lost this case. The court found that the school's reason, control of gang-related activities, justified any constitutional infringement.

In 1992, a federal district court in Virginia heard a case wherein a twelve-year-old brought suit against her school district. The student had been suspended for one day for refusing to turn her T-shirt inside out. The T-shirt carried the words "Drugs Suck." The court gave deference to the school board, asserting that the word "suck" could reasonably be considered offensive and therefore school officials acted properly in prohibiting and disciplining the student (*Broussard v. School Board of City of Norfolk* 1992). Similarly, a student's T-shirt with a caricature of three school administrators drinking alcohol and acting drunk was considered by the court to be clearly offensive (*Gano v. School District*

1987). Consequently, the school's decision to take disciplinary action was upheld and not considered violative of free speech rights.

A Dress Code That Prevailed: Sagging Pants

In the fall of 1993, Richard Bivens was a ninth grader at Del Norte High School in Albuquerque, New Mexico. During the first week of the semester the assistant principal warned Bivens that he could not wear sagging pants to school. The prohibition against wearing sagging pants was included in the dress code in response to a gang problem.

Despite the warnings, Bivens persisted in wearing sagging pants to school. He received numerous verbal warnings and was subjected to a few short-term suspensions ranging from one to three days. In late October 1993, he was given a long-term suspension. The suspension was for the remainder of the semester. Bivens, through his mother, who at one point acted as the attorney (pro se status), brought suit alleging a violation of his First Amendment right to free speech, expression, and association and his Fourteenth Amendment right to procedural due process (*Bivens v. Albuquerque Public Schools* 1995).

The court analyzed the contours of free speech and applied those principles to Biven's sagging pants. First, Judge Campos, stated that the freedom of speech, while not absolute, "is a paramount guarantee" (1995 559). Therefore, governmental constraints on the "communication of ideas must be measured against substantial and compelling societal goals such as safety, decency, individual rights of other citizens, and the smooth functioning of government" if government's restrictions on free speech are to prevail (559). While public school students enjoy some degree of freedom of speech within the schoolhouse gates, it is balanced against the need to foster an educational atmosphere free from undue disruptions.

If speech is protected but balanced against countervailing governmental claims of legitimacy, what constitutes speech is a threshold question. Judge Campos noted, "[n]ot every defiant act by a high school student is constitutionally protected speech" (1995 560). Not all conduct is labeled speech, thus bringing the act under the panoply of constitutional protection. The court in *Bivens*, citing *Tinker*, stated that wearing of a particular type or style of clothing is not seen as expressive conduct (560). The court noted that a two-part test was used to assess whether nonverbal conduct is "expressive conduct" and therefore speech protected under the First Amendment. The test was used by the United States Supreme Court in *Texas v. Johnson* (1989), the American flag burning case. According to the test, first, the actor must intend to convey a particularized message, and, second, there must be a great likelihood that the message would be understood by those who observe the conduct (*Bivens* 1995, 560).

Bivens asserted that his wearing of sagging pants to school was intended to identify his link with his black identity, black culture, and the styles of black urban youth. He argued that since sagging pants is part of a style known as "hip hop," whose roots are African American, it represents a fashion statement. If a style can be proven to have had its origins within a particular racial or ethnic group, it becomes part of that group's identity. "Such intentional identification clearly must involve freedom of expression" (*Bivens* 1995, 561). Granting that Bivens met the first prong of intentionality, the court was unpersuaded that he could prevail on the second prong, understanding the message of the expressive conduct.

The defendant school district presented evidence that Bivens' message via his sagging pants was "by no means apparent to those who view it" (*Bivens* 1995, 561). Further, the defendant argued that sagging is not necessarily identified with only one racial or cultural group and was a more generalized fashion trend throughout the United States. If sagging is just a fashion trend of adolescents, then it would be devoid of a particularized message that would have likelihood to be understood by others seeing the sagging pants.

The federal district court concluded that the plaintiff Bivens failed to meet his burden of demonstrating that sagging pants is constitutionally protected speech. There was no showing that Bivens's intentional expression by wearing sagging pants was understood. Sagging pants is understood by some to mean gang association, yet Bivens stated that he was not a member of a gang. Others may view Bivens's sagging pants as a statement of black identity, as Bivens said he intended. But others may merely see a fashion statement. With legitimate and competing views on what, if any, expression sagging pants conveys, it was difficult for Bivens' to demonstrate that there was a particularized message in the sagging pants.

Redneck T-Shirts: No Disruption

The Warren Hills School District experienced racial unrest starting in 1999 when a white student dressed for the Warren Hills Regional High School Halloween "costume day" by wearing overall jeans and a straw hat and appeared in black face with a noose around his neck. Following the incident, several students started wearing articles of clothing bearing the Confederate flag. A gang-like group known as the Hicks made their presence known on campus by being identified with the wearing and showing of the Confederate flag. Showing and wearing the Confederate flag at school precipitated a number of disruptive responses.

The school board researched racial harassment policies and implemented a policy on March 13, 2001. On March 22, 2001, Thomas Sypniewski, a student at the school, wore a Jeff Foxworthy T-shirt stating the, "Top 10 reasons you might be a Redneck Sports Fan."[8] He had worn the T-shirt before the adoption of the racial harassment policy without incident. The assistant principal gave Sypniewski the choice of turning the T-shirt inside out or being suspended. Sypniewski chose the suspension. The suspension was upheld by the school board on the basis of the dress code, which predated the racial harassment policy. The dress code prohibited mentioning alcohol (Bud Bowl) and sexual innuendo (Hooters restaurant).[9] The suspension of Thomas was upheld even though Brian, Thomas's brother, wore his Jeff Foxworthy T-shirt to the middle school and the vice principal and superintendent found that the T-shirt was neither offensive nor in violation of the dress code. The board stated that in hindsight the same action should have been taken against Brian. Thomas Sypniewski brought suit soon after his graduation (*Sypniewski v. Warren Hills Board of Education* 2002).

The plaintiffs sought a preliminary injunction against the racial harassment policy and the dress code as unconstitutional restrictions on students' free speech. They also sought damages for the suspension and defamation. The district court denied the Sypniewskis' motion for a preliminary injunction against the racial harassment policy but found that the challenged portion of the dress code might not satisfy constitutional standards and should accordingly be enjoined during the pendency of the litigation (*Sypniewski* 2002, 252). The plaintiffs appealed the court's decision not to order a preliminary injunction against enforcement of the racial harassment policy.

While racial harassment policies are beyond the scope of this chapter, the appellate court's discussion of the decision banning the Foxworthy T-shirt is instructive to our understanding of the intersection of dress and free speech. The school district did not contend that the Foxworthy shirt contained indecent language (the *Bethel* standard); nor was the shirt school sponsored (the *Hazelwood* standard); thus the wearing of the shirt was subject to the *Tinker* test of material and substantial disruption (2002, 254).

The Third Circuit discussed the disruption caused by wearing the Confederate flag and then sought to position the Foxworthy T-shirt within the context of tension that existed. The court found substantial evidence of disruption related to the Confederate flag. It acknowledged that the school could act if it is "'well-founded' where there have similar 'past incidents arising out of similar speech'" (255). The school district contended that the Foxworthy shirt was offensive—and consequently disruptive—because of the context of racial troubles in the schools. Furthermore, it maintained that the term *redneck* was directly associated with the Hicks and ongoing harassment. The court found little to no evidence that the Hicks were also known as "the rednecks" or that the word redneck had been used to harass, intimidate, or offend (256.) "Where a school seeks to suppress a term merely related to an expression that has been proven to be disruptive, it must do more than simply point to a general association" (257). This burden could not be sustained by the school district.

Thus, the wearing of a T-shirt that may have only a loose association with a known disruptive communication cannot be bootstrapped to a reasonable forecast of material and substantial disruption. Under the *Tinker* test, a well-founded inference of disruption was not established.

UNIFORMS AND THE CONSTITUTION

Uniforms in Arizona

On September 6, 1995, the Phoenix Preparatory Academy, a public inner-city middle school, instituted a mandatory uniform policy. On the day of implementation two students wore clothing that did not comply with the policy. One student wore a T-shirt with a U.S. flag and logos stating "I support my country" and "America" on it. The other student wore a T-shirt with a picture of Jesus Christ and the Bible with the words "The School of Higher Learning" on it. The parents of the students informed the school authorities that day that their children would never comply with the mandatory uniform policy and insisted that they were entitled to opt out of the policy. The school district responded by transferring the students out of the Academy school to another school, which did not have a mandatory common uniform policy. The following day, the parents and the students marched onto the Academy's campus, entered the classrooms without permission, and distributed literature to other students disparaging the dress code. Both sides soon brought suit, seeking declaratory and injunctive relief (*Phoenix Elementary School District No. 1 v. Green* 1997).

Consolidating the cases, the trial court started with the forum analysis of *Cornelius v. NAACP Legal Defense and Education Fund* (1985), a non-education case decided by the United States Supreme Court. *Cornelius* distinguishes between a public and a nonpublic forum. A traditional public forum is a place or means of communication "which by long tradition or by government fiat [has] been devoted to assembly and debate" (798). Street corners and public parks are typically perceived as public fora. Government's restriction of speech in a public forum must further a compelling state interest. Under *Cornelius*, government can restrict access to the forum "as long as the restrictions are reasonable and [are] not an effort to suppress expression merely because public officials oppose the speaker's view" (798).

The trial court's application of *Cornelius* found that the dress code regulated the medium of the message, choice of clothing, not the content of the message. It also found that the Academy was not a public forum and that the policy requiring a uniform was reasonable and an appropriate matter of concern for the school board. Finally, the trial court, balancing the interests of the entire student body, found those interests outweighing the plaintiffs' freedom of expression rights.

The court of appeals disagreed with the appellants as to whether the more stringent standard of *Tinker* was applicable and agreed with the trial court that the *Cornelius* analysis was appropriate. The appeals court further agreed with the trial court that under the *Cornelius* standard the

mandatory uniform policy's content-neutral restrictions do not contra-
vene the First Amendment. The appellate court affirmed that a school
is generally not considered a public forum. To ascertain the reasonableness of the regulation the court turned to *Hazelwood,* observing that
school officials have great latitude to regulate activities in a manner reasonably related to legitimate pedagogical concerns (*Phoenix* 1997, 839,
quoting *Hazelwood* 1988, 273). The court found the following evidence
that the mandatory uniform regulation bears a reasonable relation to the
pedagogical purpose of the school:

1. Promotes a more effective climate for learning
2. Creates opportunities for self-expression
3. Increases campus safety and security
4. Fosters school unity and pride
5. Eliminates "label competition"
6. Ensures modest dress
7. Simplifies dressing
8. Minimizes costs to parents (*Phoenix* 1997, 839)

Last of all, the court of appeals turned to the *Cornelius* analysis, which
involves consideration of whether there are alternative avenues of expression. The court noted that the dress code provided students with such alternative methods of expression as jewelry, buttons, nonuniform days, and
petitions. The court concluded that the school district's content-neutral
mandatory uniform policy "constitutionally regulates the Students' First
Amendment speech in the nonpublic forum of their school. It regulates a
method, not a message, and is reasonable in view of the pedagogical mission of the Academy" (*Phoenix* 1997, 840).

This case of first impression regarding mandatory school uniforms is
notable for what it said *and* for what it did not say. First, the court of appeals did not use a *Tinker* analysis of student speech that happens to occur at school. The focus was less on the speech of the student than on
the restrictive power of the school. The court did not explore the contours of whether the selection of clothing may meet the threshold of
speech. It may be inferred from the use of *Cornelius* that student clothing has some protected communicative properties, but the extent and
the margins of that speech are not charted. It may be that the constitu-

tional issues typically raised about dress codes are sidestepped by mandatory uniform policies because a uniform policy is content neutral. According to the decision in *Phoenix Elementary v. Green*, whether the student's clothing is speech is immaterial because the forum is content neutral.

A second issue involves the use of *Hazelwood*. The court of appeals used the legitimate pedagogical test to determine reasonableness under *Cornelius*. The court also noted that the students have alternative methods of expression, including wearing buttons. The United States Supreme Court in *Rosenberger v. Rector & Visitors of University of Virginia* (1995) made clear that *Hazelwood*'s legitimate pedagogical concern governs only when a student's school-sponsored speech could reasonably be viewed as speech of the school itself. If the mandatory school uniform becomes identified with a particular school, would anything worn on the uniform be associated with the school? In other words, would the button's message carry the imprimatur of the school, thus possibly embroiling the school in speech it may choose not to support? The alternative is that the school could disassociate itself from the speech, as per *Hazelwood*, by compelling the student to remove the button. Would this act, then, reduce the alternative methods of expression available to students, causing the school to run afoul of *Cornelius*?

Third, the decision in *Phoenix Elementary School v. Green* is conspicuous for its lack of a mandatory opt-out provision. Some have argued that an opt-out provision is necessary for a mandatory uniform policy to stand on constitutionally firm ground.[10] Judge Starr, writing for the court, argued that this lack of a need for an opt-out provision would help to overcome a major hurdle of instituting a uniform policy in high schools.

Uniforms in Louisiana

In 1997, the Louisiana Legislature amended its law to allow parish school boards the discretion to implement mandatory uniforms, provided the school board gives the students' parents written notice explaining the uniform requirements. In the 1998–1999 school year, the Bossier Parish School Board required sixteen of its schools to adopt mandatory uniforms as a pilot study to determine the effect of the uniforms on the learning

environment. After receiving favorable results, the school board implemented a mandatory school uniform policy for all of its schools beginning
in the 1999–2000 school year. The mandatory uniform was similar to the
one in Arizona and consisted of a choice of two colors of polo or oxford
shirts and navy or khaki pants.

Several parents filed suit in federal court seeking an injunction
against the enforcement of the uniform policy. The parents claimed that
the uniform policy violated their children's First Amendment rights to
free speech, failed to account for religious preferences, and denied their
children's liberty interest to wear clothing of their choice.

The parents and the school board both filed for summary judgment.
The school board offered statistics showing the reduction in disciplinary
actions and a rise in test scores after the implementation of the uniform
policy. The district court entered a summary judgment for the school
district, and the parents' appeal followed.

In *Canady v. Bossier Parish School District* (2001), the parents put
forward a two-pronged appeal. First, they argued that the trial court
erred by concluding that the enforcement of the school uniform policy
did not violate their children's constitutional rights. Second, they asserted that the trial court abused its discretion by denying them additional time to conduct discovery.

The appellate court started from the proposition that before reviewing the specifics of the uniform policy it must first be determined
whether a person's choice of attire qualifies as speech protected by the
First Amendment. For its analysis, the court cited *Texas v. Johnson*
(1989), used in *Bivens* (1995).

The court of appeals noted that the lower court relied on *Karr
v. Schmidt* (1972) and concluded that choice of clothing is a matter of
taste or style and is not afforded First Amendment protection.[11] While
Karr focused on hair length and communicative content, the district
court equated hair length and clothing as essentially the same for purposes of constitutional protection. The appellate court disagreed. It
found that a "person's choice of clothing may be predicated solely on
considerations of style and comfort, an individual's choice of attire also
may be endowed with sufficient levels of intentional expression to elicit
First Amendment shelter" (*Canady* 2001, 440). Conduct coupled with
communicative intent raises First Amendment concerns, the court

opined. "However, the First Amendment does not safeguard a limitless variety of behavior" (2001, 440).

In spite of the statement above, the court took an expansive view, asserting that a person's choice of clothing is infused with intentional expression on many levels. Words printed on clothing qualify as pure speech and are protected under the First Amendment (2001, 441). Clothing may symbolize ethnic heritage or religious beliefs. Citing *Tinker*'s armband as authority, the court argued that color patterns or styles may be speech if worn with intent to express a particular message. "The choice to wear clothing as a symbol of an opinion or cause is undoubtedly protected under the First Amendment if the message is likely to be understood by those intended to view it" (2001, 441).

Further, the court asserted that students often choose their attire with intent to signify the social group to which they belong and their attitude toward society in general and the school environment in particular. The audience for the message need not be adults, who may hold the message as of little value. The message, "has a considerable affect, whether positive or negative, on a young person's social development" (2001, 441). The court concluded that expression of one's identity and group affiliation through choice of clothing may meet the threshold for protected speech. Accordingly, the court of appeals disagreed with the district court's "blanket assertion that, like the length of a male student's hair, clothing does not contain sufficient communicative intent" (2001, 441).

Lest it appear that the court of appeals imbued any clothing choice by a public school student with First Amendment protection, the court offered several cautions regarding overreaching its analysis. First, in a footnote the court stated that "[w]e do not conclude that every choice of clothing expresses a particularized message."[12] Second, even if the forms of expressive conduct are protected speech, that protection is not absolute, "especially in the public school setting." The public school was carved out as a niche occupying a special place in First Amendment protection. Reducing First Amendment protections for students and increasing the autonomy of school officials, the court wrote that educators have an essential role in regulating school affairs and establishing appropriate standards of conduct. Citing the Supreme Court in *Hazelwood*, the Fifth Circuit wrote, "School boards, not federal courts, have the authority to decide what constitutes appropriate behavior and dress in public schools" (*Canady* 2001, 441).

The court in *Canady* found that the facts of the case do not readily conform to any of the three categories addressed by the Supreme Court: *Tinker*, *Bethel*, and *Hazelwood*. The Bossier Parish School Board's mandatory uniform policy is viewpoint-neutral on its face and as applied. In *Tinker*, the school regulation targeted the viewpoint of the antiwar movement. Unlike the *Bethel* case, students were not punished for lewd, obscene, or patently offensive words or pictures. Finally, a student's choice to wear certain apparel to school is neither a school-sponsored activity nor related to the school curriculum (*Hazelwood*).

Rejecting the three major student free speech Supreme Court cases, the Fifth Circuit was left with the need to fashion an appropriate test. The court argued that "because (1) choice of clothing is personal expression that happens to occur on the school premises and (2) the School Board's uniform policy is unrelated to any viewpoint, a level of scrutiny should apply that is higher than the standard in *Hazelwood*, but less stringent than the official's burden in *Tinker*" (*Canady* 2001,443). The court adopted the test used in *United States v. O'Brien* (1968).

Under the *O'Brien* analysis, the mandatory uniform policy will pass constitutional scrutiny if it furthers an important or substantial government interest, if the interest is unrelated to the suppression of student expression, and if the incidental restrictions on First Amendment activities are no more than is necessary to facilitate that interest.

First, improving the educational process is undoubtedly an important governmental interest furthered by the uniform policy. The court cited school board statistics showing that one year after implementing the school uniform policy in several schools, "discipline problems drastically decreased and overall test scores improved" (*Canady* 2001, 443). Second, the court asserted that the purpose behind the school uniform policy, reducing discipline problems and increasing test scores, is unrelated to the suppression of student speech. Students, the court noted, although restricted from wearing clothing of their choice at school, are free to wear what they want after school. Third, students are also free to "express their views through other mediums during the school day" (443). The Fifth Circuit Court of Appeals did not state what those media might be. In a two-paragraph application of the *O'Brien* test, the court affirmed the district court's order granting summary judgment in favor of the Bossier Parish School Board.

In a similar case, *Long v. Board of Education of Jefferson County* (2000), involving a restrictive dress code instead of a uniform policy, a federal district court, utilizing the *O'Brien* test, found the dress regulation to be on constitutionally firm ground. In an apparent departure from *Tinker*, the court stated that it is "unnecessary to require the School to show that the Dress Code was necessary to stop an actual disruption" (627). As with *Canady*, the *Long* court distinguished the application of *Tinker*, *Bethel*, and *Hazelwood* and opted for the "less stringent" standard of *O'Brien*. The court concluded that the dress code was reasonable and therefore did not violate the plaintiffs' First Amendment rights.

Uniforms in Texas

The Forney Independent School District, acting under the Texas Education Code, passed a mandatory school uniform policy in 1999. Prior to the implementation of the code, the school district had a dress code that prohibited certain types of clothing deemed unsafe, immodest, or otherwise inimical to the educational process. There was no reported finding that the dress code policy was ineffective. Nevertheless, the uniform policy was adopted to promote school spirit and values, promote the decorum of a school as a place of order and work, and promote respect for authority. It was also asserted that the uniform policy was designed to decrease socioeconomic tensions, increase attendance, and reduce dropout rates. The relationship between these outcomes and wearing uniforms was not stated. Failure to comply with the uniform policy resulted in disciplinary action up to expulsion.

In 2000, suit was brought against the policy claiming a violation of students' free speech rights. The plaintiffs argued that the uniform policy acts as a form of coerced speech conveying a state-approved message and that it acts as a prior restraint preventing the students from expressing any message at all through their attire (*Littlefield v. Forney Independent School District* 2001, 283–284).[13]

The defendant school district asserted that the choice of clothing is not expressive conduct protected by the First Amendment. The school district also contended "that the wearing of school uniforms does not convey a sufficiently particularized message to be considered coerced speech" (284).

Under *Canady*, a person's choice of clothing is infused with intentional expression and may amount to protected speech (*Littlefield* 285). Also following *Canady*, the court of appeals applied the *O'Brien* test. The court first easily found that the school district had the power to implement a uniform policy pursuant to state law. "Second, improving the educational process is undoubtedly an important and substantial interest of Forney and the school board" (286). Third, the plaintiffs did not establish that the school district's goal was to suppress expression. Consequently, the court of appeals found that the mandatory uniform policy "survives First Amendment scrutiny under the *O'Brien* test" (287). Thus the school uniform policy was found to be constitutional.

Uniforms in Connecticut: Liberty Not Speech

A school uniform case in Connecticut raises a constitutional question separate from the free speech argument, which has thus far dominated litigation on school uniforms. The Waterbury Public Schools approved a pilot program, in 1997, to try out a school attire policy that limited students to wearing clothing of prescribed styles and colors—basically a uniform. The following year the board of education adopted the pilot study school attire policy. The policy in the 1998–1999 school year provided an opt-out provision allowing parents to exempt their children from the requirements concerning style and color but not the list of prohibited items, which included blue jeans. In 1999–2000, the opt-out provision was eliminated, making the policy of clothing mandatory. The policy differentiated elementary and middle schools from high schools. The high school policy was less restrictive. Violations of the policy resulted in suspensions, with ten suspensions resulting in an expulsion recommendation.

Teshna Byars was expelled from school on July 20, 1999, after forty-nine suspensions for violations of the school attire policy. She was assigned to an alternative school operated by the school district. She was allowed to wear blue jeans—the basis for the suspensions—at the alternative school but was home schooled by her parents instead during the

1999–2000 school year. Teshna, through her parents, brought suit against the school district in April 1999 (*Byars v. City of Waterbury* 2001). The original complaint was amended in May 2000, after the school board eliminated the opt-out provision. Teshna claimed, among other complaints, that the mandatory uniform policy deprived her of her liberty, protected through the Fourteenth Amendment, to wear blue jeans. However, she did not allege that the uniform policy violated her right to free speech. Instead, she based "her claim on the fourteenth amendment's prohibition against actions which, in substance, rather than procedure, constitute a denial of due process of law" (361). The judicial analysis under a substantive due process claim is different than the traditional free speech analysis of *Tinker*, *Bethel*, or *Hazelwood*.

The court first decided which level of scrutiny was most appropriate. "When the right infringed is 'fundamental' the governmental regulations must be 'narrowly tailored to serve a compelling state interest'" (2001, 362). Fundamental rights are central to our concept of "ordered liberty." Speech, voting, and child bearing are examples of fundamental rights requiring the strict scrutiny of the government's intended regulation. Governmental actions reviewed under this strict scrutiny analysis must achieve a compelling state interest. Actions that do not involve fundamental rights are reviewed by a lesser standard. Under this lower standard government's actions are valid if they are rationally related to a valid governmental objective. Clearly, it is easier for governmental policies to survive the standard of rationally related to a valid governmental objective. Strict scrutiny analysis makes it more difficult for government to prevail because the action must be "necessary," a higher standard than rational, and the government objective being served by the policy must be compelling as opposed to legitimate. Government has a heavy burden when the courts employ strict scrutiny. "The court in the present case found that there is no fundamental right to wear blue jeans to school, and that only the rational relationship test applies to the challenged regulation" (364).

The court used the rational basis test to ascertain whether the mandatory uniform policy was valid under substantive due process. The analysis begins with the government goal. The court found that the goals of the uniform policy were to "reduce disruption, taunting, theft and loss of attention to course work" (2001, 363). Through testimony from the school's educators, the judge found that prohibition of blue jeans was rationally related to the stated goals.[14]

It is interesting and germane to our discussion that the court in *Byars* held that *Tinker* "approved the authority of school officials to regulate dress" (2001, 363) so long as the right to engage in specific fundamental rights such as political speech were not subject to unjustified regulations. In other words, the court asserted that the mere selection of what to wear to school does not necessarily implicate free speech. This position not only supports mandatory uniforms but also to a possibly lesser degree dress codes.

UNIFORMS AND DRESS CODES

Four mandatory uniform code cases have been adjudicated. In all four cases, the policy mandating a school uniform was upheld. Three cases used non-education Supreme Court cases as the primary tool for their analysis: *Phoenix Elementary School v. Green* used *Cornelius; Canady v. Bossier* and *Littlefield v. Forney* used *O'Brien*.[15] The *Canady* decision, followed closely by *Littlefield*, deliberately eschewed the use of any of the three major Supreme Court student free speech cases—*Tinker, Bethel*, and *Hazelwood*—and the *Phoenix Elementary* court refused to follow *Tinker* while using *Hazelwood* for the proposition that school authorities have great latitude to regulate activities related to legitimate pedagogical concerns.[16] The fourth case, *Byars*, did not use a speech analysis because the plaintiff asserted a substantive due process claim of a liberty violation. While *Tinker, Bethel*, and *Hazelwood* have long been held to be the touchstones for reviewing the constitutional protection of student speech, dress code and uniform policy litigation may be signaling a shift away from their use.

Litigation involving dress codes is considerably less consistent in its holdings. In fact, it has a tendency to be all over the board in its use of legal standards and its outcomes (DeMitchell 2001). Dress code litigation tends to look more like potpourri than a unified, articulated body of case law. "Unanimity on the issue of the constitutionality of dress codes had not been achieved, leaving a large degree of uncertainty in the courts" (DeMitchell, Fossey, and Cobb 2000, 46).[17] Thus far students have been more successful in challenging dress codes than mandatory school uniform policies. The paradox is that students have had some success contesting the lesser restrictions of a dress code and no success in contesting the more restrictive mandatory school uniform policies, either through a free speech analysis or a substantive due process analysis.

Dress codes prohibit wearing specific styles or types of clothing, leaving a large spectrum of options for student choice of wearing apparel. A school uniform, on the other hand, is mandatory, often leaving students with the choice of blue or khaki. Paradoxically, students have some success in overturning the less restrictive policy of dress codes and have been unsuccessful in three attempts concerning the more restrictive uniform policies. So far, four courts seem willing to give school uniforms the chance to transform our schools. Will other courts follow the path that says more restriction is constitutional, whereas with less restriction, the jury is still out?

④

TO UNIFORM OR NOT TO UNIFORM?
EMPIRICAL ANTECEDENTS TO
POLICY FORMATION AND ADOPTION

[T]here is a reason why "uniform" is both a noun *and* a verb.

> —a post on the Center at Georgetown University for the Study of
> Violence listserv (posted April 23, 2002, emphasis in original)

It is an interesting question how far men would retain their relative
rank if they were divested of their clothes.

> —Henry David Thoreau

INTRODUCTION

As chapter 1 illustrated, school uniform policies have been adopted in
American public schools in increasing numbers from 1987 to the present day. Through a detailed chronology of the rise of school uniform
policies in U.S. public schools, that chapter also highlighted the various
anecdotal rationales behind the decisions to implement such policies of
standardized dress. The picture that has been painted thus far points to
several important patterns in the journalistic documentation of the
school uniform movement. I wish to look closer at these patterns of anecdote as well as move away from such sketches and look at data from

the late 1990s in public elementary schools (using the Early Childhood Longitudinal Study) to investigate the empirical correlates to uniform policy formation and implementation in the United States. In the process, I will place the implications in the popular press into a more concrete empirical context of identifiable patterns from a nationally representative sample of public elementary schools. Both provide insights on their own, but together the picture they provide is richer, more informative, and, in the end, much more accurate.

This chapter provides, for the first time, an empirical analysis of the correlates to and factors associated with public school uniform policy adoption. First, we delve into the reasons that administrators and educators give for pursuing school uniform policies for their educational jurisdictions. Second, for the first time in published form, we obtain a glimpse at the empirical antecedents and correlates that distinguish those elementary schools that have adopted uniform policies from those that have not. There is a great deal of conjecture in the anecdotal literature about the type of school or community that looks into and eventually adopts a uniform policy; however, no empirical evidence exists to verify these claims. This important analysis and discussion will give us unique insight into the growing phenomenon of school uniform policies. The various factors implicated in this analysis are demographic variation, socioeconomic variation, the political climate, the types of schools, student body characteristics, etc. Third, this chapter looks closely at the various methods of implementation adhered to by the adoptees as well as the legal, educational, communal, and student-level pitfalls and promises experienced throughout the implementation process. Finally, several districts and individual schools recently have repealed their uniform policies for a variety of reasons—reasons that are, in large part, inherent to the form and content of this particular reform effort. This chapter explores the reasons behind the breakdown of these policies and, in so doing, helps us understand to a much greater extent the school uniform movement in the U.S. public school system.

DESCRIPTIVE DATA: UNIFORM POLICIES IN THE UNITED STATES

Several accounts of the degree of uniform policy adoption in public schools can be unearthed if one looks across the almost twenty years of discussion surrounding the movement in the United States. As early as the fall of 1988, there were at least fifty published, individual cases of school adoption of uniform policies (New Haven School 1988). Almost a decade later, by the end of the 1996–1997 school year, a figure was tossed around in the media estimating that approximately *half* (50 percent) of all urban public schools had adopted some sort of uniform policy (Lewis 1997). In addition, in 2000, the Centers for Disease Control found that uniforms were required in about 20 percent of public and Roman Catholic elementary and middle schools and 10 percent of high schools (Zernike 2002). In addition to this published guess work (typically based on extremely sketchy data and selective [il]logic), it is apparent from even a cursory look at the periodical and newspaper coverage of this movement that such policies have been implemented consistently in suburban and, indeed, rural schools—although the coverage of policy adoption procedures and trajectories in these areas leaves much to be desired. The bottom line is that even as recently as 2000, we have no reliable estimates of the number of public schools with uniform policies and, even more interesting, the number of public school children who must wear school uniforms. It is my hope to remedy that to some degree in this chapter.

I primarily approach the empirical investigation of these questions through an analysis of the Early Childhood Longitudinal Study (ECLS) data from the National Center for Education Statistics (NCES). This data set is utilized instead of the National Educational Longitudinal Study (NELS) for several important reasons. First, the years of the data collection for the first two waves of NELS was 1988 (cohort of eighth graders) and 1990 (those eighth graders in the tenth grade), when the school uniform movement was in its infancy and *very* few public schools had uniform policies. Second, due to the infancy of the movement as well as the fact that the earliest public school uniform adoptions were in elementary schools, NELS is not the most appropriate data set for looking at patterns of uniform adoption. Third, because the uniform movement was just beginning during the late 1980s and early 1990s in public elementary schools, there are really not enough cases of public school uniforms being required in middle and high schools to look for patterns in the data. Therefore, NELS, although providing interesting possibilities for discovering patterns in the effectiveness of uniform policies *across all school sectors* of America's educational system (see chapters 5 and 6), does not provide useful information for looking into the distribution of *public* school uniform policies and therefore is limited in the analysis of the empirical correlates to uniform policy adoption.

Table 4.1 shows the distribution of school uniform policies by school sector, region, and urbanicity using the ELCS-K (kindergarten base year) and follow-up data representative of elementary schools in both the 1998–1999 and 1999–2000 school years. Overall, in 1998–1999, 19.5 percent of American elementary schools had school uniform policies; by the next school year this figure had risen to 26.7 percent. This is roughly in line with, albeit somewhat higher than, the CDC report that estimated 20 percent of elementary and middle schools had uniform policies (Zernike 2002). Although no reliable data are available for understanding the prevalence of uniforms in public middle and high schools, it is presumably much lower than that for elementary schools—maybe as much as 50 to 75 percent lower—somewhere in the 8 to 10 percent

Table 4.1. Distribution of School Uniform Policies in Elementary Schools by Sector, Urbanicity, and Region, 1998–1999 and 1999–2000 School Years

	1998–1999		1999–2000	
	Uniformed	Nonuniformed	Uniformed	Nonuniformed
Sector				
Catholic	65.7% (65)	34.3% (34)	89.9% (116)	10.1% (13)
Private (Rel.)	25.8% (16)	74.2% (46)	44.9% (35)	55.1% (43)
Private (Nonrel.)	25.0% (10)	75.0% (30)	41.4% (12)	58.6% (17)
Public	11.5% (74)	88.5% (566)	15.5% (138)	84.5% (753)
	$\chi^2 = 162.88^{***}, df = 3$		$\chi^2 = 336.98^{***}, df = 3$	
Urbanicity				
Urban	28.5% (92)	71.5% (231)	36.0% (164)	64.0% (292)
Suburban	18.2% (59)	81.8% (264)	24.6% (105)	75.4% (321)
Rural	7.2% (14)	92.8% (181)	26.7% (301)	73.3% (826)
	$\chi^2 = 882.85^{***}, df = 2$		$\chi^2 = 76.76^{***}, df = 2$	
Region				
Northeast	14.1% (22)	85.9% (134)	22.0% (48)	78.0% (170)
Midwest	11.5% (25)	88.5% (192)	19.9% (56)	80.1% (226)
South	23.6% (68)	76.4% (220)	31.0% (122)	69.0% (272)
West	27.3% (50)	72.7% (132)	31.7% (73)	68.3% (157)
	$\chi^2 = 25.70^{***}, df = 3$		$\chi^2 = 21.68^{***}, df = 3$	
TOTALS	19.5% (165)	80.5% (678)	26.7% (301)	73.3% (826)

Note: $^{***}p < .001$, $^{**}p < .01$, $^{*}p < .05$; df = "degrees of freedom"; χ^2 = "Chi-Square"; Rel. = "Religious"; Nonrel. = "Non-Religious".

range. Still, these basic descriptive data from ECLS show that the media coverage of the uniform movement in public schools has been almost consistently *overestimated*.

As one can see in table 4.1, between 1998 and 1999 school uniforms were found most prominently in Catholic elementary schools (65.7 percent and 89.9 percent respectively). About one-quarter of other private schools (religious or nonreligious) had school uniform policies for their K–6 students. This had gone up, a year later, to over 40 percent for these private schools. In the 1998–1999 school year, some 11.5 percent of public elementary schools had uniform policies; this number had risen to 15.5 percent by the end of the 1999–2000 academic year. Across all types of schools in the United States, school uniform usage increased quite dramatically between 1998 and 2000.[1]

Across all sectors of schooling, school uniforms have been used most prominently in elementary schools in urban areas (28.5–36.0 percent) but have also been used quite frequently in suburban (18.2–24.6 percent) as well as rural areas. The most dramatic increase in uniform usage between these years was in rural areas of the United States, where, in 1998–1999, 7.2 percent of these elementary schools had such policies and by the end of the next school year, 26.7 percent had them. Rural public school uniform adoption practices are rarely discussed in the media. Table 4.1 also shows an interesting issue regarding the concentration of such policies in various regions of the United States. If one peruses the anecdotal literature and traces the amount of coverage given to uniform usage in various parts of the country, one walks away from that experience with a view that uniforms are concentrated in the Northeastern United States (New York City, Washington, D.C., Maryland, Connecticut, etc.)—but this is inaccurate. The implementation and employment of school uniform policies in American elementary schools is actually most concentrated in the Western and Southern United States, distantly followed by the Northeast and the Midwest. These findings are quite intriguing given the different demographic and socioeconomic status of the South and the West vis-à-vis the Northeast and Midwest (in terms of size of minority population, numbers of families in poverty, average educational attainments, and a host of other factors) (McNiece and Jolliffe 1998; Parcel and Geschwender 1995; Sernau 2001; Triest 1997). This pattern held in 1999–2000.

Table 4.2 reports results similar to those in table 4.1, but this time the data are for *public schools only*. This is more in line with the objectives of this book. What is the degree of school uniform utilization in American public elementary schools in the late 1990s? Revisiting the crucial data from table 4.1, one can see that in 1998–1999, 11.5 percent of public elementary schools had school uniform policies; this had increased to 15.5 percent by the end of the next school year (1999–2000). This shows, I believe, that the media have indeed overestimated the degree of school uniform implementation in American schools, not by much in some cases, but overall the media representation of the sweep of school uniform policy adoptions across the United States has been exaggerated.[2]

Table 4.2. Distribution of School Uniform Policies in Public Elementary Schools by Region and Urbanicity, 1998–1999 and 1999–2000 School Years

	1998–1999		1999–2000	
	Uniformed	Nonuniformed	Uniformed	Nonuniformed
Northeast				
Urban	3.1% (1)	96.9% (31)	10.7% (6)	89.3% (50)
Suburban	—	100% (31)	—	100% (75)
Rural	—	100% (26)	—	100% (30)
Totals	0.9% (1)	99.1% (103)	3.9% (6)	96.1% (155)
Midwest				
Urban	11.5% (6)	88.5% (46)	13.9% (10)	86.1% (62)
Suburban	1.7% (1)	98.3% (57)	3.9% (3)	96.1% (73)
Rural	—	100% (52)	1.6% (1)	98.4% (61)
Totals	4.5% (7)	95.5% (155)	7.1% (14)	92.9% (196)
South				
Urban	23.8% (19)	76.2% (61)	30.7% (43)	69.3% (97)
Suburban	17.3% (17)	82.7% (81)	20.7% (25)	79.3% (96)
Rural	11.1% (6)	88.9% (48)	12.1% (7)	87.9% (51)
Totals	22.1% (42)	77.9% (190)	30.7% (75)	69.3% (244)
West				
Urban	25.8% (16)	74.2% (46)	28.6% (22)	71.4% (55)
Suburban	16.3% (8)	83.7% (41)	18.8% (12)	81.2% (52)
Rural	11.1% (6)	88.9% (48)	5.4% (2)	94.6% (35)
Totals	22.2% (30)	77.8% (135)	25.4% (36)	74.6% (142)
Total				
Urban	18.6% (42)	81.4% (184)	23.5% (81)	76.5% (264)
Suburban	10.4% (26)	89.6% (225)	11.9% (40)	88.1% (296)
Rural	3.7% (6)	96.3% (156)	5.3% (10)	94.7% (177)
TOTALS	11.5% (74)	88.5% (566)	15.5% (138)	84.5% (753)

An example of the journalistic reporting and newspaper coverage discussing the pervasiveness of school uniforms in public schools is Lewis (1997), who reported that by 1997, 50 percent of urban public schools had school uniforms. This is seriously misleading; if we look at the totals in table 4.2, it is clear that only somewhere between 18.6 percent and 23.5 percent of urban public elementary schools had uniform policies. For the media to make a statement like that above is patently ridiculous, for even if we used 1998–1999 data (for elementary public schools only) and assumed that something like 10 percent of urban middle and high schools may have had uniforms, we would only arrive at an estimation of 28.6 percent of all urban public schools having school uniforms. This mismatch between the discourse and the actual structure of implementation is discussed in more depth in chapter 7.

It is interesting to note the degree of growth in school uniform policy adoption between just these two years (albeit very important years in the movement). Both urban areas and rural areas increased their scope of implementation between 1998–1999 and 1999–2000. Suburban implementation grew as well, but not nearly as much as that seen in the other two contexts. It may be the case that suburban parents, due to their higher average economic standing and education levels, have thwarted implementation more readily (or driven compliance rates downward) than their urban or rural counterparts in similar situations. This hypothesis is worth pursuing as we search for underlying streams of ideology and structural imbalances that have permitted the uniform movement to grow in the way that it has, in the contexts that it has.

WHY UNIFORMS? WHY NOT?: ANECDOTAL REASONS GIVEN FOR THE IMPLEMENTATION OF UNIFORM POLICIES

Looking at the anecdotal literature on the reasons given by administrators, educators, parents, and politicians for the implementation of school uniform policies in their schools, seven basic clusters of reasons come to the fore:

1. reducing violence and behavioral problems,
2. fostering school unity and improving the learning environment,

3. reducing social pressures and leveling status differentials,
4. increasing student self-esteem and motivation,
5. saving parents money on clothing for their children,
6. improving attendance, and, ultimately,
7. improving academic achievement.

I examine these in turn and illustrate each facet with examples from the anecdotal literature from which it comes.[3]

The number one reason given for the implementation of uniform policies in public schools is that they will work to somehow decrease the incidence of school violence and misbehavior at the school building. This reason was given in slightly over a third of the articles (34.4 percent) and represents the original impetus behind the uniform movement. Specifically, these reasons span the terrain of violence and delinquent behavior—from school shootings, general school violence, gang affiliations and activities on campus, to the need to recognize outsiders and a whole host of behavioral and disciplinary problems. Consider this representative example of how this aspect of the discourse is framed in the media:

[After referencing an incident in which a car drove up and four men pointed a shotgun at some boys on the corner, asking them to show them their shirt colors, the mother states:] . . . My sons could have been killed that day, but they did not have on any red or blue; they were dressed in uniform—a white shirt and tie and black/grey pants. Wearing a uniform is one of the ways to keep our children safe to and from school or while they are in school. I, for one, am a witness that it may save a child's life, and I thank God every day . . . [the article continues]. . . . Young people, 18 and under, commit about half of the violent crimes today. Disruptions and violence are a growing problem in our schools and communities. Violence is rampant; kids are getting killed over designer jackets, shoes or just because they are wearing a certain color. As *Time* magazine tells us, more than 100,000 students carry a weapon to school each day. Public school uniforms have become the latest rage. Parents, teachers, school administrators and politicians feel that uniforms may be a new tool for reducing violence in schools. There are many claims that, as a result of uniforms, disciplinary incidents and violence have declined, students' attitudes have improved and a more serious learning environment has resulted. Parents and teachers are positive about a uniform policy. (Merritt 1996)

It is both interesting and discouraging to see the absolute lack of sociological insight and/or critical questioning into the social and cultural *causes* of gangs, violence, fashion consumption, etc.[4] This discursive line is one of the most prominent in the movement to uniform public school students without understanding the complexities of social and educational structures.

Closely following these anecdotal reasons for uniform policies is the argument that such policies will produce increased unity and school spirit, thereby, through some unnamed mechanism, enhancing the learning environment. Roughly one-quarter of the reports give such explanations and justifications for uniform policies. The assumption has been that uniforms will augment the orderliness and general level of morale of the student (and staff) body, leading to an increased firmness of social connections and camaraderie. There is little doubt that this is lacking in many public schools—yet it first is lacking in the wider society (Putnam 2000). Furthermore, after almost two decades of research, we now know the importance of social capital for student achievement and success in school (Carbonaro 1998; Coleman 1988; McNeal 1999; Putnam 1995, 2000; Stanton-Salazar and Dornbusch 1995); however, from quotes and arguments one reads in the newspaper, like the following, it is unclear how increases in unity, spirit, and social capital in general are supposed to actually occur:

The uniform program aims to promote school spirit and unity and encourage better discipline, said Lemasters Principal George Wilson. It also helps keep students from fighting about whether or not they are wearing name brand clothing, he said . . . . "We hope the kids will learn to work together, and identify with their school," Wilson said. (Hopgood 1996)

[Said a sixth graders' mother:] "I think it's a good idea. . . . School uniforms formulate school spirit and school unity while giving a positive school image. School uniforms also make it easier on parents and break barriers between the haves and the have-nots. They help kids to judge each other by what's on the inside instead of by what they wear . . . [Said later school board member Philip Enright:] "I believe that school uniforms give students a sense of purpose and pride in themselves and their school. . . . Especially in a school district with a diverse population . . . uniforms help to bring a sense of unity." (Saslow 1998)

A third set of reasons typically given for the creation and implementation of such policies is that uniforms will level economic disparities and reduce social pressures. This discursive positioning (seen in 12.5 percent of the published reports) usually encompasses assumptions about school uniforms erasing status distinctions of all kinds—usually centered around clothing (designer clothing, name brands, etc.) and socioeconomic class—and even possibly (though completely illogically) diminishing race, ethnic, and even gender distinctions. For instance:

> [Referring to a Phoenix school:] They thought uniforms would improve the climate for learning by eliminating "label competition" and other peer pressure concerning clothing; by eliminating gang clothing and enabling security personnel to identify trespassers instantly; by instilling school spirit and pride; and by equalizing at least one sphere of life for children from different socioeconomic settings. (At one California school that requires uniforms, a teacher told a visitor to a classroom that one student was the child of a wealthy movie producer, another lived in a shelter for the homeless. The visitor was asked if he could tell which was which. He could not.) (Will 1996)

The idea, it appears, is that standardized dress policies like school uniforms will produce a commonality, unity, conformity, and sameness among the students that will obliterate the very distinctions that schools have dealt with for half a century at least.[5]

Slightly less than 10 percent (9.4 percent) of the news coverage on public school uniforms cites increasing student self esteem levels and a general sense of creating public school students who feel good about themselves and their place in the school system—and perhaps in the wider society. This desired social-psychological effect of a school reform or specific policy like uniforms is not new (Hirsch 1999; Sykes 1995). As if schools did not have enough to do, the charge of increasing individual student self-esteem levels goes back almost three decades. The literature is littered with statements from administrators, teachers, parents, and even students regarding this supposed effect of uniforms on students, as illustrated by the following reports:

> School uniforms is an idea whose time has come [said Governor William F. Weld of Connecticut]. . . . Little things add up to a lot. . . . Uniforms

may seem like a little thing, but I think they're relevant to self-esteem, possibly even to confidence."(Aucoin 1997)

Joseph Copeland, elementary school principal in Columbus, Ohio, was quoted as saying:

> The reason we went to uniforms is to try to equalize things for our kids. . . . You get away from worrying about who has and who doesn't have, and build up a little bit of self-esteem. (Doulin and Sternberg 1996)

These examples are representative of the almost nonchalant manner in which those who discuss the effects of uniforms seem to just throw in another (and another) effect, like increased self-esteem, without giving much thought to how, exactly, such linkages are made, or how, in practice, such outcomes will be enhanced through educational restructuring.

The remaining aspects of the discourse surrounding reasons why school uniform policies are established are threefold, each equally weighted in frequency (6.25 percent each). First, it is argued that such policies are implemented to save parents money on the purchase of school clothing for their children. To this day, this remains a central point of contention in the empirical literature (see chapter 2), yet the argument is consistently pushed in the media. This argument was much more prominent earlier in the discourse as it tied itself closely to the need to reduce competition for designer clothing in school. Kathi Marotta, PTA president at New York City's P.S. 71, stated:

> [F]amilies would save money. A uniform set for a boy, consisting of three pairs of pants, three shirts and a sweater with a school emblem, costs $135. The price for girl's skirts or jumpers is comparable. With shoes, the cost might be $170 to $180. Expensive at first, but that's it for the whole year. (Stewart 1997)

Of course, many families in New York City's system, and thousands of other families across the country, would not spend this amount for clothing anyway.

Second, it is assumed and presented to parents that school uniforms will increase attendance rates and, similarly, reduce tardiness, truancy, and absenteeism. Though the mechanisms are unclear, it appears to be the case that this outcome will occur through previously mentioned premises, such as increased commitment to the organizational norms of the school, unity and spirit, and an improvement in the educational climate of the school. Students will somehow come ready to learn if in uniform, even if they have little support or direction in that effort. Finally, no educational reform effort would be complete without some consideration given to the possibility that uniform policies could improve academic achievement. Academic achievement is the ultimate goal of any educational strategy in the era of high stakes testing and standardization (Orfield and Kornhaber 2001; Sacks 2001). That school uniforms could improve a student's grades and overall academic success is a theme that also rings throughout the discourse on school uniforms in American public schools.

EMPIRICAL CORRELATES TO POLICY ADOPTION IN PUBLIC SCHOOLS

Given some understanding of where school uniforms are found throughout the United States as well as some anecdotal reasons given by administrators for the implementation of uniform policies, it is of considerable interest to investigate, with available data, empirical patterns distinguishing between those schools that have uniform policies and those that do not. Using ECLS data from the 1998–1999 and 1999–2000 school years, we can achieve an empirical glimpse into the factors that are associated with uniform policies at the school level. I am concerned here with *public schools only,* and tables 4.3 and 4.4 report the correlations between a variety of factors and policy adoption in American public elementary schools between 1998 and 2000.

From the brief anecdotal exposition above, as well as my reading of countless news accounts and publications about school uniform policies in the United States, several possible correlates emerge as potential explanations behind the movement, now in its sixteenth year. First, as uniforms appear to be, in many cases, a reactionary policy aimed at alleviating a variety of problems at the school building, I look at several factors touching on these issues: school enrollments, decreasing levels of funding, the general safety and educational climates of these schools,

Table 4.3.   School-Level Correlates to School Uniform Policy Adoption in Elementary Schools, 1998–1999

Independent Variable	Correlation with Uniform Policy
Average Socioeconomic Status	−.24***
School Enrollment	+.14***
Percentage of Minority Students	+.40***
Percentage of Students Receiving Free Lunch	+.42***
Is School a Magnet School? (1 = yes, 2 = no)	+.23***
Is School a Choice School? (1 = yes, 2 = no)	+.02
Does School Have a Focus? (1 = yes, 2 = no)	−.15***
Are Classes Team-Taught? (1 = yes, 2 = no)	−.06
Have Funding Levels Decreased? (1 = yes, 2 = no)	+.03
Does School Have Security Guards? (1 = yes, 2 = no)	−.13**
Does School Have Metal Detectors? (1 = yes, 2 = no)	−.31***
Does School Lock Doors during the Day? (1 = yes, 2 = no)	+.16***
Is There a Sign-In Policy? (1 = yes, 2 = no)	−.09*
Is There Limited Restroom Time? (1 = yes, 2 = no)	−.09*
Do Teachers Patrol Hallways? (1 = yes, 2 = no)	+.03
Percentage of Students Reading at Level	−.27***
Percentage of Students at Mathematics Level	−.23***
Gender of Principal (1 = Female, 2 = Male)	+.10**
Urban School	+.16***
Rural School	−.14***
Parental Involvement Levels	−.22***
Safety Climate of School	−.29***
Educational Climate of School	−.17***

Note: ***p <.001, **p <.01, *p <.05

and aggregate measures of achievement levels (reading and mathematics) at these elementary schools. Second, the anecdotal literature illuminates several unspoken potential demographic correlates to the adoption of such policies that beg an empirical investigation: a socioeconomic class factor (i.e., average SES levels of the students' families as well as the proportion of students whose families fall below the poverty line), a racial composition of the student body factor (as these policies appear to be implemented to a greater extent in predominantly minority educational contexts), and urbanicity measures. Third, it is consistently discussed throughout the literature that parental involvement is key in the adoption of uniform policies; however, there is also abundant anecdotal evidence that many schools do not actually adequately survey the parents in a reliable and methodologically sound manner and, if opt-outs are permitted, rarely grant them. Therefore I look into the levels of

Table 4.4.   School-Level Correlates to School Uniform Policy Adoption in
Elementary Schools, 1999–2000

Independent Variable	Correlation with Uniform Policy
Average Socioeconomic Status	−.15***
School Enrollment	+.16***
Percentage of Minority Students	+.32***
Percentage of Students Receiving Free Lunch	+.15***
Is School a Choice School? (1 = yes, 2 = no)	−.10
Does School Have a Focus? (1 = yes, 2 = no)	−.05
Does School Have Security Guards? (1 = yes, 2 = no)	−.12***
Does School Have Metal Detectors? (1 = yes, 2 = no)	−.22***
Does School Lock Doors during the Day? (1 = yes, 2 = no)	+.12***
Is There a Sign-In Policy? (1 = yes, 2 = no)	−.05
Is There Limited Restroom Time? (1 = yes, 2 = no)	−.16***
Do Teachers Patrol Hallways? (1 = yes, 2 = no)	−.05
Percentage of Students Reading at Level	−.16***
Percentage of Students at Mathematics Level	−.11**
Gender of Principal (1 = Female, 2 = Male)	+.12*
Urban School	+.17***
Rural School	−.17***
Parental Involvement Levels	−.22***
Safety Climate of School	−.07*
Educational Climate of School	−.09*

Note: ***p <.001, **p <.01, *p <.05.

parental involvement at these schools. Fourth, I analyze several other
dimensions of the school structure and climate to assess their relationship with school uniform policies in elementary schools: the gender of
the principal and whether the schools are magnet, choice, or schools
that have clear foci (i.e., mission statements or charters). Finally, I also
look at the correlation of other policies that have been implemented to
curb violence and increase safety at schools, such as security guards,
metal detectors, locked door policies, limited restroom time, teachers
patrolling hallways, etc., and their association with school uniforms. Do
schools that have uniforms also implement other zero-tolerance types of
policies?

    Table 4.3 presents the results of the correlates to uniform policy
adoption in elementary schools for the 1998–1999 school year. Concerning school-level quandaries, it does appear that those elementary
schools that had significant "problems" were also the ones more likely to
have uniform policies. As the results indicate, high enrollments and

lower percentages of students achieving at grade level possibly prompted administrators to pursue and eventually adopt a school uniform policy. Also, if both the safety and the educational climate of the school are perceived as poor, the administration is more likely to adopt a uniform policy in these schools. Of course, it has been well documented for decades that success in schools and successful schools are highly related to income, which is itself related to race and urbanicity. The results for the demographic and socioeconomic factors associated with uniform policies show that more affluent schools are less likely to have uniform policies, while more disadvantaged schools are more likely to have such policies. Schools with high levels of poverty and a high proportion of minorities comprising their student body also have a much higher propensity for school uniform policy adoption—a possibility that is quite clear, though to this day it remains essentially unstated in the anecdotal literature. We now have some important empirical confirmation of that hypothesis. In addition, urban schools are more likely than suburban schools to have such policies, but rural schools are the least likely of all to have such policies (see also tables 4.1 and 4.2).

Elementary schools that have low levels of parental involvement in schooling are more likely to have school uniform policies. This finding is intriguing, given the fact that parents *must* support such policies for them to be implemented with any respectable degree of compliance. Yet, as is clear from these results, we know from previous research that urban, minority, and poor parents are much more likely to defer educational authority to the school and its staff (Seeley 1989; Wells and Crain 1997), and, therefore, are less likely to be involved in schooling and their children's education, for structural and cultural reasons (Lareau 1987). Other factors associated with uniform policy implementation in elementary schools are that female principals are more likely to implement uniform policies than male principals and that schools with an explicit focus and/or mission statement are less likely to have uniforms.[6]

Looking at the relationship between other zero-tolerance policies and school uniform policies in 1998–1999 (table 4.3), one sees that these policies overlap a good deal of the time. Elementary schools with uniform policies are also more likely than schools that do not have such policies to have security guards, metal detectors, sign-in policies, and limited restroom time. Furthermore, according to a recent study (Educational

Testing Service 2000) such policies actually do not deter delinquency and deviance on campus (see chapter 2).

Turning now to the following school year, 1999–2000, table 4.4 shows the correlates to uniform policy adoption in elementary public schools during this year. Of course, we saw (table 4.2) that between these two school years the use of uniforms in public elementary schools increased, there was less distinction between regions, and a growing number of rural and suburban schools, with quite different student profiles, were implementing them. In 1999–2000, the patterns of empirical correlates to uniform use in these schools in 1999–2000 are very much the same as the relationships were the previous year, with a few minor exceptions.

FROM IDEA TO PRACTICE: PROTOCOL, PROMISES, PITFALLS, AND PERILS

It is clear that the idea of the school uniform has deep historical, political, and cultural roots (see chapter 1). In the U.S. public school system, the recent institutional push to append "school uniforms" to the set of ideas that comprise the way we "do public education" in this country came from the trenches of teaching and administration of increasingly diverse and socially complex student bodies. The idea of uniforming students became solidly ensconced as a possible "reform" strategy between 1994 and 1996. Given this set of ideas, what is the modus operandi for taking such ideas from the drawing board to the halls of our public schools?

When considering the protocol of implementing school uniforms in public schools, one must really start with two key sets of documents. First is the policy devised by the Long Beach Unified School District (LBUSD), in California, as well as their *Guidelines and Regulations for Implementing the Mandatory Uniform Policy in Grades Kindergarten through Eight*, from the Office of the Superintendent. Second, one must look at the *Manual on School Uniforms*, published and distributed to over 16,000 school districts across the United States in 1996, by the Department of Education under the Clinton administration. These two sets of documents set the original tone and were the original "guidebooks" for schools and districts interested in pursuing the idea of school uniforms.

Looking at the two sets of documents, it is clear that the protocol intended by these early pioneers of the school uniform movement sought to travel down a common path, with the following obligatory stops along the way:

1. Communicate intentions behind the policy, the policy itself, and the logistics of the policy to parents and allow parents various opportunities to have input into the policy.
2. Provide some form of financial assistance procedures for families who cannot afford uniforms.
3. Develop measures and training, if necessary, to ensure the enforcement of the policy, with clear guidelines for disciplinary actions that will be taken against those who do not comply with the policy—all in a concerted effort to warrant policy compliance.
4. Allow means for families to exempt their children from the uniform policy or to "opt out" for varying religious, philosophical, and freedom of speech/expression reasons.
5. Prepare the district and/or school for legal challenges to the uniform policy.
6. Conduct annual evaluations of the policy to assess its effectiveness in obtaining the intended goals and outcomes.

The *Manual* also includes a final section on making school uniforms just one *part* of an overall "safety program" in a district or a specific school.[7] Using this general road map of "how to implement a school uniform policy," I take each point in turn and discuss the caveats, pitfalls, fulfilled promises, and perils that each has phase has encountered (from my reading of the vast literature, both anecdotal and empirical).

Parents and School Uniform Policies: Gauging or Ignoring?

In many schools and school districts, a typical chain of events early in the adoption of a school uniform policy includes sending a "survey" to all parents whose children attend the school(s) to gauge their support for pursuing a school uniform policy. A letter usually goes out to the parents stating the intention of the board or principal (or, in some instances a group of parents) to pursue the institution of a uniform policy, often including the policy itself (or a working draft), and perhaps the survey at this point as well. Though this procedure appears levelheaded, and, in theory, it is, parents across the country have raised concerns that this stage in the protocol is less than informative and often misleading. The media play an enormous role at this stage as well, as they report "results" from these "surveys" and the level of parental (and sometimes student) support based on what are usually shady and methodologically unsound surveying practices.

Concerning the survey stage, several problems arise that are rarely, if ever, attended to. First are the misleading questionnaires on which parents, in the end, are not at all exactly clear what it is that they are supporting or not supporting. Given the media's attention to school uniform policies, the plethora of anecdotal meanderings on the effectiveness of such policies, as well as the fact that the *idea* of school uniforms and what *might* be the result of such a policy are quite simplistic and rest nicely in the heads and "common sense" of most Americans who want the best for their children, one ultimately is unsure what an approval rate of 77 percent (for instance) means. Second, the correspondence to parents (or worse, the sending of the survey and other information on the proposed uniform package home with the students), varies widely in the degree of detail given about the policy, the clarity of sanctions for noncompliance, a mandatory versus a voluntary program, what this means exactly, the reasons behind the pursuit of the policy, etc. This all can lead to serious misinterpretation. Furthermore, given the lack of voice that most parents have in schooling matters, they are, in the end, given very little opportunity to ask pertinent and relevant questions. Third, with a mailing to 10,000 parents with a return rate (which is rarely given in published news reports) of, say, 60 percent, which "results" in an "approval rating" of 78 percent—what exactly does this mean? The effects of nonresponse on statistical parameters as simplistic as percentages and proportions can be enormous. The following excerpts illustrate published reports of parental surveying procedures and subsequent newspaper reporting tactics; they are quite typical:

> Last week, several board members expected to hear the full results of the parent questionnaire distributed last month at parent-teacher conferences. . . . All administrators would divulge was that 72 percent of parents—or

about 12,000—filled out the questionnaire and that 69 percent of them indicated they liked the uniform concept. (Nygren 1996)

More than half the parents surveyed in Cherokee County want uniforms for
elementary students. . . . According to results of a survey released Wednes-
day, 58 percent of parents and 68 percent of teachers said uniforms should
be mandatory for children in elementary school. . . . About 49 percent of the
26,000 surveys sent home to parents were returned. (Reinolds 2001)

Not only is nonresponse a serious issue for gauging parental support, so
is the construction of the surveys themselves.[5]

The manner in which questions are worded can have an *enormous*
impact on parental attitudes, their responses, their interpretations, and
therefore on the vast dimensions of meaning one could glean from a
"yes" or a "no" response. Following is a sampling of questions from a variety of parent surveys conducted to gauge the level of parental support
for implementing a uniform policy at their children's school:

1. From a Bloomington, Illinois school district in 2000–2001: "Other
   school districts in the state have students wear school uniforms.
   Do you favor having a school uniform in [name of student]'s
   school?"
2. From a Hawaiian elementary school: "Would you be in favor of a
   school uniform for the students of [school]?"
3. From a school in Castroville, California: "I would approve of a
   school uniform."

A few comments are in order regarding these three questions (which are
quite representative of the array of questions asked on such surveys).

The first question is a fantastic example of one of the prime suspects
in poor survey questionnaire item construction—the leading question.
Parents reading this could perhaps feel strong social pressure from
knowing the "fact" that other schools in Illinois have uniforms. Also, in
this particular instance (which is quite typical) as well as in the other
two, the parents were not given a copy of the policy and therefore had
to rely on their knowledge and opinions about the purpose and potential effectiveness of such policies. Given the media attention and the

almost sole use of anecdote in such coverage, parents who have any familiarity with uniform policies at all most likely derived their understanding of them from the media. In the end, regardless of the way in which the question is constructed, a "yes" response usually is interpreted as "yes, I support the policy" and a "no" as a "no, I do not support the policy"—even though these interpretations may be seriously flawed.

Financial Assistance for the Disadvantaged: Crisis and Consumption

It is clear that school uniform policies have been disproportionately implemented in schools with higher poverty rates and greater contextually rooted social problems, and where the student body is more likely to be predominantly minority or non-white. Since its inception, public education was to be free of charge to work toward the societal goal of equality of educational opportunity (Coleman 1990a). Given this cultural, political, and social ideal and the empirical reality that uniform policies are disproportionately implemented in poor and minority schools, schools that do implement such policies run the risk of being seen as attempting to charge a fee for public education from a group of students and their families in American society who are the most unable to pay. The constitutional issues aside (which have not yet been fully decided), this appears to be quite unfair in a "good society" (Bellah et al. 1985). Because of these issues, the protocol of uniform adoption in public schools is encouraged to provide some form of financial aid to those who cannot afford uniforms but are forced to wear them by their schools.

To address this potential problem, some schools create programs and set aside monies to help disadvantaged families purchase the required uniforms, while others seek out business and/or corporate sponsorship or donation of uniforms for underprivileged children. Still other districts and schools might allow parents to opt out of the uniform policy for financial hardship reasons. Others do nothing. An example of such a policy follows:

> Severe, *bona fide*, *demonstrated* financial hardship *may* be considered or exemption from a mandatory school uniform program *if, and only if, other*

means to provide uniforms free of charge or at a nominal charge are *not available*. Such a *request* should follow the procedures set forth in the Procedures For Exemption. (from St. Tammany Parish in Louisiana, emphasis added)

Imagine having to *prove* your economic hardship, in several ways, to school authorities. Think of the student(s) who must attempt to opt out because of their socioeconomic status and then have to come to school without a uniform. In policies such as this not only can the uniform stigmatize various schools in an area as poor and minority, but within a given school they can stigmatize students for not wearing the uniform because of financial hardship. A more humanistic, clearer policy can be seen in the following:

It is the responsibility of district and school staff to adequately communicate to parents information concerning financial hardship guidelines in reference to the [school's] uniform policy. In many cases, school uniforms are less expensive than the clothing that students typically wear to school. Nonetheless, the cost of purchasing a uniform may be a burden on some families. . . . No student will be denied attendance at school, penalized, or otherwise subject to compliance measures for failing to wear a uniform by reason of financial hardship. The principal will establish a committee to assist those families in need. Parents of students who cannot afford uniforms should complete a Uniform Policy Application and submit to the Supervisor of Child Welfare and Attendance. The District Uniform Oversight Committee (members appointed by the Superintendent) will review these applications and, if appropriate, issue a voucher for the appropriate school uniform. No money is to exchange hands and school funds cannot be used. (from St. Charles Parish Public Schools in Louisiana)

This is a much better policy. It provides accountability to the school and school administration for the implementation of a clear policy to assist families in financial need. It provides a uniform voucher so that the student may obtain the appropriate uniform and thereby remain in compliance. However, as good as any policy can sound in writing, in practice we have seen a variety of pitfalls surrounding the implementation of policies providing financial help for uniform costs[9]—the classic, and widening, gulf between de jure and de facto.

One of the perennial claims about the potential effects of school uniform policies is that they will eradicate distinctions of social class. From
the empirical data reported in this chapter as well as from the varying
problems associated with clothing the disadvantaged students at these
schools, the argument could be made, quite convincingly, that uniforms
in public schools in the United States are, on a macro level, actually at-
tenuating the social class distinctions because poor and minority students
are more likely to be in uniform in our public schools. Furthermore, on
a micro level, given that students who need financial assistance are often
given hand-me-downs and/or one or two uniforms, they are more likely
to be wearing school uniforms that are not as crisp and clean as more affluent students. Having only one (or two) uniforms for a school year will
not go very far in terms of wear and tear on the clothes. In other words,
on a microlevel interactional basis, daily distinctions between who has
and who does not have will remain salient. We are reminded of the
Christ's Church Hospital children in England, whose uniforms were a
marker of disadvantage. On average, the face of the uniformed student
in American public schools, regardless of what policies are put in place
to deal with disparities, is one of poverty and minority status.

Enforcing the Uniform: "Cops," Compliance, and Control

Another crucial component of the protocol for adopting a uniform in
an individual public school and/or a public school district is how the new
policy will be enforced. How will a school ensure that the vast majority
of its students are conformists to such a policy and minimize deviations
from the uniform code? Who will police the policy? Parents? Teachers?
Administrators? Peers? These are all questions of social control and policy enforcement procedures. Such procedures are compulsory for the
school that wishes to test the uniform waters in public education. This
issue is of great importance to the policy, for, after all, if no one wears
the uniform, or if compliance rates are exceedingly low, is not such a
state of affairs antithetical to the stated goals and ideals of the policy?
The answer is an emphatic yes! Compliance is key; thus, enforcement
and methods of social control also become central factors.

Policies of standardized dress vary quite widely across the country.
What clothing is mandated to be worn by students is usually painstak-

ingly detailed within the policy itself. An example of a policy from the Waterbury, Connecticut, school district follows:

BOYS:

    5.1.1. Pants, shorts (colors: solid navy blue, gray, or khaki)—must be "dress" or "docker" style pants or knee-length shorts—worn or belted at the waist.

    5.1.2. Tops (colors: solid white or light blue)—must be oxford, polo, or turtleneck style with sleeves (short or long) and collar. Must be tucked into the pants/shorts at all times. Individual schools may choose a third color from the following: solid yellow, pink, navy blue or black. Please contact individual school for their choice.

    5.1.3. Optional—sweater (v-neck or cardigan), blazer, suit jacket or vest—worn over top (color: solid navy blue, white, gray or same color as top).

GIRLS:

    5.1.4. Jumpers, skirts, pants, shorts, skorts (colors: solid navy blue, gray or khaki)—must be "dress" or "docker" style pants or knee-length shorts. Pants, shorts, skirts and skorts must be worn or belted at the waist.

    5.1.5. Tops (colors: solid white or light blue)—must be oxford, polo, or turtleneck style with sleeves (short or long) and collar. Must cover waistline when arms are raised. Individual schools may choose a third color from the following: solid yellow, pink, navy blue or black. Please contact individual school for their choice.

    5.1.6. Optional—sweater (v-neck or cardigan), blazer, suit jacket or vest—worn over top (color: solid navy blue, white, gray or same color as top).

    5.1.7. SHOES (Boys and Girls):

        1. Sneakers are not considered shoes. Sneakers are only to be worn in gym class, except as stated below under Gym Day Attire.

        2. Sandals are not permitted. (*Byars v. City of Waterbury* 2001)

Procedures for noncompliance are also given, though these are usually not as painstakingly meticulous and often remain sketchy. The sanctioning procedures for not wearing the appropriate, policy-mandated clothing can often be vague, and there have been a variety of methods and mishaps regarding the punishments doled out to noncompliant students.

Of course this is the fodder for many a lawsuit from parents against districts (see chapter 3). An examples of such procedures from Waterbury, Connecticut, follows:

> School Attire Violation as per Board Rules: *High School—First Offense:* Removal from class with opportunity to correct and return to class. If not corrected, immediate in-school suspension and notification of parent. *Second Offense:* In-school suspension and after-school detention. *Third and All Subsequent Offenses:* Out of school suspension, one day. *Middle School—First Offense:* Removal from class with opportunity to correct and return to class. If not corrected, immediate in-school suspension and notification of parent. *Second Offense:* In-school suspension and after-school detention. *Third and All Subsequent Offenses:* Out of school suspension, one day. *Elementary School:* Verbal Warning. *Second Offense:* Notify Parent/Guardian. *Third Offense:* In-house suspension, recess or lunch suspension as determined by Principal. (*Byars v. City of Waterbury* 2001)

This example is a sort of middle-of-the road approach. Other policies are *much* more Draconian, at all levels of schooling; some are more lenient. Some schools deal with infractions of their uniform codes as in the example, other schools "offer alternative schooling" to these students, and still other schools continue to suspend students from school indefinitely.[10]

As one peruses the literature on school uniforms, it becomes quite obvious that teachers must become "fashion police" to look for policy infringements on a daily basis. Indeed, this was a worry from early on in the debate on student appearance. The constitutional issues aside, a school uniform policy that does not have clear guidelines for sanctioning procedures aimed at those who do not comply with the mandated dress will be perpetually besieged with and plagued by noncompliance. Noncompliance is strongly related to another facet of implementation, the opt-out clause. It is to this we now turn.

Opting Out: Myths and Realities

The Manual on School Uniforms and years of documentation from the ACLU and other state affiliates have made it exceedingly clear that a mandatory school uniform policy that does *not* provide a bureaucratic mechanism that allows parents to "opt out" of the uniform policy will be faced with serious legal challenges. Through such opt-out policies, a district creates a space for families and parents with religious, philosophical, financial, and other "justifiable" objections to a uniform policy to exempt their children from the policy. Typically these exempted children must follow the previous dress code of the school. Simply by having an "opt-out" clause within the uniform policy, public school districts can avoid legal challenges because they have, within the text of a given policy on standardized dress, given parents the option of exemption from the policy. This said, there has been much debate and controversy over several issues concerning these "opt-out" clauses:

1. Parents may not know the details of the policy and may not understand the procedures involved in pursuing an exemption for their child.
2. There is a mismatch between the written possibility of an exemption from the policy (de jure) and the actual incidence of submitted requests ultimately receiving administrative approval (de facto).
3. There is a stigma and consequences of opting out for children and parents in the public educational domain.

If one considers the information vacuum at the surveying stage and the responsibility of the school and/or district to provide detailed and accurate information to parents so that they may make a knowledgeable decision to support the policy or not support it, the situation of information impotency becomes even more questionable at the stage of implementation and follow-through. I have had countless conversations with journalists, parents, and community members regarding the fact that, in a number of circumstances, opt-out requests are denied or not even addressed by school officials. Though concrete numbers are difficult to acquire, there is no shortage of examples of this kind of mismatch between stated possibilities and actual incidences of accepted waivers.

Preparing for Legal Challenges

Adopting a uniform policy for many districts also means adopting a defensive posture against those parents and students who may challenge the legality of the policy through the court system.[11] These preparations typically take the form of setting aside monies in the event that the district must go to trial.[12] It also has meant that educators, educational administrators, and board members can often manipulate the process, semantically construct the policy, and preemptively hedge any challenges before they foment. Chapter 3 highlights the key legal battles that have been waged and the results of those arguments; however, as of this writing, there are many, many other court cases on the dockets across this country, some that have been going on for years, others that have been filed, and others that are currently in appellate processes. A number have yet to materialize because of financial restraints and/or lack of adequate representation.

Concerning legal issues and the constitutionality of school uniforms, one is of course struck by the similarities between this issue and the banning of long hair and other modes of appearance in the 1960s and 1970s. In that movement, there were "widespread protests and litigation that resulted in 35 reported federal and state court cases and an expenditure by the schools of over $10 million in legal costs to expel long-haired boys—many with straight A averages" (Klahr n.d.). Regarding the current movement, hard data are difficult to find regarding the amount of money that has been spent by districts and individuals in the legal pursuit of defending a uniform policy or attempts to challenge the constitutionality of such a policy. As Polk County (Florida) School Superintendent Glenn Reynolds stated regarding the legal battles and uniform policies, mirroring the feeling (though possibly not the pocketbooks) of many district and school leaders: "We never want to spend taxpayers' money fighting lawsuits, but this is an issue worth fighting for" (Sager 1999). Two years after this statement, and two years into Polk County's school uniform policy, the district had spent more than $250,000 on litigation, and these fees were discounted by their law firm, Holland & Knight. In addition, this is only what was spent by the district, not what the parents spent (Alberto 2001).[13]

A school in Arizona has spent at least $260,000 on litigation, and this does not include the costs incurred by the plaintiffs in that case (*Phoenix Elementary District No. 1 v. Green* 1997). In DeKalb County, Georgia, costs for the plaintiffs were largely kept within the ACLU's overhead. By the end of 2002, it was the threat of legal action against the DeKalb County board and superintendent that eventually led to their compromise in that system. In the Houston area, legal costs are between $30,000 and $40,000 (but when asked to provide information on compliance rates, opt-out requests/acceptances, etc., the system will charge those persons inquiring up to $4,000 to comply with that request). In Mount Carmel, Pennsylvania, plaintiff costs are well over $250,000 and quite immeasurable, as of this writing, the Mount Carmel Area School District has not been forthcoming about their incurred costs since 1999, which promise to be quite large (see *Greco v. Mount Carmel Area School Board* 2001).

What cannot be measured in dollars and cents is the cost to the families and the children involved in disputes over uniform policy compliance. These are incalculable. As evidence of this problem, following is an electronic communication I received from a student who (along with his family), has been heavily involved in challenging their area's school uniform policy:

> All these things we have been fighting has taken a great toll on our family and has almost caused divorce a couple of times, only because [name] focuses so intensely on the subject that [name] almost loses [themselves] in it. Don't misunderstand though, [name] still has a great passion for the issue, as do I. We have just moved our focus back to our family now and things at home are the best they have been in a couple of years. . . . As far as legal costs are concerned . . . [it has] cost us as far as traveling all over for conventions, research costs, costs to get information from the school districts . . . .in the thousands.

Nothing can replace the time that this issue has taken away from thousands of children and families as they challenge and/or try to work within the policy of school uniforms in their public schools.

Assessing Effectiveness:
Evaluations and the Empiricization of Anecdotes

One aspect of the protocol of implementing school uniforms has, in many ways, been consistently assumed but rarely accomplished: the occasional evaluation of uniform policy effectiveness on outcomes of interest to the district and/or the individual school. It is completely sensible for a district to wonder whether a policy is having the desired impact, and, if not, whether there are unintentional and unaddressed problems with the process of implementation that might require more fine-tuning of the policy in question. In the end, few schools that have implemented uniform policies in the last ten years or so have done any kind of evaluation whatsoever.[14] This is a curious state of affairs given the complete overhaul of a school community that a uniform policy is intended to achieve (and often does accomplish—for better or worse). It is as if the new policy becomes the status quo with little or no critical study and/or insight into its actual operations and effectiveness.

The preeminent example of the problematic assessment process is that of the Long Beach Unified School District (Stanley 1996). The results of the district's "evaluation" have been severely criticized in this book as well as in other publications (see chapter 2). The results of the LBUSD evaluation of its districtwide policy, however, were actually leaps and bounds more rigorous than many other methods of evaluation. These modes often amount to the quantification of anecdotal information, which is far from a methodologically sound or rigorous attempt at assessing uniform effectiveness. A good deal of the evaluation of specific uniform policies in specific locations is in unpublished dissertations (Britt 2001; Creel 2000; Davidson-Williams 1997; Dussel 2001; Fosseen 2002; Gregory 1998; Jones 1997; Kim 1999; McCarty 2000; Murphy 1998; Pate 1998; Sher 1995; Shimizu 2000) and typically relies on extremely small samples, weak survey instruments, and often incomparable or, worse, *no* comparison groups (as in the case of LBUSD). We also have seen anecdotal meanderings on various attempts at evaluations across the country in the news media. It is becoming clear that many districts do not have in-house statisticians or individuals skilled in evaluation research who could actually construct and conduct the necessary research to determine the effectiveness of policies such as school uniforms.

FROM PRACTICE TO THE COMPOST HEAP

In the fall of 2002, Kate Zernike of the *New York Times* published an article that was a first of its kind, "Plaid's Out, Again, As Schools Give Up Requiring Uniforms." The piece cited several schools that have given up on the uniform idea in public schools: "In California alone, . . . , at least

50 schools have abandoned uniforms in the last two years. In and around Salt Lake City, 16 of the 40 schools that once required uniforms have dropped them. School officials report defections in Florida, Kansas and New Hampshire" (Zernike 2003 A1). This came as quite a surprise to many given the strong push for some ten years to require school uniforms in American public schools. To others this was not surprising at all given their experiences of failure and the pitfalls of such policies. However intriguing Zernike's piece may be, it does not, from my research, represent a trend. In fact, it is extremely difficult to find other media coverage of public schools running away from their policies of standardized dress adopted in the past decade or so. On the contrary, media coverage still focuses on adoptions, not abandonments.

It is excruciatingly difficult to obtain data regarding the number of schools and districts that have dropped their uniform policies in the last five years or so. Simply no one has collected those data. Despite the fact that the media are not covering policies that have failed, one can find evidence of reasons why various schools may be considering dropping their uniform policies. We actually are not sure why some schools are getting rid of their uniform policies, nor do we know how many schools may fall in this category; however, from a survey of the scant literature, there are a few prime suspects for the downfall of uniform policies at certain schools in certain systems.

First, and, I think, foremost, are the correlated issues of noncompliance and "opt-outs." Schools that struggle with the implementation and follow-through of a school uniform policy typically face a scenario in which a significant proportion of the parents opt out of the policy and are actually given waivers and exemptions for their children to attend school without wearing a school uniform; these students are usually counted in the noncompliance statistics (when generated) that are given in media accounts and district-level data. As an example, I use one of the few collections of compliance data readily available, from Polk County, Florida. This district's experience with uniform policies and the resulting issues of exemptions and noncompliance are discussed in the following section.

Compliance in Polk County elementary schools in 1999, ranged from a high of 95 percent to a low of 10 percent. Overall the compliance rate for these Polk County elementary schools in 1999 was 65 percent, with 22.5 percent of students' parents opting out of the policy. In the middle schools the situation was, as expected, quite different. Compliance rates in Polk County middle schools ranged from a low of 5 percent to a high of 90 percent (across thirteen middle schools). These middle schools had an overall compliance rate of 28 percent, with 51.5 percent of families opting-out of the policy (Tillman 1999). Another interesting calculation by Tillman (1999) from this compliance data is the "Blow-Off Factor" or BOF. The BOF is calculated by dividing the percent of students who have opted out of the policy into the percent of students out of uniform; thus, if BOF is greater than one, more students are out of uniform than have officially opted out (and this is a measure of the social effects of large amounts of opt-outs); if the BOF is less than one, fewer students are out of uniform than have officially opted out (a less likely scenario). The BOF for elementary schools in Polk County averaged 1.89 (SD = 1.38), with a range from 0.68 to 9.63. For middle schools, the average BOF was 1.49 (SD = 0.70), ranging from a low of 0.81 to a high of 3.63. This unique set of data illustrates that opt-outs can and do lead to higher levels of noncompliance than the sheer number of students opting out would indicate. Furthermore, these two issues combined provide a difficult context in which to effectively enforce a uniform policy. Most school officials facing this state of affairs, it is my guess, would begin to look into significantly revamping and/or doing away with the policy altogether.[15]

Related to opting out and noncompliance in the possibility that a school might revisit the decision to have a school uniform policy is the lack of parental knowledge and, ultimately, support of such policies. There has been some acknowledgment in the last two years that school boards are recognizing the faulty methods of surveying parents to gauge parental support. Parents have claimed that not all schools, most particularly within the same district, follow the districtwide policy in similar ways; there is a lack of consistency in sanctioning procedures, interpretations of the policy, leniency, etc., between schools. I have seen reports that *within* schools the policies are not consistently applied, with specific children being held more strictly to the uniform rule than other students *in the same school*. Also, it has been parents, speaking at board meetings across the county for almost five years now, who have brought to the board members' attention what little academic and scholarly research there is on the effectiveness of school uniform policies, and it appears that in some (albeit very few) cases the research is beginning to be utilized in board decisions about whether to implement a policy in their jurisdictions.

Contrary to the assumptions in the anecdotal literature, some schools have faced significant increases in student absenteeism, behavioral problems, and a general sense of student (and parental) rebellion against the policy. During the daily process of "doing schooling" in our public schools, there are quite a few reports of teachers' complaints that they must spend an inordinate amount of time policing the policy; figuring out which students have exemptions/waivers and which do not; determining who is or is not in uniform and should be; and figuring out who, among those who are exempted from the policy, is dressing according to the original dress code. This is a tall order for overworked and underpaid public school teachers (Wragg 2002) who work in schools and districts often with little to no consensus on what the purpose of education is (Hirsch 1987; Kozol 1992; Postman 1996).

Finally, for some schools the potential legal issues involved in a school uniform policy may be more than they are willing to (or can, financially) handle. As time goes on and more cases are decided on students' freedoms of expression and speech, appearance and dress, and rights when inside the "schoolhouse gate," more precedents will be set, and the terrain of these precedents will make navigating the legality of uniform policies (especially those with no opt-out possibilities) much more difficult.

These and, perhaps, several other issues form the problematic side of the uniform movement and have possibly led to the repeal of such policies at various public schools across the country. However, I do not think all of this amounts to a trend away from the school uniform. Donna Wells, former director of school safety programs for the state of Virginia, disagrees, stating: "I think uniforms have peaked for now. If there are a couple of school shootings tomorrow, we may see it again. But my sense is that right now people are focused on larger issues" (Zernike 2002).

DISCUSSION: TO UNIFORM OR NOT TO UNIFORM? IS THAT THE QUESTION?

We have seen that the usage of school uniforms in American public schools has increased quite dramatically in the last twenty years. The data on the proportion of elementary public schools that have uniforms are quite reliable, whereas those estimates for middle and high-schools are less reliable, but we can be certain that they have increased at those levels of schooling as well. The variety of anecdotal reasons for administrators to pursue the idea of a school uniform policy have been examined; to summarize, they include

1. reducing of violence and behavioral problems;
2. fostering school unity and improving the learning environment;
3. reducing social pressures and leveling status differentials;
4. increasing student self-esteem and motivation;
5. saving parents money on clothing for their children;
6. improving attendance; and, ultimately,
7. improving academic achievement.

The primary goal of this chapter is to investigate the empirical correlates to uniform policy adoption at the elementary school level. We found that school uniforms were more likely to be adopted in public schools that

1. had more low-achieving students,
2. had a higher percentage of minority students,
3. had higher levels of economically disadvantaged students,
4. were in urban areas, and
5. had low levels of parental involvement.

These were associations—not perfect—but statistically significant. Finally, we looked at the various problems associated with the process of implementing and enforcing uniform policies.

There has been a great deal of anecdote and speculation about why some schools adopt and implement school uniform policies. Some policies are designed and laid out with specific purposes, but with little or only a vague idea of the mechanisms that will affect the school and its students. Others adopt such policies with the sole purpose of reacting against national, regional, or even local pressures and fears; however, some of these schools do not have the problems associated with violence, gangs, delinquency, etc., that have led other districts to try uniforms on for size. The larger point, however, is this: Regardless of the reasons behind implementing uniform policies, if they do not actually do anything, why implement them? It is to this question (of effectiveness) that the next two chapters turn.

❺

THE EFFECTS OF SCHOOL UNIFORMS
AND DRESS CODES
ON EDUCATIONAL PROCESSES
AND OUTCOMES

There is much to support the view that it is clothes that wear us and not we them; we may make them take the mould of arm or breast, but they would mould our hearts, our brains, our tongues to their liking.

—Virginia Woolf

It's always the badly dressed people who are the most interesting.

—Jean Paul Gaultier

INTRODUCTION

This chapter reports the findings of recent research conducted using nationally representative samples of elementary, middle, and high school students as well as the results of several case studies I have been involved in analyzing over the past several years. These analyses investigate the effect of school uniforms and dress code policies on a variety of educational outcomes that are of immense interest to those involved in the school uniform debate in particular and the education of American children in general: academic achievement, truancy, pro-school attitudes and preparedness, etc.

In addition to these new analyses, I present a longitudinal analysis of the educational effects of switching from a nonuniformed school to a uniformed school (eighth grade to tenth grade, as well as kindergarten to first-grade switches). This is an exciting empirical proxy for what happens when a school goes from no uniforms to uniforms. These findings will fill a significant gap in the literature to this point: the lack of over-time data. I look at both the individual *and* the school level for the general educational effects of this kind of switch (i.e., what happens to *students* undergoing the switch *and* what happens to *schools* when undergoing this switch). Because much of the sociological literature on educational outcomes has implicated the role of school climate (Griffith 1999; Welsh 2000; Wren 1999) in providing a space for students to succeed or fail, I will also look, first, at the role of school uniform policies in increasing the probability of a school possessing a positive school climate, as measured in a variety of ways.

UNIFORMS AND SCHOOL CLIMATE VARIABLES

A great deal of conjecture has been devoted to the relationship between the implementation of school uniform policies and some idea of school climate, school spirit, or school unity. It is through this mechanism of school climate that school uniform policies are assumed to affect other outcomes like achievement and behavior. Though these links appear commonsensical, the anecdotal literature is really relying on "magical thinking" in the sense that no mechanisms for *how* and *why* uniforms would create a safer environment, a more focused and positive educational climate, or a greater sense of school pride and unity are ever offered. Couple these mysterious relationships with no empirical grounding for such claims, and one is left wondering why so many administrators and advocates continue to *take for granted* the effects of uniforms on school climate. Not surprisingly, very little empirical research has been dedicated to exploring these assumptions.[1] Both NELS and ECLS provide a plethora of questionnaire items designed to obtain a sense of the safety and educational climate in American schools. The results presented below assess the contribution that uniform policies may or may not make to improving school climate.

Data are available for the eighth-grade sample from NELS:88 to test the overall effectiveness of uniform policies on school climate across school sectors. The most interesting analyses are those that utilize the ECLS data, since they are more recent, as well as at the elementary school level, where climate has a large impact on student learning.

Uniforms and Eighth-Grade Student and Principal Perceptions of School Climate

To explore the impact of uniform policies on measures of middle school climate, two sets of scales were constructed. NELS:88 contains items that measure how students and principals perceive the various facets of their school's climate. The first set measures how students and principals view the *safety* climate of their school in terms of the degree to which tardiness, absenteeism, physical conflicts, theft, vandalism, substance use, weapons possession, and physical/verbal abuse of teachers are problems. To the degree that they are not problems, one could consider the school to have a "positive" safety climate. The second set of scales quantify the degree to which students and principals view the *educational climate* as a positive one. This includes the degree to which students get along, school spirit, quality of teaching, quality of teacher–student relationships, etc. The specific measures and the codings utilized in these scales are detailed in appendix A.

Do school uniform policies have an impact on student and principal perceptions of the safety and educational climates of their schools? Since school climate is a property of schools and not of individuals, the regression models include school-level variables to predict both types of school climate. Table 5.1 displays the results for the four models predicting the four school climate measures in these middle schools in 1988. Looking at the first column of that table, *school uniform policies do not significantly alter eighth-grade students' perceptions of their schools' safety climate.* All of the variables taken together explain these student perceptions of safety quite well ($R^2 = .41$). The factors that *do* positively affect student perceptions of safety at their schools are the aggregate achievement levels of the student body, attending Catholic or private schools, and having a stronger parental involvement network. High enrollments and the percentage of minorities in a school negatively affect students' perceptions of the safety climate. Despite opinions and hypotheses to the contrary, uniforms, however, do not play a role in perceptions of safety.

Table 5.1. Effects of Uniforms and Other Variables on Eighth-Grade Perceptions of School Climate (OLS Models, Standardized Betas)

Variables	Student Perceptions of Safety Climate	Student Perceptions of Educational Climate	Principal Perceptions of Safety Climate	Principal Perceptions of Educational Climate
Policy				
School Uniforms	−.08	−.01	−.09*	.01
Student Factors				
Minority	−.12***	.07	−.02	.05
Aggregate SES	−.05	−.30**	.15	.08
Aggregate Parent Ed.	−.08	.08	.04	.03
Aggregate Achievement	.11*	.38***	.10*	.09
School Controls				
Urban	−.04	−.03	−.03	.03
Rural	−.02	.07*	.07*	−.03
Catholic	.32***	.18***	.28***	.16**
Private	.27***	.35***	.08*	−.01
Parent Involvement	.10***	.13***	.08*	.05
Enrollment	−.29***	−.03	−.16***	−.07
Attendance Rate	.03	.10***	.10***	.10**
Student/Teacher Ratio	.06*	−.05	.04	−.06
Constant	26.44***	21.99***	19.87***	35.75***
Adjusted R^2	.41	.35	.31	.12
Standard Error	2.67	1.59	3.96	5.80
F-Value	54.57***	42.32***	35.26***	10.80***
Total N	993	993	993	993

Note: ***$p < .001$, **$p < .01$, *$p < .05$.

Even more contrary to anecdotal musings on these subjects are the results contained in column 3 of table 5.1—the factors influencing principals' perceptions of the safety climate of their schools. Controlling for a variety of factors, *school uniforms have a significant negative effect on principals' perceptions of the safety climate of their schools.* This finding contradicts the usual discussion in the anecdotal literature on school uniforms and principal perceptions and therefore is worth discussing further below. Other factors that alter principals' perceptions of the safety climate are similar to those that play a role in students' perceptions, with the exception that rural principals, on average, are more likely to view the safety climate of their middle schools more positively than suburban middle school principals. This model explains about one-third (31 percent) of the variation in these principals' perceptions. Even though these data do not allow us to understand the negative effect of uniform policies on principals' perceptions of their schools' safety climate, it could well be the case that schools that have uniform policies have higher rates of incidents that may call into question the safety of their environment.

Concerning the educational climate of these middle schools, columns 2 and 4 of table 5.1 offer results for student and principal perceptions respectively. In both cases, school uniform policies do not affect student or principal perceptions of the educational climate of their schools. A high-achieving student body, rural schools, Catholic and private schools, high levels of parental involvement at the school, as well as a high attendance rate are all factors that help create positive student images of the educational climate of a school, while principals' perceptions are most affected by the attendance rate at their schools.

Uniforms and Elementary School Principals' Perceptions of School Climate

A similar set of scales (though with different components—see appendix A) were constructed using ECLS-K and the school administrator file. These scales allow a multivariate examination of the effects of school uniform policies on both the safety climate and the educational climate of a nationally representative sample of elementary schools. Little research is done on elementary schools and school uniform policies. This is unfathomable given the increase in elementary schools that have adopted school uniforms since the early 1990s (see chapter 4). This data set finally gives us the opportunity to test the assumptions in the literature on a representative set of data from elementary schools.

Tables 5.2 and 5.3 highlight the results of the effects of uniforms and other school-level variables on elementary principals' perceptions of the safety and educational climates of the school in kindergarten and first grade respectively. Looking at column 1 and the safety environment, there is no significant effect of uniform policies on principals' perceptions of the safety climate of their elementary schools. These variables explain 36 percent of the variation in these perceptions; however, uniforms

Table 5.2. Effects of Uniform Policies and Other Variables on Elementary School Principals' Perceptions of School Climate (OLS Models, Standardized Betas)

Variables	Principals' Perceptions of the Safety Climate	Principals' Perceptions of the Educational Climate
Policy		
School Uniforms	−.08	.01
Student Factors		
Percent Minority	−.36***	−.04
Percent Free Lunch	−.23***	−.13*
Parent Involvement	.12**	.21***
School Factors		
Urban School	.09	−.02
Rural School	.06	−.17***
Private School	−.06	.04
Total Enrollment	−.05	−.23***
Average Daily Attendance	.05	.15***
Constant	11.93**	3.65
Adjusted R^2	.36	.22
Standard Error	2.05	2.94
F-Value	25.26***	15.99***
Total N	384	468

Note: ***$p < .001$, **$p < .01$, *$p < .05$.

add nothing to this model. Only parental involvement levels, so important at elementary schools, affect principals' perception of the degree of safety in their schools. Elementary schools with a high proportion of minority and poor students are more likely to have principals who express concerns about the safety of their schools. However, uniform policies do not have an impact on these principals' views.

Again, uniforms have no effect on elementary school principals' perceptions of the educational climate. Parent involvement levels and high attendance rates boost these principals' perceptions of the educational environment, while principals in schools with many poor students, rural schools, and/or schools with high enrollments are likely to have a more negative view of the educational climate of their elementary schools. This model explains 22 percent of the variation in these perceptions. In table 5.3, the results are from first-grade ECLS data. The results are very much the same for the previous year (1998–1999). Uniform policies have no effect on elementary school principals' perceptions of the safety or educational climates of these public schools.[2]

Table 5.3.   Effects of Uniform Policies and Other Variables on Elementary School Principals' Perceptions of School Climate (First-Grade Data, OLS Models, Standardized Betas)

Variables	Principals' Perceptions of the Safety Climate	Principals' Perceptions of the Educational Climate
Policy		
School Uniforms	−.07	.06
Student Factors		
Percent Minority	−.22***	−.08
Percent Free Lunch	−.37***	−.22***
School Factors		
Urban School	−.11*	.03
Rural School	.03	−.08
Private School	−.01	−.05
Total Enrollment	−.07	−.26***
Average Daily Attendance	.06	.12**
Constant	12.33**	10.27
Adjusted R^2	.35	.15
Standard Error	2.01	3.00
F-Value	32.46***	11.65***
Total N	460	471

Note: ***$p <.001$, **$p <.01$, *$p <.05$.

In addition, one must understand that these tests go beyond the assumption that uniforms affect these processes—they actually test whether they do or not. This vastly improves upon the earlier research, which tested the effects of school uniforms, for example, on school climate by asking administrators, teachers, and principals if they think uniforms do affect the climate of their schools. This chapter tests whether uniforms do indeed affect the climate of these schools and the other social-psychological processes while controlling for other key variables that may help explain variations in school climate. I find that uniforms do not play a significant role.

Aggregate Analyses of School Climate and Changes in School Climate

The results for school-level effects of uniforms on aggregate student and principal perceptions of the safety climate of the schools paint a picture similar to what we found in the individual-level analysis of the same. In the individual analyses (see table 5.1), we saw that uniform policies had no impact on eighth-grade students' perceptions of the safety climate while it had negative effects on principals' views concerning how safe their schools are. Columns 2 and 3 of table 5.4 replicate these analyses at the middle school level. The results show that *uniforms negatively affect aggregate student and principal perceptions of the safety climate of their schools.* Again, this is a finding very much contrary to expectations. Even after controlling for other factors that also have an impact on these perceptions, students and principals in uniformed schools view their schools as less safe than those who are in nonuniformed middle schools. Catholic and private schools, as well as schools whose students positively perceive the educational climate of their school, have safer perceptions of their middle schools than public school students and schools whose students do not have a positive view of the educational climate.

Table 5.4. School-Level Effects of Uniform Policies and Other Variables on Eighth-Grade Behavior and Perceived Safety Climate (OLS Models, Standardized Betas)

Variables	Aggregate Perceptions of Safety Climate (S)	Aggregate Perceptions of Safety Climate (A)
School Characteristics		
Percent Minority	−.23***	−.13***
Aggregate SES	−.13***	.15***
Catholic	.42***	.33***
Private	.26***	.16***
Urban	−.08**	−.06
Rural	−.04	.07*
Policy		
Uniform	−.14***	−.10*
School Climate		
Aggregate Student Climate Perception	.31***	.09**
Constant	15.27***	10.98***
Adjusted R²	.36	.22
Standard Error	1.08	1.58
F-Value	73.15***	35.49***
Total N	1012	1010

Note: ***p <.001, **p <.01, *p <.05.

The data from ELCS provide a much more rigorous test of the effects of school uniform policies on educational and safety climates and their correlate climate of parental involvement. Tables 5.5 through 5.7 present models that regress 1999–2000 levels of climate measures on the previous year's levels to model change from the first year (1998–1999) to the second, at the aggregate level, *in public schools only*. What we are looking for in these three sets of analyses is whether the impact of previous-year climate levels on subsequent-year climate levels (which should almost certainly be positive and quite strong) is partially explained by uniform policy changes of several kinds:

1. those public schools that had uniforms in 1998–1999 (the first year of the data collection) and still had them in the subsequent school year (Uniform → Uniform);
2. those public schools that did not have a uniform policy the first year but adopted one the following year (Non-Uniform → Uniform); and
3. those public elementary schools that had uniforms the first year of the ECLS study but dropped the policy in the subsequent year (Uniform → Nonuniform)—three "dummy variables," all in comparison to the fourth type, which is those public schools that did not have a uniform policy the first year and still did not have one the second year.

These analyses also look at the effects of other school-level changes on the climate changes in public elementary schools across these two years.

Table 5.5 reports the results of such an analysis of the effects of changes in uniform policies at the elementary school level on changes in the aggregate levels of safety climate in these schools. As one can see, in Model 1 there indeed is a strong trend between these two years in that schools with positive educational climates tended to remain that way, but this coefficient is far from perfect (.45). In fact, previous administrator perceptions of the educational climate of their elementary schools predicted 21 percent of the subsequent year's distribution of educational climate levels. Furthermore, this trend is not explained by changes in uniform policies across these two years in these schools. Changes in uniform policies, either way, had no impact whatsoever on changes in educational climate. One primary factor seemed to be implicated in decreasing educational climate levels

Table 5.5. School-Level Effects of 1999 Educational Climate, Changes in Uniform Policies, and Other Changes on 2000 Educational Climate (Public Schools Only, OLS Models, Standardized Betas)

Variables	Model 1	Model 2
Educational Climate	.45***	.50***
Policy Changes		
Uniform → Uniform		-.01
Nonuniform → Uniform		.03
Uniform → Nonuniform		-.05
School Controls		
Urban		.06
Rural		-.01
School-Level Changes (K→1)		
Safety Climate Changes		-.04
Enrollment Changes		-.18**
Percent Minority Changes		-.01
Percent Free Lunch Changes		-.07
Attendance Rate Changes		.12*
Agg. App. to Learn. Changes		.09
Parent Involvement Changes		.14*
Constant	13.02***	11.86
Adjusted R^2	.21	.31
Standard Error	2.74	2.64
F-Value	54.66***	6.68***
Total N	211	211

Note: ***$p < .001$, **$p < .01$, *$p < .05$.

across these two years: if the school went through enrollment increases. Rising attendance rates as well as more parental involvement between these two years were responsible for some significant improvement in the educational climate of these public elementary schools.

Turning now to changes in the safety climate of these public elementary schools in the late 1990s, table 5.6 shows the impact of changes in uniform policies on changes in the safety climate. The first prominent difference between the results shown in table 5.5 and those presented in table 5.6 is that explaining the changes in elementary schools' safety climates is much more difficult and a potentially much more complicated endeavor. Whereas previous educational climate levels explained 21 percent of subsequent educational climate levels in elementary schools, in the case of safety climate changes, the explanatory power of

Table 5.6. School-Level Effects of 1999 Safety Climate, Changes in Uniform Policies, and Other Changes on 2000 Safety Climate (Public Schools Only, OLS Models, Standardized Betas)

Variables	Model 1	Model 2
Safety Climate	.34***	.35***
Policy Changes		
Uniform ➔ Uniform		.14
Nonuniform ➔ Uniform		.01
Uniform ➔ Nonuniform		−.03
School Controls		
Urban		−.05
Rural		−.05
School-Level Changes (K➔1)		
Educational Climate Changes		−.02
Enrollment Changes		.06
Percent Minority Changes		.02
Percent Free Lunch Changes		.03
Attendance Rate Changes		−.02
Agg. App. to Learn. Changes		.01
Parent Involvement Changes		.06
Constant	7.68***	7.34**
Adjusted R^2	.12	.15
Standard Error	4.12	4.17
F-Value	27.92***	2.56**
Total N	211	211

Note: ***$p < .001$, **$p < .01$, *$p < .05$.

previous levels on later levels is 12 percent. In the end, one can see that changes in school uniform policies were not significant predictors of 1999–2000 safety climate levels and that the addition of other changes in the schools added only 3 percent more explanation of the variation in safety climate levels in these public elementary schools.

Finally, I want to look at changes in aggregate parental involvement levels across these two years in these public elementary schools, since much of the anecdotal debate focuses on two facets regarding parents: 1) that their support of a uniform policy is an absolute imperative, and 2) that uniform policies can possibly increase the level of parental involvement and parental communality. Table 5.7 looks at the effects of elementary school uniform policy changes on aggregate changes in the levels of parental involvement. Model 1 indicates a strong pattern: that

Table 5.7. School-Level Effects of 1999 Parent Involvement Levels, Changes in Uniform Policies, and Other Changes on 2000 Parent Involvement Levels (Public Schools Only, OLS Models, Standardized Betas)

Variables	Model 1	Model 2
Parent Involvement	.51***	.51***
Policy Changes		
Uniform → Uniform		−.05
Nonuniform → Uniform		−.03
Uniform → Nonuniform		.05
School Controls		
Urban		−.11
Rural		−.07
School-Level Changes (K→1)		
Safety Climate Changes		.04
Enrollment Changes		.03
Percent Minority Changes		−.06
Percent Free Lunch Changes		−.09
Attendance Rate Changes		−.01
Agg. App. to Learn. Changes		.19***
Educational Climate Changes		.15*
Constant	−.02	.16
Adjusted R^2	.26	.36
Standard Error	.92	.88
F-Value	73.41***	8.37***
Total N	211	211

Note: ***p <.001, **p <.01, *p <.05.

parental involvement tends to remain strong in schools that have high levels (and, conversely, tends to be low in elementary schools that have low levels) of parental involvement. Model 1 explains 26 percent of the variation in subsequent levels of parental involvement. However, *changes in school uniform policies have no significant impact on aggregate parental involvement levels in public elementary schools.* Those factors that do seem to affect parent involvement levels are the aggregate performance of the children as well as the educational climate.

According to these analyses, school uniforms do not have an impact on schools' climates either through individual-level investigations or in these school-level, aggregate analyses. These findings are much more rigorous than previous studies of school climate (see Murray 1997) and certainly contrary to the contemporary discourse on school uniform policies' potential effects. Such analyses, and their results, are detrimental to the reigning assumptions of enhancing school unity and safety through common, standardized dress policies. In fact, it is in these two areas—safety climate and educational climate—that most anecdotal advocates of school uniforms "theorize" uniforms will affect many of the other assumed outcomes like student self-esteem and behavior (see chapter 6) and academic achievement. It is to the latter outcomes, the goal of most reform efforts in American public education, that we now turn our empirical eye.

UNIFORMS AND ACADEMIC ACHIEVEMENT

The original Brunsma and Rockquemore (1998) publication found a small negative effect of school uniforms on a standardized composite test of reading and mathematics. This report utilized the tenth-grade student-level sample from NELS:88 for the analysis. Finding a negative effect of uniform policies on achievement was one of the first statistically significant findings concerning the effects of uniforms in the empirical, peer-reviewed literature. In this section, the original analyses are reevaluated using standardized tests for specific subject matter to more fully understand the effects of uniform policies on achievement in specific areas. These student-level analyses are conducted on tenth, eighth, and elementary school samples. School-level analyses are also presented to look at aggregate changes in academic achievement. The aim is to problematize the original findings to more exactly present the specific effects of the policy.

Student-Level Analyses: Effects of Uniform Policies on Tenth-Grade Standardized Achievement

Table 5.8 replicates the results from the earlier study (Brunsma and Rockquemore 1998), this time utilizing standardized beta coefficients to more appropriately secure models (across all types of subject matters) that are directly comparable to each other. Model 3, the final model, reiterates what was found earlier: Controlling for student and school factors, school uniform policies have a *negative* effect on academic achievement.

Table 5.8. Effects of Uniform Policies and Other Variables on Tenth-Grade Standardized Achievement (OLS Models, Standardized Betas)

Variables	Models		
	1	2	3
Student Controls			
Female	.05**	.05**	.02
Minority	−.14***	−.14***	−.15***
SES	.40***	.40***	.40***
School Controls			
Catholic	.04*	.08***	.08***
Private	.02	.03	.02
Rural	−.01	−.01	-.02
Urban	.01	.01	.01
Policy			
Uniform		−.06**	−.06*
Student Process			
Academic Preparedness			.05**
Pro-School Attitudes			.08***
Peer Pro-School Attitudes			−.01
Constant	51.72***	51.71***	41.79***
Adjusted R^2	.22	.22	.23
Standard Error	8.62	8.61	8.56
F-Value	118.97***	105.15***	81.20***
Total N	7,854	7,854	7,854
Effective N	2,964	2,964	2,964

Note: ***p −.001, **p −.01, *p <.05.

The dependent measure of achievement in this analysis is a standardized composite of tenth graders' reading and mathematics scores. There are a few key questions at this point:

1. Do the negative effects of uniforms on academic achievement hold up in separate analyses of reading and mathematics?
2. Does the effect hold up across all types of standardized mastery of other key subject areas?
3. What explanation, if any, does the analysis give of *how* uniforms negatively affect student-level academic achievement?

Four models were constructed in table 5.9 to analyze the effect of school uniform policies on four separate standardized achievement

Table 5.9. Effects of Uniforms and Other Variables on Tenth-Grade Reading, Math, Science, and History Achievement (OLS Models, Standardized Betas)

Variables	Standardized Achievement			
	Reading	Math	Science	History
Student Controls				
Female	.08***	−.04*	−.15***	−.09***
Minority	−.13***	−.15***	−.18***	−.13***
SES	.35***	.39***	.35***	.35***
School Controls				
Catholic	.09***	.07**	.05	.07**
Private	.03	.01	−.01	.01
Rural	−.01	−.02	.01	−.01
Urban	.02	−.01	−.02	−.01
Policy				
Uniform	−.07**	−.04	−.04	−.05
Student Process				
Academic Preparedness	.04*	.06***	.04*	.05**
Pro-School Attitudes	.08***	.06***	.06***	.06**
Peer Pro-School Attitudes	−.02	.01	−.01	−.01
Constant	41.92***	42.85***	45.88***	44.98***
Adjusted R^2	.19	.22	.21	.18
Standard Error	8.84	8.62	8.76	8.89
F-Value	62.18***	78.32***	73.16***	58.71***
Total N	7,841	7,841	7,838	7,837
Effective N	2,959	2,958	2,948	2,943

Note: ***p <.001, **p <.01, *p <.05.

tests at the tenth grade: reading, mathematics, science, and history. Columns 1 and 2 present the results for the individual components of that original composite: reading and mathematics achievement. Looking at the effects of school uniforms on these tests separately, one can see that the impact of uniforms *remains* for tenth-grade reading achievement and is *not* a significant predictor of mathematics achievement. This indicates that the original negative effect on academic achievement was specifically a *negative effect of school uniforms on student-level reading achievement*, while mathematics achievement is unaffected by whether or not tenth graders wear uniforms. Columns 3 and 4 of that table show that, after controlling for other factors, *school uniform policies do not have an effect on science or history achievement among tenth graders.*

At this point it is important to delve a bit deeper and try to understand the effects and *noneffects* of uniforms on these specific tenth-grade achievement levels. If one looks simply at the bivariate effects of uniforms on each of the achievement tests (e.g., the correlation between the uniform variable and one of the tests *before* controlling for other factors influencing that achievement), there is, in fact, a positive relationship between uniform policies and reading achievement (.04**), mathematics achievement (.05**), and history achievement (.04*).[3] However, this is precisely why multivariate models are so important, because these bivariate relationships may be explained by other variables that also are correlated with school uniform policies and/or the outcomes of interest. Knowing these bivariate associations is important because, as we see in table 5.9, after the controls are properly added to the equation, there are no effects in most cases of academic achievement and a significant *negative effect on reading.*

How can a correlation switch signs from significantly positive to significantly negative? This happens because when the important control variables are put in place, one is looking at the "purer" effect of school uniforms on reading achievement that is *not* due to other factors such as student gender, student minority status, student family SES, school type, and other student process variables. Indeed, looking across these models it is these other social and educational process and organizational variables that affect achievement, not uniform policies. The negative effect on reading achievement is a real effect and quite significant. It is not large, but it exists after controls. Why and how uniforms might negatively affect a student's reading achievement is not known. What is known, however, is that these models include more than adequate controls, and we can know with certainty that uniform policies *do not have positive effects on tenth-grade student reading aptitude and uniform policies and offer no significant contribution to the other subjects.*

As in the original Brunsma and Rockquemore (1998) article, it is interesting to note here that it is possible for uniforms to affect academic achievement through increasing those factors that *do* have an impact on achievement according to our models: academic preparedness, proschool attitudes, and peer pro-school attitudes. I encourage readers to go back to that original article (Brunsma and Rockquemore, 1998) to see the results that answer this question. In fact, uniform policies *do not* affect these other important factors; therefore, any effects of school uniforms on academic achievement are direct until shown to be otherwise. Uniforms do not, according to these results, indirectly affect academic achievement through these variables.

Student-Level Analyses: Effects of Uniform Policies on Eighth-Grade Standardized Achievement

Table 5.10 closely replicates the model used in the original tenth-grade analysis of standardized composite academic achievement, with slight modifications.[4] As one can see from looking across the models in the table, *school uniforms do not significantly affect eighth-grade student*

Table 5.10. Effects of Uniform Policies and Other Variables on Eighth-Grade Standardized Achievement (OLS Models, Standardized Betas)

	Models		
Variables	1	2	3
Student Controls			
Female	.05***	.05***	.03***
Asian	.01	.01	.01
Black	−.16***	−.16***	−.16***
Hispanic	−.10***	−.10***	−.09***
SES	.40***	.40***	.39***
School Controls			
Catholic	.03**	.03	.02
Private	.04***	.04***	.03**
Rural	.01	.01	.01
Urban	−.03***	−.03*	−.02*
Policy			
Uniform		−.01	.01
Student Process			
Academic Preparedness			.11***
Perceived Educ. Climate			.06***
Constant	51.57***	51.57***	41.59***
Adjusted R²	.25	.25	.26
Standard Error	8.67	8.67	8.57
F-Value	280.21***	252.16***	230.20***
Total N	20,336	20,336	20,336
Effective N	7,674	7,674	7,674

Note: ***p <.001, **p <.01, *p <.05.III

composite achievement levels. Similar variables do have an impact on achievement in this sense as in tenth grade: student gender, socioeconomic status, attending a private school, coming to school prepared with paper and pencil, and a perception of a positive educational climate. However, uniforms are not a part of this process; they do not help distinguish those eighth graders who achieve from those who do not.

Regarding uniform policy impacts on specific subject matter, table 5.11 shows that *uniforms do not have an impact on academic achievement among eighth graders in any subject matter.* Again, as with the tenth-grade analysis, there are positive bivariate correlations between uniform policies and these specific tests: reading (.09°°°), mathematics (.06°°°), science (.04°°°), and history (.11°°°). However, to drive the

Table 5.11. Effects of Uniforms and Other Variables on Eighth-Grade Reading, Math, Science, and History Achievement (OLS Models, Standardized Betas)

	Standardized Achievement			
Variables	Reading	Math	Science	History
Student Controls				
Female	.10***	−.03**	−.09***	−.07***
Asian	−.02	.03**	−.01	−.01
Black	−.14***	−.16***	−.18***	−.12***
Hispanic	−.09***	−.09***	−.09***	−.09***
SES	.34***	.38***	.33***	.35***
School Controls				
Catholic	.05*	−.02	−.01	.03
Private	.04***	.02*	.01	.01
Rural	.01	.01	.03**	.01
Urban	−.02	-.03*	−.04**	−.03*
Policy				
Uniform	−.01	.01	.01	.03
Student Process				
Academic Preparedness	.09***	.11***	.09***	.10***
Perceived Educ. Climate	.06***	.06***	.05***	.05***
Constant	41.64***	42.82***	44.11***	43.52***
Adjusted R²	.21	.25	.21	.21
Standard Error	8.83	8.73	8.88	8.81
F-Value	174.60***	210.60***	172.35***	171.16***
Total N	20,336	20,336	20,336	20,336
Effective N	7,665	7,660	7,637	7,615

Note: ***p <.001, **p <.01, *p <.05.

point home again: *Bivariate correlations do not imply causation.* This methodological truism is even more important when one acknowledges the complex process of schooling American children. One *needs* to control for other factors that these students bring to their educational experience, other factors that schools have that parameterize and contextualize this experience, etc. Uniform policies, contrary to popular, unsubstantiated belief, do not offer the contextualization and situation that those implementing such policies assume they do, particularly for one of the most crucial variables for all educators: academic achievement.

Student-Level Analyses: Uniform Policies and Kindergartners' Reading, Math, and General Knowledge

ECLS, in providing the first nationally representative sample of elementary school students (i.e., kindergartners in the first wave of data collection), has given researchers an important tool to assess the impact of particular policies aimed at bettering the educational environment and student success. For our purposes here, looking at the effects of uniforms on kindergartners is a unique enterprise, because if uniform policies act to distinguish students' academic achievement and readiness from elementary schools that do not have uniform policies, these effects should be witnessed in the entry into the K–12 system: kindergarten. Tables 5.12 and 5.13 provide the results for this new test of uniform effects for the fall and spring semesters respectively. These results assess the impact of uniform policies on kindergartners' reading and mathematics achievement/readiness as well as their level of general knowledge as they enter the educational system from a wide variety of social, cultural, and economic backgrounds. Do uniforms affect kindergartners' academic achievement?

Again, because the results for the fall and spring semesters mirror each other, the findings are presented in tandem. Looking at the results, *uniform policies do not affect kindergartners' reading readiness scores.* The models for reading explain roughly 30 percent of the variation in these scores. Older students, students from higher socioeconomic backgrounds, students who attend private schools, and students who have positive approaches to learning all are more ready to read, on average, than others

Table 5.12. Effects of Uniform Policies and Other Variables on Kindergarten Reading, Math, and General Knowledge Scores (OLS Models, Standardized Betas)

Variables	Reading	Fall Semester Mathematics	General Knowledge
Student Controls			
Female	.01	−.05***	−.05***
Minority	−.11***	−.12***	−.22***
Age (in months)	.14***	.19***	.17***
SES	.29***	.26***	.28***
Single Parent Household	.04**	.01	.03*
School Controls			
Private	.06***	.07***	.01
Urban	.02	.02	−.02
Rural	−.01	−.02	−.01
Total Enrollment	−.02	.02	−.05***
Percent Minority	−.03	−.01	−.10***
Percent Free Lunch	−.07***	−.08***	−.08***
Policy			
Uniform	−.01	.01	−.01
Student Process			
Approach to Learning	.25***	.33***	.23***
Constant	−8.04***	−13.22***	−5.58***
Adjusted R²	.31	.36	.42
Standard Error	7.95	5.96	6.80
F-Value	193.69***	249.94***	312.04***
Total N	15,033	15,033	15,033
Effective N	5,673	5,673	5,673

Note: ***p <.001, **p <.01, *p <.05.

after controlling for all the other factors, with poor and minority children scoring lower than others. Column 2 of both tables (5.12 and 5.13) allows us to conclude that *uniform policies do not affect kindergartners' mathematical aptitude*. These models explain 36 percent of the variation in these scores. The same factors influencing reading readiness also affect mathematics in the same ways. Finally, looking at the general knowledge scores for these kindergartners, one can see that *uniform policies do not alter the general knowledge of these children*. These models even more fully explain variations in general knowledge scores among these kindergartners— about 40 percent. The bottom line is that *uniforms are not implicated in the success or failure of kindergarten students*. Furthermore, in results (not

Table 5.13. Effects of Uniform Policies and Other Variables on Kindergarten Reading, Math, and General Knowledge Scores (OLS Models, Standardized Betas)

Variables	Reading	Mathematics	General Knowledge
		Spring Semester	
Student Controls			
Female	.01	−.08***	−.07***
Minority	−.10***	−.13***	−.21***
Age (in months)	.09***	.15***	.15***
SES	.26***	.23***	.27***
Single Parent Household	.03**	.02	.02*
School Controls			
Private	.05***	.05***	−.01
Urban	.01	.04***	−.02
Rural	.00	−.01	−.02
Total Enrollment	.02	.04***	−.04***
Percent Minority	−.01	−.02	−.11***
Percent Free Lunch	−.06***	−.06***	−.09***
Policy			
Uniform	.01	.01	−.01
Student Process			
Approach to Learning	.32***	.38***	.22***
Constant	.54	−6.35***	4.52**
Adjusted R^2	.29	.36	.39
Standard Error	9.67	7.20	6.99
F-Value	171.02***	231.626***	273.01***
Total N	14,410	14,410	14,410
Effective N	5,438	5,438	5,438

Note: ***p <.001, **p <.01, *p <.05.

shown here), school uniforms do not *indirectly* affect academics among kindergartners through increasing a positive approach to learning (which *does* significantly affect their academic success).

Table 5.14 presents some very intriguing results, which are attended to in later analyses in more depth. Looking at the effect of uniform policies on first-grade students' reading, mathematics, and general knowledge scores, one sees similar patterns in the effects of other variables on these outcomes as were evident in those analyses for kindergartners. However, one set of findings stands out: *Uniforms do have a small, significant positive effect on these first graders' reading and general knowledge scores.* These standardized positive effects of uniform policies on reading and

Table 5.14. Effects of Uniform Policies and Other Variables on First-Grade Reading, Math, and General Knowledge Scores (OLS Models, Standardized Betas)

Variables	Spring Semester		
	Reading	Mathematics	General Knowledge
Student Controls			
Female	−.01	−.11***	−.07***
Minority	−.04*	−.07***	−.08***
Age (in months)	.03*	.06**	.06**
SES	.16***	.14***	.14***
Single Parent Household	.02	.03	.03
School Controls			
Private	−04	−.02	−.04
Urban	.05**	.03	.06**
Rural	−.02	−.07***	−.06**
Total Enrollment	.01	.02	−.01
Percent Minority	−.02	−.01	−.01
Percent Free Lunch	−.05	−.07***	−.08**
Parent Involvement	−.02	−.03	−.04
Policy			
Uniform	.07***	.01	.06**
Student Process			
Approach to Learning	.60***	.56***	.48***
Constant	.63*	.46	.51
Adjusted R^2	.45	.40	.32
Standard Error	.68	.68	.81
F-Value	122.56***	99.29***	68.86***
Total N	5,581	5,516	5,305
Effective N	2,102	2,076	2,007

Note: ***$p < .001$, **$p < .01$, *$p < .05$.

general knowledge scores are small when compared to the important effect of students' approach to learning, which is crucial for success in school, as well as family class background. But the positive effect is larger than, say, the effect for age. One set of crucial analyses to test this first positive effect of uniform policies is to see whether uniform policies distinguish between those who have more positive approaches to learning and those who do not—a partial explanation for this positive uniform effect—as well as to investigate whether this effect is just an artifact of the data or if these effects can hold up in over-time change models.

We have looked at the effects of uniforms on the students who wear them versus those who do not on a variety of educational outcomes. A uniform *policy*, often seen as a student-level variable, is, in fact, also an important school-level variable, distinguishing schools whose student body must wear them from schools that do not have such a policy. The analyses presented in this section move all of the previous analyses up an analytical level by focusing on *school-level* effects of uniform policies. Schools, as organizations, contextualize and provide opportunities and constraints that impinge upon the student-level processes of academic achievement. Therefore, this section focuses on aggregate measures of achievement within schools, controlling for other school-level factors that have an impact on that achievement.

The organization of these analyses parallels the analyses done in the original article (Brunsma and Rockquemore 1998) but conducts the analyses completely at the school level. This was an important component missing from that original article. Indeed, the debate over school uniforms and the anecdotal literature speak with both the student and school levels in mind. Because of this, it is important to look at the empirical relationship between uniform policies and other school-level, aggregate factors of interest to those involved in the debate. In addition to this reasoning, many of the court cases across the country that contain data analyses in their arguments usually conduct these analyses at the school-level. This situation exists because most data available to researchers regarding particular schools and schools within districts are *school-level data*.

Although some individual student-level data exist, there is a consistent problem with obtaining analogous data from other schools for comparison. Large, nationally representative data sets provide a remedy to this situation since they sample schools from the common core of data lists of all U.S. schools and then sample students within those schools (see McDowell and Sietsema 2003). Adding to this sampling feature is the bonus of a standardized, common survey of these students and administrators. Such data provide us with an opportunity to analyze the school-level effects of uniforms, inform the debate on school uniforms, and provide a nationally representative foundation for the interpretation of local and district analyses occurring at the school level.

School-Level Analyses: A Tenth-Grade School-Level Replication of Brunsma and Rockquemore (1998)

Earlier in this chapter the original tenth-grade student-level analyses of academic achievement (composite with new analyses for the specific tests) were presented in tables 5.7 and 5.8. Table 5.15 replicates these analyses at the school level using aggregations of the measurements utilized in those previous models. These aggregate variables are aggregations within each school of the variables listed in appendix A. In addition, an important variable was added to the tenth-grade school-level analyses—the percentage of the student body who are in college preparatory tracks—as this has been strongly related to academic achievement in high school in previous literature on tracking and cur-

Table 5.15. School-Level Effects of Uniform Policies and Other Variables on Tenth-Grade Academic Achievement (OLS Models, Standardized Betas)

Variables	Standardized Achievement				
	Composite	Reading	Math	Science	History
School Characteristics					
Percent Minority	−.22***	−.20***	−.23***	−.27***	−.23***
Aggregate SES	.53***	.51***	.51***	.51***	.48***
Catholic	.05	.07	.04	.03	.06
Private	.03	.02	.03	.02	.02
Urban	.05*	.08*	.03	.01	.02
Rural	.01	.02	.01	.04	.02
% in College Prep Track	.14***	.12***	.15***	.07*	.11***
Policy					
Uniform	−.06*	−.06*	−.06*	−.08**	−.08*
School Climate					
Aggregate Preparedness	.08***	.08**	.07**	.07**	.02
Aggregate Pro-School Attitudes	.02	.03	.01	−.04	.02
Aggregate Peer Pro-School Attitudes	.01	−.03	.04	.01	−.04
Constant	41.78***	42.86***	41.66***	50.22***	48.49***
Adjusted R²	.55	.48	.55	.50	.43
Standard Error	4.35	4.41	4.43	4.56	4.75
F-Value	109.47***	81.66***	106.07***	87.01***	68.10***
Total N	965	965	965	963	963

Note: ***p <.001, **p <.01, *p <.05.

riculum differentiation (Hallinan 1987, 1995; Page and Valli 1990). The explanatory power of these models is quite extraordinary, ranging from an R^2 of .43 for aggregate history achievement to .55 for both the aggregated composite measure and mathematics achievement. The findings are especially interesting at the school level; therefore, I provide a more detailed interpretation of these results than shown previously, partially because school uniforms are indeed implicated in the aggregate achievement levels of tenth graders across the nation.

The results predicting aggregate achievement for all tests are presented in table 5.15. For the composite measure of academic achievement, *uniform policies have a significant negative effect on aggregate tenth-grade achievement.* This effect withstands the explanatory power of the control variables in this school-level model. This finding indicates that high schools that mandated school uniforms have lower tenth-grade academic achievement (using the composite measure) than high schools without uniform policies. There are additional factors that influence this aggregate composite. High schools that draw their students from a higher socioeconomic level, are located in urban districts (versus suburban districts), have high proportions of their student body enrolled in college preparatory courses, and have a student body that is relatively well prepared for their classes have higher aggregate achievement rates. On the other hand, schools with a higher percentage of minority students (nonwhite) exhibit lower levels of aggregate achievement. All of these findings are quite significant (statistically) even with the control variables competing for explaining achievement.

Aggregate tenth-grade reading achievement mirrors that of the composite results (reading is a component of the composite, as is mathematics). *High schools with uniform policies score significantly lower than schools without such policies on aggregate tenth-grade reading scores.* The same set of control variables that influenced the composite measure of achievement in positive and negative ways also affects aggregate reading achievement in the same ways, with basically comparable strength. The other subject matter contained in the aggregate composite measure of achievement is aggregate mathematics achievement for the tenth grade. Column 3 of table 5.15 presents these results for school-level tenth-grade mathematics achievement. Again, *high schools with uniform policies score significantly lower than schools without such policies on aggregate tenth-grade reading scores.* As with the aggregate composite and reading scores, the same control variables exhibit the same influence on mathematics achievement, with the exception of there being no urban/suburban difference in these aggregate rates.

Two other aggregated standardized subject tests are analyzed in table 5.15: science and history. The effects are similar: *There is a negative effect of school uniform policies on aggregate science and history achievement in tenth grade.* In fact, aggregate school-level science achievement is the *most* affected by uniform policies at the secondary level ($-.08^{**}$), even after the controls are accounted for. History achievement is also negatively affected by uniforms, but the effect is less statistically significant than that for science.

What stands out across all of these models can be summed up as follows:

1. Uniform policies negatively affect all aspects of academic achievement when analyzed at the school level.
2. The socioeconomic level of the student body is a *powerful force* in increasing achievement among tenth graders.
3. School uniform policies implemented in largely minority high schools are likely to further exacerbate the academic achievement problems witnessed in these schools.
4. Academic preparedness is an important factor in increasing overall school-level achievement.

This last point begs the question of whether it is possible for school uniforms to increase the level of student preparedness to come to classes and learn and *thereby* influence academic achievement in positive ways. From previous analyses, this seems unlikely from the analyses of student-level effects; however, there are different rules and properties at the school level than at the student level. The answer to this question is revealed in table 5.16.

School-Level Analyses: Do Uniform Policies Indirectly Affect School-Level Outcomes?

Because the models discussed previously indicated that both academic preparedness and pro-school attitudes actually worked to increase aca-

Table 5.16. School-Level Effects of Uniform Policies and Other Variables on Tenth-Grade Aggregate Academic Preparedness, Pro-School Attitudes, and Peer Pro-School Attitudes (OLS Models, Standardized Betas)

Variables	Aggregate Measures		
	Aggregate Academic Preparedness	Aggregate Pro-School Attitudes	Aggregate Peer Pro-School Attitudes
School Characteristics			
Percent Minority	−.02	.21***	.22***
Aggregate SES	.06	.03	.19***
Catholic	.05	−.06	−.02
Private	.06	.06	.05
Urban	.03	.07	.05
Rural	.08*	.03	.05
% in College Prep Track	.02	−.01	.03
Policy			
Uniform	−.01	.03	.04
Constant	9.67***	64.25***	7.02***
Adjusted R^2	.01	.05	.06
Standard Error	.78	3.12	.72
F-Value	2.17*	7.11***	9.13***
Total N	971	970	966

Note: ***$p < .001$, **$p < .01$, *$p < .05$.

demic achievement, increase attendance rates, decrease student problem behavior, and decrease aggregate drug use in these high schools, it remains possible that uniform policies have an impact on all of these outcomes by increasing the level of preparedness and pro-school attitudes. This of course is the assumption made by many advocates and authors of the anecdotal literature; however, table 5.16 tells a different story.

For uniforms to indirectly affect the other outcomes through academic preparedness and pro-school attitudes, we would need to observe statistically significant effects of uniforms on aggregate levels of these mediating variables at the school level. Table 5.16 shows this is actually not the case. *School uniform policies do not have any significant effect on aggregate measures of academic preparedness, pro-school attitudes, or peer pro-school attitudes.* Therefore, since uniforms are not a part of creating a climate in which these attitudes can flourish any more than in schools without uniforms, one can conclude that uniforms neither directly (tables 5.8 and 5.9) nor indirectly (table 5.16) affect academic achievement on the aggregate school level.

Table 5.17. School-Level Effects of Uniform Policies and Other Variables on Aggregate Eighth-Grade Reading, Math, Science, and History Achievement (OLS Models, Standardized Betas)

Variables	Standardized Achievement			
	Reading	Math	Science	History
School Characteristics				
Percent Minority	−.23***	−.17***	−.28***	−.21***
Aggregate SES	.64***	.73***	.63***	.64***
Catholic	.05	−.09**	−.07*	.01
Private	.02	−.04	−.08**	−.08**
Urban	.02	.02	.01	.01
Rural	.05*	.05*	.09***	.05*
Policy				
Uniform	.01	.01	−.01	.04
School Climate				
Aggregate Student Percent	.16***	.15***	.15***	.16***
Constant	38.13***	37.41***	38.62***	36.70***
Adjusted R²	.72	.72	.65	.64
Standard Error	2.64	3.06	3.16	3.22
F-Value	328.40***	322.03***	254.79***	222.76***
Total N	1012	1013	1012	1012

Note: ***p <.001, **p <.01, *p <.05.

School-Level Analyses: Eighth-Grade School-Level Effects of Uniform Policies

Table 5.17 summarizes the results of the eighth-grade school-level analyses of aggregate academic achievement. Looking across the models for the specific tests, one can see that *there are no effects of school uniform policies on eighth-grade aggregate reading, mathematics, science, or history achievement.* These models are indeed useful, since they explain almost three-quarters of the variation in eighth-grade school-level measures of achievement on these distinct tests. However, uniform policies play no part in this process. The socioeconomic status of the middle schools' student bodies greatly influences aggregate achievement, as does the aggregate student perceptions of the educational climate in the schools. Table 5.18 also shows that uniform policies do not affect any aggregate measures of academic achievement in eighth grade. Furthermore, since we saw above that such policies do not significantly alter the safety or educational climates of these schools, it is

Table 5.18. School-Level Effects of Uniform Policies and Other Variables on Aggregate Eighth-Grade Reading, Math, Science, and History Achievement (OLS Models, Standardized Betas)

	Standardized Achievement			
Variables	Reading	Math	Science	History
School Characteristics				
Percent Minority	−.23***	−.17***	−.28***	−.21***
Aggregate SES	.64***	.73***	.63***	.64***
Catholic	.05	−.09**	−.07*	.01
Private	.02	−.04	−.08**	−.08**
Urban	.02	.02	.01	.01
Rural	.05*	.05*	.09***	.05*
Policy				
Uniform	.01	.01	−.01	.04
School Climate				
Aggregate Student Perc.	.16***	.15***	.15***	.16***
Constant	38.13***	37.41***	38.62***	36.70***
Adjusted R^2	.72	.72	.65	.64
Standard Error	2.64	3.06	3.16	3.22
F-Value	328.40***	322.03***	254.79***	222.76***
Total N	1,012	1,013	1,012	1,012

Note: ***$p < .001$, **$p < .01$, *$p < .05$.

clear that school uniforms do not directly or indirectly affect academic achievement in middle school.

School-Level Analyses: The Effects of Uniform Policies on Aggregate Elementary School Achievement

Tables 5.19 and 5.20 present the school-level results for predicting aggregate academic achievement in elementary schools. In this case, the achievement measure is the percentage of students who achieve the reading/verbal and mathematics goals (as dictated by school, district, and/or state policies). The results indicate that *elementary schools that have mandatory school uniform policies are not significantly different from those without such policies regarding the percentage of their student body that achieves the reading/verbal or mathematics goals.* The primary influences on these aggregate achievements at the elementary school level are the percent of nonwhite students and the proportion of the student body that receives free lunches.

Table 5.19. School-Level Effects of Uniform Policies and Other Variables on Elementary School Achievement (OLS Models)

Variables	Percent Achieving Reading/Verbal Goals	Percent Achieving Mathematics Goals
Total Enrollment	.01	.08
Percent Minority	−.26***	−.22**
Percent Free Lunch	−.22**	−.19*
Percent Avg. Attendance	.02	.05
Rural	−.01	−.01
Urban	.08	.10
Private	.08	.05
Parental Involvement	.04	.06
Adm. Perceived Climate	.10	.11
Adm. Perceived Safety	.11	.14*
Uniform	.04	.04
Constant	20.49	−29.91
Adjusted R^2	.33	.27
Standard Error	19.43	20.02
F-Value	13.04***	10.23***
Total N	275	272

Note: ***p <.001, **p <.01, *p <.05.

Table 5.20. School-Level Effects of Uniform Policies and Other Variables on Elementary School Achievement (First-Grade Data, OLS Models)

Variables	Aggregate Reading/Verbal	Aggregate Mathematics
Total Enrollment	−.01	.03
Percent Minority	−.05	−.17**
Percent Free Lunch	−.24**	−.21***
Percent Avg. Attendance	.09*	.11*
Rural	−.04	−.07
Urban	.10	.14**
Private	.01	−.03
Adm. Perceived Climate	−.01	−.02
Adm. Perceived Safety	.08	.02
Uniform	.02	.01
Constant	.86	.75
Adjusted R^2	.09	.11
Standard Error	.60	.56
F-Value	5.33***	6.52***
Total N	430	428

Note: ***p <.001, **p <.01, *p <.05.

UNIFORMS AND ATTENDANCE

Another variable that was analyzed in the original article on school uniforms (Brunsma and Rockquemore 1998) was attendance. Table 5.21 presents the school-level results of this analysis. The outcomes have been aggregated across the tenth- and eighth-grade schools in the NELS sample. As one can see, *school uniform policies have no statistically significant effect on attendance at the tenth-grade school level.* These findings mirror the findings from the student-level analyses. Student body socioeconomic status, enrollment in college preparatory courses, and pro-school attitudes are school-level factors that *do* increase attendance in tenth grade, while schools located in urban areas as well as those having high percentages of minorities have lower attendance rates.

Table 5.21. School-Level Effects of Uniform Policies and Other Variables on Tenth-Grade Attendance (OLS Models, Standardized Betas)

Variables	Attendance Rate
School Characteristics	
Percent Minority	−.09*
Aggregate SES	.15***
Catholic	.11*
Private	.02
Urban	−.16***
Rural	.08*
% in College Prep Track	.13**
Policy	
Uniform	−.02
School Climate	
Aggregate Preparedness	.04
Aggregate Pro-School Attitudes	.09**
Aggregate Peer Pro-School Attitudes	.02
Constant	78.63***
Adjusted R^2	.13
Standard Error	4.95
F-Value	13.34***
Total N	932

Note: ***$p < .001$, **$p < .01$, *$p < .05$.

Uniforms and School-Level Attendance in the Eighth Grade

To look into the impact of school uniform policies on school-level attendance rates in eighth grade, three variables were considered: the overall attendance rate for the school, the aggregated degree to which students view absenteeism as a problem in their school, and the aggregated degree to which administrators view absenteeism as a problem in the same schools. Table 5.22 shows the results of these three models and uniforms' effectiveness (if any) after controlling for school characteristics and school educational climate.

The results for attendance rates show that *uniforms have no impact on the attendance rates of middle schools.* Aggregate socioeconomic status levels as well as aggregate student perceptions of the educational climate *do* affect attendance rates in middle schools. This model explains 18 percent of the variation in these attendance rates. What is interesting to note is that although more objective measures of attendance rates are not affected by

Table 5.22. School-Level Effects of Uniform Policies and Other Variables on Eighth-Grade Attendance and Perceived Absenteeism (OLS Models, Standardized Betas)

	Aggregate Attendance Measures		
Variables	Attendance Rate	Degree Absenteeism Is Problem (Stud.)	Degree Absenteeism Is Problem (Adm.)
School Characteristics			
Percent Minority	−.09*	.13***	−.01
Aggregate SES	.23***	−.15***	.39***
Catholic	.07	−.38***	.27***
Private	−.03	−.30***	.07
Urban	−.11***	.07*	−.02
Rural	.06	−.07*	.12***
Policy			
Uniform	.07	.09*	−.07
School Climate			
Aggregate Student Perc.	.15***	−.19***	.11***
Constant	83.58***	3.49***	1.30**
Adjusted R²	.18	.41	.28
Standard Error	3.62	.28	.70
F-Value	26.38	89.87***	48.76***
Total N	993	1,012	1,009

Note: ***p <.001, **p <.01, *p <.05.

school uniform policies, perceptions of problem absenteeism *are*, and the effects on student and administrators perceptions are opposing (though the administrator effect of uniforms is not significant). Student aggregate perceptions of whether absenteeism is a problem at their school are affected by uniform policies. In other words, *uniform policies create an aggregate perception among eighth-grade students that absenteeism is a problem*. The coefficient for uniform effects on administrators' perceptions of problem absenteeism is negative, though not statistically significant.

THE BIG QUESTION: UNIFORMS VERSUS DRESS CODES

The extant literature on the effects of standardized dress appears to focus primarily on school uniform policies. Many of the writings, debates, and discussions on this issue, however, fail to make the distinction between dress codes and school uniforms. They are different. A school uniform policy tells students what they *must* wear while at school, whereas a dress code specifies what students *may not* wear to school. Interestingly enough, this oversight has led researchers to investigate the effects of school uniforms without ever (to my knowledge) empirically testing the effects of the more common dress codes.[5] Without knowing the effects (if any) of dress codes on the outcomes of interest, those involved in the debate as well as those charged with making sensitive decisions about whether to implement a school uniform policy are assuming that uniforms are the answer without understanding the relationship between enforcing a dress code policy and student outcomes. In other words, it is entirely possible that dress codes *simply need to be enforced* to produce desired effects. Yet it is unclear at this stage in the research whether dress codes actually affect the very things that advocates of school uniforms assume mandatory uniform policies will.

This analysis is readily accomplished by simply replacing the variable indicating whether a school has a uniform policy with a new variable that distinguishes between those schools that have dress code policies and those that do not. In the interest of space, it is not practical, nor does it make sense, to reproduce all the previous tables to compare the effects of uniform policies with dress code policies on the outcomes of interest. Instead, two tables will suffice to show the differential effects of these two types of standardized dress policies. Table 5.23 summarizes the effects of uniforms for the all the previous *student-level analyses*, while table 5.24 does the same for all previous *school-level analyses*. The columns include the effects of uniforms (column 1) and dress codes (column 2). The rows indicate the dependent variable and the referent table from which the uniform effect was drawn. The columns present the standardized beta coefficients from the regression models for the effects of uniforms (column 1) and dress codes (column 2) *after controlling for the exact same factors as in the parallel uniform analysis*. These coefficients are directly comparable to each other because they are standardized effects.

The Differential Effects of School Uniform Policies and Dress Code Policies

Comparison of the Student-Level Effects of Uniforms and Dress Codes   Table 5.23 shows the variable effect comparisons for uniforms and dress codes on all previous student-level analyses. Because most of the results for *both* uniforms and dress codes are not significant, I focus only on the comparisons where one of the effects is statistically significant. The first comparison of note is that predicting student perceptions

Table 5.23.   Comparison of Uniform and Dress Code Effects for All Student-Level Analyses (Standardized Betas)

Analysis (Table)	Uniforms	Dress Codes
Tenth-Grade Self-Concept (3.1)	.04	.01
Tenth-Grade Locus of Control (3.2)	.02	.01
Eighth-Grade Self-Concept (3.3)	.02	.01
Eighth-Grade Locus of Control (3.4)	.01	.01
Eighth-Grade Perceptions of Safety Climate (S) (3.7)	−.08	.03*
Eighth-Grade Perceptions of Educational Climate (S) (3.7)	−.01	.01
Eighth-Grade Perceptions of Safety Climate (A) (3.7)	−.09*	−.06*
Eighth-Grade Perceptions of Educational Climate (A) (3.7)	.01	.05
Tenth-Grade Composite Achievement (4.1)	−.06*	−.03*
Tenth-Grade Reading Achievement (4.2)	−.07**	−.02
Tenth-Grade Mathematics Achievement (4.2)	−.04	−.04*
Tenth-Grade Science Achievement (4.2)	−.04	−.03
Tenth-Grade History Achievement (4.2)	−.05	−.03
Eighth-Grade Composite Achievement (4.3)	.01	−.01
Eighth-Grade Reading Achievement (4.4)	−.01	−.01
Eighth-Grade Mathematics Achievement (4.4)	.01	−.02
Eighth-Grade Science Achievement (4.4)	.01	−.02
Eighth-Grade History Achievement (4.4)	.03	−.01

Note: ***p <.001, **p <.01, *p <.05.

of the safety climate. School uniforms had no significant effect on these perceptions; however, *dress codes do have a positive effect on perceptions of the safety climate of middle school students.* In another pair of significant effects, both uniforms and dress codes had significant negative effects ($-.09$* and $-.06$* respectively) on eighth-grade principals' perceptions of the safety environment. The other three comparisons of note all deal with tenth-grade academic achievement. Both dress codes and uniform policies negatively affect the composite achievement of these tenth graders, while uniforms affect reading achievement negatively and dress codes affect mathematics achievement negatively.

Comparison of the School-Level Effects of Uniforms and Dress Codes Table 5.24 contains the comparisons of uniform and dress code effects on all previous school-level analyses. Like uniform policies, dress code policies have very little effect on the processes and outcomes of interest in these analyses. This fact alone may be the most significant finding

Table 5.24. Comparison of Uniform and Dress Code Effects for All School-Level Analyses (Standardized Betas)

Analysis (Table)	Uniforms	Dress Codes
Tenth-Grade Composite Achievement (5.1)	$-.06$*	$-.03$
Tenth-Grade Reading Achievement (5.1)	$-.06$*	$-.01$
Tenth-Grade Mathematics Achievement (5.1)	$-.06$*	$-.04$
Tenth-Grade Science Achievement (5.1)	$-.08$**	$-.04$
Tenth-Grade History Achievement (5.1)	$-.08$*	$-.01$
Tenth-Grade Attendance Rates (5.2)	$-.02$	.03
Tenth-Grade Aggregate Perceptions of Behavior (5.2)	.05	.01
Tenth-Grade Aggregate Drug Use (5.2)	.01	.01
Tenth-Grade Aggregate Academic Preparedness (5.3)	$-.01$	$-.01$
Tenth-Grade Aggregate Pro-School Attitudes (5.3)	.03	$-.01$
Tenth-Grade Aggregate Peer Pro-School Attitudes (5.3)	.04	$-.01$
Eighth-Grade Aggregate Reading Achievement (5.5)	.01	$-.02$
Eighth-Grade Aggregate Mathematics Achievement (5.5)	.01	$-.03$
Eighth-Grade Aggregate Science Achievement (5.5)	$-.01$	$-.03$
Eighth-Grade Aggregate History Achievement (5.5)	.04	.01
Eighth-Grade Attendance Rates (5.6)	.07	.02
Eighth-Grade Aggregate "Absenteeism is a Problem" (S) (5.6)	.09*	.06*
Eighth-Grade Aggregate "Absenteeism is a Problem" (A) (5.6)	$-.07$	.08***
Eighth-Grade Aggregate Perceptions of Drug Use (S) (5.7)	.06	$-.07$*
Eighth-Grade Aggregate Perceptions of Drug Use (A) (5.7)	$-.06$	$-.06$*
Eighth-Grade Aggregate Student Behavior (5.8)	$-.03$	.01
Eighth-Grade Aggregate Perceptions of Safety Climate (S) (5.8)	$-.14$***	.01
Eighth-Grade Aggregate Perceptions of Safety Climate (A) (5.8)	$-.10$*	$-.07$*

Note: ***p <.001, **p <.01, *p <.05.

of this brief report on these comparisons. A few significant differences deserve attention. First, while uniform policies *significantly and negatively* affect all aspects of tenth-grade aggregate academic achievement scores, *dress codes do not affect tenth-grade school-level achievement rates at all.* Second, in both middle schools with dress codes and those with uniforms, aggregate student perceptions of problematic absenteeism among the student body are likely to be higher than in those schools without such dress policies. Administrators (principals) are more likely to perceive absenteeism as a problem in schools with dress codes than in those without such policies. Third, though uniforms have no effect on eighth-grade aggregate student and administrator perceptions of student drug use on campus, *dress code policies appear to lead to a view among both students and principals that their school does not have a drug problem.* Finally, in middle schools with mandatory uniform policies, students were less likely to perceive their schools as safe. On the other hand, this negative effect is not apparent with dress code policies, though there is no positive effect either. Principals of both uniformed schools and those with dress codes are more likely to have a negative view of the safety climate of their middle schools than principals at schools without these policies.

These comparisons point to a sobering and obvious culmination of evidence that policies of dress, whether they be uniforms or dress codes, do not make a difference in the complex and interwoven society of the school. Such policies, it appears, have the political benefit of being commonsensical enough that parents and educators buy into them; however, these policies do not include a notion of exactly how complicated and multifaceted the social world in general is and how equally complex the process of schooling is. *There is no evidence from this set of analyses that dress codes or uniforms positively affect the school or its students in discernible ways, nor do they influence the very processes that do affect schools and students (i.e., climate, pro-school attitudes, etc.).*

IS IT TOO EARLY TO TELL? PROSPECTS FOR THE LONGEVITY OF UNIFORM POLICIES

The need for longitudinal data to assess the impact over time of school uniform policies on a variety of educational and social-psychological outcomes is currently at an all-time high. Coupled with this demand is the always-present problem of collecting such data. I have previously discussed the dilemma of wanting to use data collected from individual schools that are currently involved in legal battles over school uniforms but at the same time needing generalizability. The problem is needing certain specific measures of particular processes implied in the discourse surrounding the effects of school uniforms but not finding such data available at the local, district, or state level in many cases. These issues intersect with the desire researchers have to obtain longitudinal data that reliably and validly measure processes and outcomes of interest before the implementation of the uniform policy and after and to have for controlling purposes comparable data across a wide variety of both schools that have uniform policies and those that do not. Unfortunately, the foresight involved and the exorbitant costs of collecting such a data set have made such a collection effort impossible and impractical. The National Center for Educational Statistics can only collect these amazing, representative data sets with the complete help and backing of the U.S. government. Therefore, researchers interested in having rigorous and broad educational data sets useful to assess effectiveness of policies, such as uniforms, should look toward these data sets to try to implement research designs and methodological proxies for the kinds of data that we simply do not have in the United States.

This section conceptualizes the longitudinal issue in a slightly different manner. Because NELS and ECLS include two waves of in-school data collection (eighth and tenth grades and kindergarten and first grade, respectively), and in lieu of the kinds of data we need and want to test these longitudinal ideas about the effects of uniforms, we can pose the question of whether students who move from eighth to tenth grade (and from kindergarten to first grade), which typically (but not necessarily) involves a move from one school to another, also switch from a school that did not have a uniform policy to one that does. Furthermore, we can assess through empirical analysis whether or not the individual student-level and/or the institutional/organizational switch from a nonuniform school to a uniform school is related to changes in standardized achievement scores and other educational outcomes. We can further compare these effects (if any) to baseline effects of remaining in a uniform school from eighth to tenth grade *and* kindergarten to first grade, of moving out of a uniformed school, and of staying in a nonuniformed school (the most prevalent situation, especially in the middle and secondary levels of schooling in the United States). This is the methodological and empirical proxy I am proposing to test these ideas of longitudinal swath and change. This first-time analysis is carried out in the following section.

Effects of Middle School to High School Switches under Uniform Policies

Before looking into the empirical relationships between student and/or school switches from schools with one type of policy to schools with another, it is important to get a sense of how prevalent such moves are. Of the entire NELS eighth- to tenth-grade panel sample (12,706 students with valid cases), 1.1 percent (136 cases) made a move from a nonuniformed middle school to a uniformed high school. Almost 5 percent (4.7 percent or 597 students) moved from a uniformed middle school to a nonuniformed high school. Another 5.3 percent (673) stayed in uniformed schools from eighth through tenth grades. Finally, the majority of students (88.9 percent) stayed in nonuniformed schools for these years of their schooling. The low number of students who moved from nonuniformed to uniformed schools—the move we are particularly interested in for this report—can make statistical inferences difficult; however, this is a nationally representative data set, and, therefore, 1.1 percent of the eighth-grade population in 1988 moved from a nonuniformed middle school to a uniformed high school in 1990. If there is any relationship between this change and changes in the outcomes of interest, the data analysis should pick it out.[6]

If we look just at those students who remained in the public school system through the move from the eighth to the tenth grade, the percentages shift greatly. The total number of sampled students who remained in the public system throughout this shift is 10,258. Out of this public panel sample size, 0.5 percent (48 students) made the move we are interested in, from nonuniformed to uniformed schools. The same percentage went the other direction, from uniformed to nonuniformed schools. Because of the very small number of public schools with uniform policies in the late 1980s and early 1990s, only 0.1 percent of these public panel sample members remained in public uniformed middle and high schools. Finally, the vast majority of public school students (98.9 percent) remained in nonuniformed schools.

The first step in this analysis is to see if there are any correlations between switching schools (and policies) and changes in the outcomes of interest over the same period of time. If there are correlations that are statistically significant and moderate (.10 or higher), *then* we can look into modeling these effects. However, if the correlations are only mildly suggestive of a relationship (significant correlations of .01 to .09), then, from the previous analyses in this report, these bivariate correlations will most certainly disappear once we control for other changes occurring alongside these changes. So, are there indeed correlations between students being switched to schools with different dress policies and other student educational and social-psychological changes? Table 5.25 reports these results.

Table 5.25 summarizes the results of the correlational analysis described above. The results are broken down into two samples: the entire eighth- to tenth-grade panel sample and the eighth- to tenth-grade public school panel sample only. Looking at the total sample, it is clear that the switch of interest to us here (N ➔ U) is unrelated to any of the dependent changes under scrutiny. In other words, among all school types, *there is no correlation between students who switch from nonuniformed to uniformed schools and changes in their academic achievement or perceptions of the safety climate of their schools.* The other, less interesting move (U ➔ N) does appear to be correlated very slightly with increased mathematics achievement, decreased history achievement, and increased perceptions of the safety climate; however, based on our previous analyses, these correlations are very small and unlikely to remain as significant predictors after the introduction of control variables into the models. Readers should not give these any weight.

Movements from a middle school to a high school that keep students in the same type of dress policy (U ➔ U and N ➔ N) show some interesting, though sideline, issues. Remaining in a uniformed (typically Catholic or private) school appears to have cumulative effects for perceptions of the safety climate (.10°°°), while remaining in a nonuniformed (usually public) school appears to lessen these perceptions. These results are, I believe, not a function of the uniform policies (or

Table 5.25. Correlations between Eighth- to Tenth-Grade Policy Changes and Eighth- to Tenth-Grade Achievement and Perception of Safety Climate Changes

Dependent Changes Eight to Tenth Grades	Total Panel				Public Panel			
	U→U	U→N	N→U	N→N	U→U	U→N	N→U	N→N
Composite Achievement Changes	n.s.	n.s.	n.s.	n.s.	n.s.	.03**	n.s.	n.s.
Reading Achievement Changes	n.s.	n.s.	n.s.	n.s.	n.s.	.03**	n.s.	−.02*
Mathematics Achievement Changes	.03**	.02*	n.s.	−.03***	n.s.	.02*	n.s.	n.s.
Science Achievement Changes	n.s.	n.s.	n.s.	n.s.	n.s.	n.s.	n.s.	n.s.
History Achievement Changes	n.s.	−.02*	n.s.	.02**	n.s.	n.s.	n.s.	n.s.
Perceptions of Safety Climate Changes	.10***	.03***	n.s.	−.09***	n.s.	n.s.	−.03***	.02*

Note: ***p <.001, **p <.01, *p <.05; "n.s." = not statistically significant.

Table 5.26. Correlations between Eighth- to Tenth-Grade Policy Changes and Tenth-Grade Achievement and Perception of Safety Climate

Tenth-Grade Outcomes	Total Panel				Public Panel			
	U→U	U→N	N→U	N→N	U→U	U→N	N→U	N→N
Composite Achievement	.10***	.06***	n.s.	−.12***	−.02*	n.s.	n.s.	n.s.
Reading Achievement	.10***	.07***	n.s.	−.12***	n.s.	n.s.	n.s.	n.s.
Mathematics Achievement	.09***	.05***	n.s.	−.10***	−.02*	n.s.	n.s.	n.s.
Science Achievement	.05***	.05***	n.s.	−.07***	−.02*	n.s.	n.s.	n.s.
History Achievement	.07***	.06***	n.s.	−.10***	n.s.	n.s.	n.s.	n.s.
Perceptions of Safety Climate	.07***	.03**	n.s.	−.07***	n.s.	n.s.	−.03**	n.s.

Note: ***p <.001, **p <.01, *p <.05; "n.s." = not statistically significant.

lack thereof) but rather the more pertinent effect of moving from *middle school* to *high school*, a change that can have significant effects on students.

If we look solely at the correlations for the public-only panel sample we see a slightly different pattern of relationships. The move of interest for us here (N → U) is slightly negatively correlated with a decrease in student perceptions that their schools are safe. Remaining in a nonuniformed school in the public system is weakly, though significantly, correlated with lower reading achievement and safer perceptions of schools. On the other hand, remaining in a uniformed school within the public school system from the eighth to the tenth grade has no association with other relevant changes. Finally, leaving a middle school that has a uniform policy and going into a high school that does not is correlated, again very weakly, with increased academic achievement over this period of time. It is important to note that though there appear to be some minor patterns in these associations and relationships, these are extremely weak correlations and would never withstand the adequate controls for other significant changes across this time span for these students.

One can also look at the relationships of such switches with tenth-grade outcomes only instead of eighth- to tenth-grade *changes* in those outcomes (though this is a much less robust comparison than the previous one). Table 5.26 presents these results. Almost all of the tenth-grade outcomes are significantly correlated with all of the types of switches except one, nonuniformed to uniformed. More important is to look at the *public-only panel sample,* which is much more relevant for the purposes of these reports.

Looking only at the public school panel sample (i.e., students who make these four types of moves *within the public school system*), there are more telling results. Remaining in a uniformed school while at the same time remaining in the public school system is negatively correlated with academic achievement changes from the eighth to the tenth grade. The move of interest (N → U, although all of these moves are important to look at) shows a small, weak, but significant negative correlation with perceptions of the safety climate of a school. However, these relationships, although their pattern of directions leads to a bit more consensus on an interpretation, are not very strong.

Effects of Kindergarten to First-Grade Switches in Uniform Policies

The data from ELCS also provide us with a way to longitudinally proxy the potentiality of longer term effects of uniform policies on elementary students' academic achievement (reading, math, general knowledge, etc.) as they move from kindergarten to first grade. Tables 5.27 through 5.29 present these over-time results. What we are looking for in these three sets of analyses is whether the impact of previous year achievement levels on subsequent year climate levels (which should almost certainly be positive and quite strong) is partially explained by uniform policy changes of several kinds, again, for

1. those public schools that had uniforms in 1998–1999 (the first year of the data collection) and still had them in the subsequent school year (Uniform ➔ Uniform, 11 percent of all public schools were in this scenario);
2. those public schools that did not have a uniform policy the first year but adopted one the following year (Non-Uniform ➔ Uniform, 4.3 percent of all public schools were in this scenario); and
3. those public elementary schools that had uniforms the first year of the ECLS study but dropped the policy in the subsequent year (Uniform ➔ Nonuniform, 0.8 percent of all public schools were in this scenario).

These are three "dummy variables" all in comparison to the fourth type, which is those public schools that did not have a uniform policy the first year and still did not have one the second year (83.9 percent of all public elementary schools were in this scenario). These analyses will also look at the effects of other school-level changes on the achievement changes among public elementary students across these two years.

Tables 5.27 through 5.29 present the results of previous achievement on subsequent achievement for elementary school students and the possibility that changes in uniform policies are implicated in any way in that process. For reading scores (table 5.27), we can see that the overall trend is very strong and positive (kindergarten reading levels are highly associated with first-grade reading abilities). However, there is *no effect*

Table 5.27. Effects of Kindergarten Reading/Literacy, Uniform Policies, and Other Changes on First Graders' Reading/Literacy Scores (OLS Models, Standardized Betas)

Variables	First-Grade (Spring) Reading Achievement		
	Model 1	Model 2	Model 3
Kindergarten Achievement	.60***	.60***	.62***
Policy Changes			
Uniform → Uniform		.04	.03
Nonuniform → Uniform		.03	.03
Uniform → Nonuniform		−.01	.03
Student Controls			
Female			.03
Minority			−.04
Age (in months)			.02
SES (changes in)			−.04*
Household (changes in)			−.02
Student Moved K→ 1st			.03
School Controls			
Private			−.01
Urban			−.02
Rural			−.09***
Enrollment (changes in)			−.02
% Minority (changes in)			.02
% Free Lunch (changes in)			.01
% Parent Involv. (changes)			−.01
Educ. Climate (changes)			−.01
Safety Climate (changes)			−.01
Student Process			
App. to Learning (changes)			.28***
Constant	.98***	.97***	.66***
Adjusted R²	.36	.36	.46
Standard Error	.73	.72	.67
F-Value	722.81***	181.69***	52.51***
Total N	3,380	3,380	3,380
Effective N	1,271	1,271	1,271

Note: ***p <.001, **p <.01, *p <.05.

of uniform changes on explaining these kindergarten to firstgrade trends in reading levels among elementary school students. What does affect this trend is if there are corresponding changes (in the positive direction) in these students' approaches to learning (and, conversely, those students whose approach to learning radically plummets between

Table 5.28. Effects of Kindergarten Math Achievement, Uniform Policies, and Other Changes on First Graders' Math Scores (OLS Models, Standardized Betas)

Variables	First-Grade (Spring) Math Achievement		
	Model 1	Model 2	Model 3
Kindergarten Achievement	.48***	.48***	.50***
Policy Changes			
Uniform → Uniform		.01	.02
Nonuniform → Uniform		.03	.04
Uniform → Nonuniform		−.01	−.02
Student Controls			
Female			−.03
Minority			−.08***
Age (in months)			.04
SES (changes in)			−.04
Household (changes in)			−.01
Student Moved K→ 1st			.02
School Controls			
Private			−.01
Urban			−.06*
Rural			−.14***
Enrollment (changes in)			−.02
% Minority (changes in)			.01
% Free Lunch (changes in)			.01
% Parent Involv. (changes)			−.01
Educ. Climate (changes)			.01
Safety Climate (changes)			−.04
Student Process			
App. to Learning (changes)			.25***
Constant	1.53***	1.53**	.94*
Adjusted R^2	.23	.23	.32
Standard Error	.78	.78	.74
F-Value	363.43***	55.99***	15.56***
Total N	3,306	3,306	3,306
Effective N	1,243	1,243	1,243

Note: ***p <.001, **p <.01, *p <.05.

kindergarten and first grade will also see a corresponding decrease in their reading improvement).

Elementary school improvements in mathematics achievement levels are summarized in table 5.28. We can see, as with reading, that the trend toward improvement in these early grades is again strong (but not

Table 5.29. Effects of Kindergarten General Knowledge, Uniform Policies, and Other Changes on First Graders' General Knowledge Scores (OLS Models, Standardized Betas).

Variables	First-Grade (Spring) General Knowledge		
	Model 1	Model 2	Model 3
Kindergarten Gen. Knowledge	.42***	.42***	.43***
Policy Changes			
Uniform → Uniform		.01	.02
Nonuniform → Uniform		.03	.03
Uniform → Nonuniform		−.03	−.04
Student Controls			
Female			.02
Minority			−.09***
Age (in months)			.05*
SES (changes in)			−.02
Household (changes in)			−.02
Student Moved K → 1st			−.02
School Controls			
Private			−.01
Urban			.01
Rural			−.10***
Enrollment (changes in)			−.01
% Minority (changes in)			.03
% Free Lunch (changes in)			.01
% Parent Involv. (changes)			.03
Educ. Climate (changes)			.03
Safety Climate (changes)			−.03
Student Process			
App. to Learning (changes)			.21***
Constant	1.69***	1.69***	.72
Adjusted R^2	.17	.17	.23
Standard Error	.88	.88	.85
F-Value	197.37***	49.86***	13.87***
Total N	3,205	3,205	3,205
Effective N	1,205	1,205	1,205

Note: ***$p < .001$, **$p < .01$, *$p < .05$.

nearly as strong as for reading) and that *uniform policy changes from kindergarten to first grade (or elementary schools that changed policies between 1998–1999 and 1999–2000) have no effects on mathematics improvement.* Again, the crucial factor is for schools to increase students' desire and approach to *learning how to learn* (approaches to learning). The findings regarding these elementary students' progress in their

Table 5.30. Effects of Kindergarten Approaches to Learning, Uniform Policies, and Other Changes on First Graders' Approaches to Learning Scores (OLS Models, Standardized Betas)

Variables	First-Grade (Spring) General Knowledge		
	Model 1	Model 2	Model 3
Kindergarten Approach To Learning	.52***	.52***	.49***
Policy Changes			
Uniform → Uniform		.01	.01
Nonuniform → Uniform		.03	.04
Uniform → Nonuniform		.02	.02
Student Controls			
Female			.10***
Minority			−.04
Age (in months)			.02
SES (changes in)			-.01
Household (changes in)			−.05*
Student Moved K → 1st			.01
School Controls			
Private			.01
Urban			.01
Rural			−.03
Enrollment (changes in)			.01
% Minority (changes in)			.02
% Free Lunch (changes in)			.06*
% Parent Involv. (changes)			.06*
Educ. Climate (changes)			.06*
Safety Climate (changes)			−.02
Constant	1.34***	1.33***	1.18***
Adjusted R²	.27	.27	.29
Standard Error	.61	.61	.60
F-Value	495.87***	124.54***	28.97***
Total N	3,520	3,520	3,520
Effective N	1,323	1,323	1,323

Note: ***p <.001, **p <.01, *p <.05.

general knowledge, not surprisingly, mirror the previous two findings for reading and mathematics. In the end, *changes in school uniform policies do not affect improvement in general knowledge in elementary schools.* The crucial factor for all three types of involvement improvements in these early years of schooling is inculcating the love of learning. It is to this which we now turn.

Table 5.31.   School-Level Effects of 1999 Aggregate Approach to Learning Levels, Changes in Uniform Policies, and Other Changes on 2000 Aggregate Approach to Learning Levels (Public Schools Only, OLS Models, Standardized Betas)

Variables	Model 1	Model 2
Approach to Learning	.53***	.53***
Policy Changes		
Uniform ➔ Uniform		−.06
Nonuniform ➔ Uniform		.03
Uniform ➔ Nonuniform		.02
School Controls		
Urban		−.03
Rural		−.10
School-Level Changes (K ➔ 1)		
Safety Climate Changes		−.02
Educational Climate Changes		−.01
Enrollment Changes		.01
Percent Minority Changes		.07
Percent Free Lunch Changes		.07
Attendance Rate Changes		.07
Parent Involvement Changes		.20***
Constant	1.42***	1.44***
Adjusted R^2	.28	.35
Standard Error	.40	.39
F-Value	81.11***	8.11***
Total N	211	211

Note: ***$p < .001$, **$p < .01$, *$p < .05$.

Perhaps uniform policies (and changes in uniform policies) work to improve academic outcomes through the improvement of the individual-level desire to learn and/or the organizational climate of the school of loving to learn. Tables 5.30 and 5.31 present the results testing this possibility using individual increases in approaches to learning as well as school-level changes in approaches to learning. Concerning individual student-level increases in their approach to learning from kindergarten to first grade, table 5.30 shows that uniform policies do not affect improvements in approaches to learning. The key variable for increasing individual approaches to learning, year to year in elementary school, is enhancing the level of parental involvement in the school as well as increasing the general educational climate (both of which are related, but distinct enough to have separate effects on such improvements). What about at the school level? Do uniforms increase an overall, contextual-level approach to learning (this is one of the supreme assumptions of the uniform movement)? Table 5.31 shows that uniform policies do not have a significant effect on school-level approaches to learning, but that parental involvement levels are crucial. In the end, these analyses show that *uniform policies (and changes in uniform policies) in elementary schools do not affect academic achievement over time directly or indirectly through an increase in approaches to learning. Uniforms do not affect approaches to learning changes either.*

SUMMARY

In the end, the analyses in this chapter have painted a fairly clear picture: *School uniform policies do not significantly affect students' educational outcomes, and, in some cases, they may be more harmful than previously thought.* In all, school uniform policies do not significantly alter middle or high school students' perceptions of the educational and safety climates of their schools, but such policies do appear to affect principals' perceptions of these important climate variables. Uniform policies did not help us differentiate between higher performing students and higher performing schools; however, such policies were associated with lower achievement in some subjects—though the effects were negligible. Overall, school uniform policies did not directly affect academic achievement in elementary, middle, or high schools. Nor did uniforms show any possibility of affecting these outcomes indirectly, through parental involvement, climate variables, enhancing academic preparedness and pro-school attitudes, or elementary students' approaches to learning levels. Thus, uniform policies neither directly nor indirectly influence academic achievement.

THE EFFECTS OF SCHOOL UNIFORMS AND DRESS CODES ON BEHAVIORAL AND SOCIAL PROCESSES AND OUTCOMES

> When you can't do anything truly useful, you tend to vent the pent up energy in something useless but available, like snappy dressing.
>
> —Lois McMaster Bujold

> Dress is at all times a frivolous distinction, and excessive solicitude about it often destroys its own aim.
>
> —Jane Austen

INTRODUCTION

In this chapter, I test the prominent assumptions of school uniform advocates that school uniform policies will affect student behavior, self-perception, self-esteem, and other behavioral and social psychological outcomes at the individual level. Furthermore, I conduct analyses to assess whether uniformed schools have greater school pride and school unity than nonuniformed schools, another untested assumption of the school uniform movement. Using ECLS data on elementary school students and NELS data on eighth and tenth graders, I assess the effects of such a policy on these important social-psychological and school climate variables using nationally representative data. Both NELS and ECLS data allow researchers to compare the effects of dress code policies and school uniform policies—an analysis that has heretofore not been done *and* whose results have only been assumed but never tested.

When one peruses the literature, it remains unclear whether school uniforms affect these processes. Do school uniforms have an impact on student self-concepts, loci of control, and other measures of social-psychological well-being? Does standardized dress have an impact on how elementary school students externalize and/or internalize problems? It is to these questions that this chapter is devoted.

The results of the data analyses that explore these questions are presented below. The results for tenth-grade student self-concept and locus of control models are discussed first. This is followed by a summary of the results for eighth grade. Finally, the relationship between school uniform policy effects on elementary students' degree of self-control and the externalization/internalization of problem behaviors is presented.

As do the majority of the analyses in this book, each begins with a set of control variables that are known to affect both self-concept and locus of control (i.e., gender, minority status, socioeconomic status, etc.), thereby eliminating these influences from the possible impact on school uniform policies. Second, the school uniform variable is introduced to assess its impact on the dependent variables. Next, student process and school climate variables are entered into the equation to possibly account for mechanisms through which uniform policies affect self-concept and locus of control (if they do at all).[1]

UNIFORMS AND SELF-ESTEEM/SELF-CONCEPT

An assertion that has surfaced again and again in the anecdotal literature on the effects of school uniforms is that such standardized policies will somehow decrease the impact of in-school social-psychological stressors such as interpersonal comparison, status competition, and other sources of diversity and difference. The assumption is that school uniforms will minimize these processes; "level the playing field"; provide a context in which students can reflect on themselves and their relationship to others without the distraction of comparison and competition; and, through some unnamed mechanism, increase student self-esteem (or self-concept) in particular. In general, the literature also presupposes that a variety of psychological benefits can derive from the implementation of a school uniform policy, creating an overall positive atmosphere for students of all levels to feel good about themselves and their schooling experiences.

Although some empirical research has been conducted on this link between uniforms and self-esteem, the findings are inconclusive and the methodologies are questionable (see chapter 2 for more detailed summaries). Though the literature hypothesizes a positive effect of uniforms on student self-esteem through the above "logic," it may be the case that uniforms actually stifle and redirect the very factors that are implicated in the construction of a positive self-concept through a leveling of individual differences (though there is no evidence that uniforms actually do this), a decreasing of interpersonal comparison based on clothing, and an overall message that individualism and personal expression do not matter, thus, creating a negative self-image.

The Impact of School Uniforms on Tenth Graders' Self-Esteem

Table 6.1 presents the results of wearing a uniform on tenth-grade students' sense of self-esteem.[2] Looking across the models, it is important to point out from the start that *uniforms have no significant impact on tenth-grade student self-concepts*. Model 2 is the most important model to discuss in this regard since it represents the first time that the uniform variable is entered into the equation. As one can see, the coefficient is weak (.02) and not statistically significant. Therefore, any other variables added to the model are irrelevant for answering our first research question: Do uniforms have an impact on tenth graders' self-concept? The answer is no.

It is interesting to briefly discuss, however, which variables *do* affect tenth-grade students' self-concept. Looking at Model 4, after all the variables have been entered into the model, it is clear that uniforms do not have an impact on self-concept. Females have lower self-concepts than males, while minorities have higher self-concepts than whites—two

Table 6.1. Effects of Uniform Policies and Other Variables on Tenth-Grade Students' Self-Concept Levels (OLS Models, Standardized Betas)

Variables	Model 1	Model 2	Model 3	Model 4
Student Controls				
Female	−.14***	−.14***	−.20***	−.09***
Minority	.08***	.08***	.09***	.09***
SES	.08*	.08*	−.03	−.02
Parent Education	−.01	−.01	−.03	−.03
School Controls				
Urban	.03	.03	.02	.02
Rural	−.01	−.01	−.01	−.02
Catholic	.01	−.01	−.03	−.05*
Private	.01	−.01	−.01	−.03
Policy				
School Uniforms		.02	.03	.04
Student Process				
Discuss w/ Parents			.19***	.16***
Parent Involvement			.06**	.04
Acad. Preparedness			.05*	.04
Pro-School Attitude			.12***	.04
Acad. Achievement			.15***	.11***
Student Behavior			.01	.03
School Climate				
Peer Pro-School				.06**
Educational Climate				.23***
Constant	−.07	−.07	−1.88***	−0.25***
Adjusted R^2	.03	.03	.12	.17
StandardError	.66	.66	.63	.61
F-Value	10.39***	9.32***	25.26***	32.35***
Total N	10,212	10,212	10,212	10,212
Effective N	2,609	2,609	2,609	2,609

Note: ***$p < .001$, **$p < .01$, *$p < .05$.

findings that are consistent with the literature on self-esteem (Howard 2000; Utsey, Ponterotto, and Reynolds 2000; Zaff, Blount and Philips 2002). Attending a Catholic school appears to diminish one's self-concept somewhat. Several student process and school climate variables do indeed affect student self-concept positively. Students who have high academic achievement as well as those who discuss schooling with their parents have higher self-concepts than those who do not. In addition, the educational climate of a school positively affects self-concept among its students; existing in a school with a positive educational environment with positive relationships and existing within a network of peers who value education appears to quite significantly affect student self-concept. The full model explains 17 percent of the variation in self-concept scores—uniforms add no explanatory power to the equation. One lingering question is whether school uniforms actually have an impact on the school climate and thereby *indirectly* influence self-concept through the creation of a positive school climate. The answer to this question appears below.

The Impact of School Uniforms on Eighth Graders' Self-Esteem

The results for predicting self-concept scores for eighth graders are given in table 6.2. After taking into account student and school control variables, if one looks at Model 2, *school uniform policies have no effect on the self-concept scores of eighth graders.* The effect of going to a school that mandates the wearing of a school uniform is insignificant and adds nothing to the explanation of self-concept scores among this sample (R^2 for Model 1 and Model 2 is the same). The full model (Model 4) shows that 16 percent of the variation in eighth graders' self-concept scores is explained by these variables. The patterns are very similar to those of the tenth-grade models (table 6.1), and since the effects of uniforms are the main concern of this book, I will only briefly touch on these. It appears that females as well as those who have behavior problems are more likely to have lower self-concepts than males and those with fewer or no behavioral problems at school. Previous research (Brunsma and Rockquemore 1998; Educational Testing Service 2000), however, found no relationship between uniform policies and decreased behavioral problems; therefore, there is unlikely to be an indirect effect of uniforms on student self-concept through a decrease in student behavior problems. As with tenth grade, academic achievement, minority status, parent involvement, academic preparedness, and a positive educational environment all boost eighth-grade students' self-concept.

In sum, school uniforms have no statistically significant impact on self-concept scores or locus of control scores for either tenth-grade or eighth-grade students. Furthermore, there is no indirect effect of school uniform policies on these social-psychological outcomes through some

Table 6.2. Effects of Uniform Policies and Other Variables on Eighth-Grade Students' Self-Concept Levels (OLS Models, Standardized Betas)

Variables	Model 1	Model 2	Model 3	Model 4
Student Controls				
Female	−.17***	−.17***	−.23***	−.22***
Minority	.09***	.09***	.10***	.10***
SES	.07**	.07**	−.02	−.01
Parent Education	.04	.04	.02	.02
School Controls				
Urban	.03	.03	.03*	.04**
Rural	.01	.01	−.02	−.02
Catholic	.02	.01	−.02	−.04
Private	.02	.01	−.01	−.03*
Policy				
School Uniforms		.02	.02	.02
Student Process				
Discuss w/ Parents			.13***	.11***
Parent Involvement			.07***	.05***
Acad. Preparedness			.15***	.13***
Acad. Achievement			.06***	.06***
Student Behavior			−.09***	−.06***
School Climate				
Safety Climate				−.02
Educational Climate				.19***
Constant	.02	.02	−1.031***	−1.864***
Adjusted R^2	.05	.05	.13	.16
Standard Error	.66	.66	.63	.62
F-Value	35.13***	31.28***	59.06***	67.60***
Total N	14,252	14,252	14,252	14,252
Effective N	5,626	5,626	5,626	5,626

Note: ***$p < .001$, **$p < .01$, *$p < .05$.

positive change in the perceptions of the educational climate. In other words, uniforms do not even affect the factors that do have an impact on self-concept and locus of control between the eighth and tenth grades.

UNIFORMS AND MEASURES OF LOCI OF CONTROL

One social-psychological variable that is related to, yet distinct from, self-esteem seems to be a relevant candidate for exploring the linkages between mandatory uniform policies and social-psychological benefits: locus of control (Ang and Weining 1999; Kulas 1996). Locus of control refers to the extent to which individuals feel that they are in control of their lives and that what they do in their everyday actions has an impact on their lives; this type of control is called "internal locus of control." Individuals can also feel that no matter what they do, someone or something is always trying to stop them or keep them down, that their actions have little to do with their successes and failures in life; this type of control is located externally and therefore is referred to as "external locus of control." Though the anecdotal meanderings and literature have not specified locus of control as one of the social-psychological advantages that uniforms may offer, interesting hypotheses can be derived from this connection. It may be the case, as with self-esteem, that though the ideal is individuals with internal locus of control, school uniforms may foster a sense among a student body (and particular students) that their desires and ideas as an individual do not matter and/or are controlled by external others dictating their reality.

The Impact of School Uniforms on Tenth Graders' Locus of Control

What of the effects of uniforms on tenth-grade students' internal locus of control (the belief that what you do matters)? Table 6.3 shows these results.[3] Moving across the table focusing on the uniform variable's effects on locus of control, one can note up front that: *school uniforms do not significantly affect tenth graders' sense of internal locus of control.* Students who do have a more internal locus of control

1. discuss schooling with their parents,
2. come to school prepared for class,
3. value schooling through pro-school attitudes,
4. have peers who value school,
5. achieve academically, and
6. perceive the educational climate positively.

Table 6.3.   Effects of Uniform Policies and Other Variables on Tenth-Grade Students' Locus of Control Levels (OLS Models, Standardized Betas)

Variables	Model 1	Model 2	Model 3	Model 4
Student Controls				
Female	.04*	.04*	−.04*	−.03
Minority	−.01	−.01	.01	.01
SES	.16***	.16***	.03	.03
Parent Education	−.04	−.04	−.07*	−.07*
School Controls				
Urban	.01	.01	−.01	−.01
Rural	−.01	−.01	−.02	−.03
Catholic	.01	.01	−.02	−.04
Private	.05*	.05*	.03	.01
Policy				
School Uniforms		−.01	.02	.02
School Process				
Discuss w/ Parents			.18***	.15***
Parent Involvement			.05*	.03
Acad. Preparedness			.07***	.06**
Pro-School Attitude			.18***	.11***
Acad. Achievement			.24***	.20***
Student Behavior			−.01	.01
School Climate				
Peer Pro-School				.05**
Educational Climate				.21***
Constant	.07	.07	−2.44***	−1.01***
Adjusted R^2	.02	.02	.18	.22
Standard Error	.62	.62	.57	.55
F-Value	7.92***	7.04***	39.23***	44.43***
Total N	10,211	10,211	10,211	10,211
Effective N	2,609	2,609	2,609	2,609

Note: ***$p < .001$, **$p < .01$, *$p < .05$.

These variables explain 22 percent of the variation in tenth-grade locus of control scores. Again, one wonders whether uniforms might affect the educational climate positively or create academically oriented tenth graders? Many who add to the anecdotal literature believe that uniforms may indirectly affect outcomes through such paths. These questions are answered in the following section and in chapter 5, respectively.

Table 6.4. Effects of Uniform Policies and Other Variables on Eighth-Grade Students' Locus of Control Levels (OLS Models, Standardized Betas)

Variables	Model 1	Model 2	Model 3	Model 4
Student Controls				
Female	−.02	−.02	−.10***	−.09***
Minority	−.02	−.02	.02	.01
SES	.21***	.21***	.08***	.09***
Parent Education	−.01	−.01	−.04	−.04
School Controls				
Urban	−.01	−.01	.01	.01
Rural	.01	.01	−.01	−.02
Catholic	.03*	.03**	−.01	−.02
Private	.04***	.04**	.02	−.01
Policy				
School Uniforms		−.01	.01	.01
Student Process				
Discuss w/ Parents			.15***	.13***
Parent Involvement			.05***	.04**
Acad. Preparedness			.16***	.15***
Acad. Achievement			.18***	.18***
Student Behavior			−.11***	−.09***
School Climate				
Safety Climate				−.01
Educational Climate				.16***
Constant	.08	.05	−1.30***	−1.98***
Adjusted R²	.05	.05	.18	.20
Standard Error	.60	.60	.56	.55
F-Value	36.22***	32.20***	88.76***	90.77***
Total N	14,251	14,251	14,251	14,251
Effective N	5,626	5,626	5,626	5,626

Note: ***$p < .001$, **$p < .01$, *$p < .05$.

The Impact of School Uniforms on Eighth Graders' Locus of Control

Table 6.4 presents the results for eighth-grade students' locus of control. Again, mirroring the results for tenth grade, *uniforms have no statistically significant effect on eighth grade student locus of control scores*. Whether a student attends a school with a mandatory school uniform policy or not does *not* differentiate those with internal and external locus of control. What does foster more internal locus of control for these eighth graders? Students from a higher social class (SES), who discuss educational matters with their parents, whose parents are involved in their schooling, who are prepared for classes, who do well in school, and who perceive their schools as having a positive educational climate, are more likely than their counterparts to have internal locus of control. The final model (Model 4) explains 20 percent of the variation in eighth-grade locus of control; school uniform policies explain *none* of that variation.

Effects of Uniform Policies on Kindergartners' Self-Control and Coping Skills

ECLS contains several measures of psychological well-being and developmental assessments. There were no direct assessments of kindergartners' self-esteem or locus of control scores; however, three variables in particular stood out as extremely relevant for our purposes here. Since there is an overriding assumption that school uniform policies somehow act as a catalyst for a more disciplined and self-aware student body, three teacher-assessed variables were considered important in testing these assumptions at the elementary school level through the use of ECLS data. Teachers directly assessed the degree of self-control that each kindergartner in the sample exhibited on a daily basis. In addition to this measure, teachers were also asked to describe the coping skills of the children: When these children act out and have problematic behaviors, do they place the blame on themselves (internalize it) or on others in their social environment (externalize it)? These assessments were made during the fall of 1998, spring of 1999, and spring of 2000. Tables 6.5 through 6.7 present the student-level results of the effectiveness of school uniforms and other variables on these social-psychological indicators.

Because the results for fall and spring kindergarten semester parallel each other, I will simply discuss the results for both tables 6.5 and 6.6 in general. The models presented in these tables are full models predicting each of the three outcomes: self-control, externalizing problem behavior, and internalizing problem behavior. According to these regression results, *there is no effect of school uniform policies*

Table 6.5. Effects of Uniform Policies and Other Variables on Kindergarten Students' Self-Control and Externalization and Internalization of Problem Behavior (OLS Models, Standardized Betas)

Variables	Fall Semester		
	Student's Self-Control	Externalizing Problem Behavior	Internalizing Problem Behavior
Student Controls			
Age (in months)	.06***	−.02	−.02
Female	.17***	−.21***	−.03*
Minority	−.03*	.01	−.02
Single Parent Household	−.08***	.09***	.07***
SES	.07***	−.05***	−.08***
School Controls			
Private	−.07***	.06***	.01
Urban	.03	−.02	−.01
Rural	.01	−.01	−.03
Total Enrollment	.01	−.01	.01
Percent Minority	−.03	.01	−.01
Percent Free Lunch	−.06***	.07***	.02
Policy			
Uniform	.01	−.01	−.01
Constant	2.60***	1.88***	1.67***
Adjusted R^2	.06	.06	.01
Standard Error	.60	.63	.53
F-Value	32.50***	32.89***	7.19***
Total N	10,279	10,358	10,313
Effective N	5,498	5,618	5,553

Note: ***p <.001, **p <.01, *p <.05.

on kindergartners' level of self-control, externalization of problem behavior, or internalization of problem behavior. Students who exhibit self-control are typically female and older (in months) and come from families with higher levels of social and economic resources. Children from single-parent households, students who attend private schools, and students who attend poorer schools (i.e., higher percentage who receive free lunch) are more likely to externalize their problems and blame others. Students from single-parent households are also more likely than those from intact families to internalize problem behavior as well. Other factors are significant *negative* predictors of these social-psychological variables; however, in the end, *school uniform*

Table 6.6. Effects of Uniform Policies and Other Variables on Kindergarten Students' Self-Control and Externalization and Internalization of Problem Behavior (OLS Models, Standardized Betas)

Variables	Spring Semester		
	Student's Self-Control	Externalizing Problem Behavior	Internalizing Problem Behavior
Student Controls			
Age (in months)	.05***	−.03*	−.01
Female	.18***	−.21***	−.04**
Minority	−.05**	.04*	.01
Single Parent Household	−.09***	.09***	.07***
SES	.08***	−.06***	−.07***
School Controls			
Private	−.06***	.03	−.01
Urban	.01	−.02	−.01
Rural	−.01	−.03	−.04**
Total Enrollment	−.01	−.01	.01
Percent Minority	−.05*	.01	−.01
Percent Free Lunch	−.04	.05**	.03
Policy			
Uniform	−.01	.01	−.01
Constant	2.80***	1.96***	1.61***
Adjusted R^2	.07	.07	.02
Standard Error	.61	.63	.53
F-Value	35.81***	35.63***	8.58***
Total N	10,209	10,222	10,198
Effective N	5,416	5,428	5,408

Note: ***$p < .001$, **$p < .01$, *$p < .05$.

policies do not significantly affect any of these outcomes at the elementary school level.

The results shown in table 6.7, reflecting these same processes in first grade, almost completely mirror those from kindergarten (tables 6.5 and 6.6). Given this, the next question is whether changes in self-control and externalization and internationalization processes between kindergarten and first grade might be attributed to changes in school uniform policies. The next section presents the results testing this idea.

Table 6.7. Effects of Uniform Policies and Other Variables on First-Grade Students' Self-Control and Externalization and Internalization of Problem Behavior (OLS Models, Standardized Betas)

	Spring Semester		
Variables	Student's Self-Control	Externalizing Problem Behavior	Internalizing Problem Behavior
Student Controls			
Age (in months)	.03	−.04*	−.04
Female	.20***	−.24***	−.03
Minority	−.03	.04	−.03
Single Parent Household	−.11***	.12***	.13***
SES	.12***	−.08***	−.12***
School Controls			
Private	−.03	.01	.03
Urban	−.02	.02	−.04
Rural	−.04	.03	.01
Total Enrollment	−.02	.02	.04
Percent Minority	.01	−.05	−.02
Percent Free Lunch	−.01	.03	.01
Parental Involvement	.04	−.02	−.01
Policy			
Uniform	.02	−.02	−.02
Constant	2.69***	2.38***	2.01***
Adjusted R^2	.08	.09	.04
Standard Error	.60	.62	.52
F-Value	15.27***	17.03***	7.06***
Total N	5,749	5,187	5,169
Effective N	2,173	2,172	2,169

Note: ***p <.001, **p <.01, *p <.05.

Policy Changes and Changes in Self-Concept, Locus of Control, and Measures of Children's Control and Coping Strategies

As seen in other analyses in this book, assessing longitudinal effects requires data collected from at least two points in time. For both NELS and ECLS, the data are available for two school years. This section investigates the possibility that *changes* in social-psychological variables from point one to point two might be associated with school-level changes (or individual student moves) to uniform policies. I highlight the NELS results for eighth- to tenth-grade changes, then the kindergarten to first-grade changes using ECLS data.

In looking at students who move from middle school to high school who experience a change in dress policies, table 6.8 shows the correlations between the various kinds of shifts and eigth- to tenth-grade student-level changes in self-esteem locus of control scores using both the full, across-school sector data set as well as the public-only paneled data set. We can see that *there is indeed no significant correlation between students who switch from nonuniformed to uniformed schools and changes in their self-concept or their type of locus of control.* Another way to test this claim of change over time is to predict tenth-grade levels of self-esteem and locus of control using eighth-grade levels of each and to assess whether a change in uniform policy is implicated in this change as well. Table 6.9 shows these results. The change of interest (N → U) is not significant in either the full-data set or the public-only set. Interesting enough, if one looks at the cases where students switched from schools that had uniforms to those that did not (U → N), we see that there are very small and weak, yet statistically significant, *increases* in self-esteem and locus of control when students move out of uniformed school climates.

Elementary changes in social-psychological variables may operate differently, given the nature of these aspects in children of this age. Tables 6.10 through 6.12 present the results from analyses of kindergarten to first-grade changes of self-control and externalization and internalization coping skills respectively in an attempt to empirically investigate whether changes in uniform policies across these two early educational points in time also affect these processes.

Regarding the growth in self-control levels between kindergarten and first grade in elementary schools, table 6.10 shows that the trend of growth is strong between these two years. Those with more self-control in kindergarten continue to grow in this direction in first grade (and the converse is also true). Looking at schools that changed within this time frame (1998–1999 to 1999–2000), we see that children in this situation actually *increased their self-control levels* more than those who stayed in nonuniformed schools between these two years. The more robust test is those children who stayed in uniform for both years, since the coverage of the movement has most recently begun to suggest that if schools start children early enough in uniform, the policy will be more effective for these children. However, the results do not give support to this way of thinking.

Table 6.8.   Correlations between Eighth- to Tenth-Grade Policy Changes and Eighth- to Tenth-Grade Self-Concept and Locus of Control Changes

Dependent Changes 8th to 10th	Total Panel				Public Panel			
	U → U	U → N	N → U	N → N	U → U	U → N	N → U	N → N
Self-Concept Changes	n.s.	n.s.	n.s.	n.s.	n.s.	n.s.	n.s.	n.s.
Locus of Control Changes	n.s.	n.s.	n.s.	n.s.	n.s.	n.s.	n.s.	n.s.

Note: ***p <.001, **p <.01, *p <.05; "n.s." = not statistically significant.

Table 6.9.   Correlations between Eighth- to Tenth-Grade Policy Changes and Tenth-Grade Self-Concept and Locus of Control Scores

Tenth-Grade Outcomes	Total Panel				Public Panel			
	U → U	U → N	N → U	N → N	U → U	U → N	N → U	N → N
Self-Concept	.02*	.02*	n.s.	−.03**	n.s.	n.s.	n.s.	n.s.
Locus of Control	.03**	.03**	n.s.	−.04***	n.s.	.02*	n.s.	−.03*

Note: ***p <.001, **p <.01, *p <.05; "n.s." = not statistically significant.

Table 6.10.   Effects of Kindergarten Self-Control, Uniform Policies, and Other Changes on First Graders' Self-Control Scores (OLS Models, Standardized Betas)

Variables	First Grade (Spring) Self-Control		
	Model 1	Model 2	Model 3
Kindergarten Self-Control	.45***	.45***	.57***
Policy Changes			
Uniform → Uniform		.01	.01
Nonuniform → Uniform		.05*	.05*
Uniform → Nonuniform		.02	.01
Student Controls			
Female			.07***
Minority			−.05*
Age (in months)			.03
SES (changes in)			.02
Household (changes in)			.01
Student Moved K → 1st			.02
School Controls			
Private			.02
Urban			−.03
Rural			−.07**
Enrollment (changes in)			.01
% Minority (changes in)			.03
% Free Lunch (changes in)			.01
% Parent Involv. (changes)			.01
Educ. Climate (changes)			−.01
Safety Climate (changes)			.01
Student Process			
App. to Learning (changes)			.47***
Constant	1.78***	1.77***	1.07***
Adjusted R^2	.20	.20	.41
Standard Error	.56	.56	.48
F-Value	328.67***	83.62***	47.25***
Total N	3,471	3,471	3,471
Effective N	1,310	1,310	1,310

Note: ***p <.001, **p <.01, *p <.05.

Looking at processes of internalizing and/or externalizing problem behavior among children in their first two years of schooling, table 6.11 and 6.12 present the results for these analyses. The method of analysis is the same as that above for self-control. We can see that in both cases, children who internalize/externalize (blame themselves/blame others

Table 6.11.   Effects of Kindergarten Externalization, Uniform Policies, and Other Changes on First Graders' Externalization Scores (OLS Models, Standardized Betas)

	First-Grade (Spring) Externalization		
Variables	Model 1	Model 2	Model 3
Kindergarten Externalization	.58***	.58***	.60***
Policy Changes			
Uniform → Uniform		−.03	−.01
Nonuniform → Uniform		−.01	.01
Uniform → Nonuniform		−.03	−.02
Student Controls			
Female			−.09***
Minority			.04
Age (in months)			−.05*
SES (changes in)			−.03
Household (changes in)			.01
Student Moved K → 1st			−.01
School Controls			
Private			−.03
Urban			.01
Rural			.05*
Enrollment (changes in)			.01
% Minority (changes in)			−.01
% Free Lunch (changes in)			.02
% Parent Involv. (changes)			−.03
Educ. Climate (changes)			.01
Safety Climate (changes)			−.01
Student Process			
App. to Learning (changes)			−.27***
Constant			
Adjusted R^2	.34	.34	.42
Standard Error	.53	.53	.50
F-Value	674.95***	48.26***	12.13***
Total N	3,472	3,472	3,472
Effective N	1,314	1,314	1,314

Note: ***p <.001, **p <.01, *p <.05.

for) problem behavior were also likely to do so in first grade. Changes in uniform policies did not add to our understanding of these trends in either case. In all three childhood social-psychological measures, approaches to learning were again a key factor in affecting these aspects of strategies for coping.

Table 6.12. Effects of Kindergarten Internalization, Uniform Policies, and Other Changes on First Graders' Internalization Scores (OLS Models, Standardized Betas)

Variables	First-Grade (Spring) Internalization		
	Model 1	Model 2	Model 3
Kindergarten Internalization	.29***	.29***	.33***
Policy Changes			
Uniform → Uniform		.01	.02
Nonuniform → Uniform		−.03	−.02
Uniform → Nonuniform		−.03	−.02
Student Controls			
Female			−.02
Minority			.01
Age (in months)			−.04
SES (changes in)			.01
Household (changes in)			.02
Student Moved K → 1st			.02
School Controls			
Private			−.02
Urban			.01
Rural			.06*
Enrollment (changes in)			.03
% Minority (changes in)			−.05
% Free Lunch (changes in)			.01
% Parent Involv. (changes)			.01
Educ. Climate (changes)			.05
Safety Climate (changes)			−.01
Student Process			
App. to Learning (changes)			−.25***
Constant	1.14***	1.15***	1.46***
Adjusted R^2	.09	.09	.14
Standard Error	.49	.49	.48
F-Value	123.78***	7.62***	2.72***
Total N	3,471	3,471	3,471
Effective N	1,310	1,310	1,310

Note: ***p <.001, **p <.01, *p <.05.

UNIFORMS, BEHAVIOR PROBLEMS, SUBSTANCE USE, AND ATTENDANCE

The assumption that uniforms will create a safer environment with less distraction, less delinquency, less interpersonal violence, and less substance use is a clear component of the school uniform discourse in the

Table 6.13.   School-Level Effects of Uniform Policies and Other
Variables on Tenth-Grade Behavior and Perceived Drug Use
(OLS Models, Standardized Betas)

	Aggregate Behavior	Aggregate Drug Use
School Characteristics		
Percent Minority	.22***	.14***
Aggregate SES	−.01	−.13**
Catholic	−.12**	−.02
Private	−.01	.02
Urban	.07*	.01
Rural	−.11***	−.02
% in College Prep Track	−.05	−.02
Policy		
Uniform	.05	.01
School Climate		
Aggregate Preparedness	−.14***	−.06
Aggregate Pro-School Attitudes	−.48***	−.06
Aggregate Peer Pro-School Attitudes	−.10***	−.01
Constant	19.76***	18.41***
Adjusted R^2	.38	.05
Standard Error	1.08	5.88
F-Value	54.14***	34.62***
Total N	964	965

Note: ***p <.001, **p <.01, *p <.05.

United States. In our original empirical investigation of school uniform
policies (Brunsma and Rockquemore 1998), we found no significant effect of uniform policies on student-level behavioral problems or substance use. Because those analyses are contained in that publication and
they were conducted at the individual level, I will look at the effects of
uniform policies on aggregate school levels of behavioral issues and substance use.

Uniforms, Behavior, and Substance Use in High Schools

Table 6.13 looks at the effects of uniform policies on aggregate
tenth-grade behavior and drug use using NELS data. In both cases
*uniforms do not significantly affect school levels of drug use or be-
havioral problems.* This finding, at the school level, mirrors the individual analysis previously published (Brunsma and Rockquemore
1998). Urban and a higher proportion of minority students increases

the potential for behavioral problems and drug use on campus. However, uniforms do not add any more to our understanding of these
outcomes of particular interest to these schools—in fact, these are the
types of schools that are most likely to implement uniforms. Unfortunately, according these analyses the roots of the problems do not re-
side in student dress.

Uniforms and Substance Use in Middle Schools

Concerning eighth-grade substance use, table 6.14 presents results
that look into the possibility that uniform policies alter the students'
and/or principals' perceptions of drug use as a problem on campus. We
can see that uniform policies do not significantly affect either of these
educational actors' perceptions of drug use on their middle schools'

Table 6.14. School-Level Effects of Uniform Policies and Other Variables on Aggregate Eighth-Grade Perceptions of Drug Use (OLS Models, Standardized Betas)

Variables	Aggregate Student Perceptions of Student Drug Use	Aggregate Principal Perceptions of Student Drug Use
School Characteristics		
Percent Minority	−.01	.14***
Aggregate SES	.18***	.02
Catholic	−.44***	.31***
Private	−.27***	.13**
Urban	.05	.01
Rural	.06*	−.01
Policy		
Uniform	.06	−.06
School Climate		
Aggregate Student Perc.	−.21***	.07*
Constant	7.10***	4.92***
Adjusted R^2	.26	.10
Standard Error	.74	1.20
F-Value	44.39***	14.88***
Total N	1,012	1,013

Note: ***p <.001, **p <.01, *p <.05.

campuses. What is striking from these side-by-side analyses is that student and administrator perceptions regarding an issue like drug use are *quite mismatched*. The two perceptions are contrary to each other. How is this possible? And what does this say about the gulf between students and the principals who run their schools? Furthermore, what might this say about the potential for uniform policy to have an impact in public schools?

Finally, table 6.15 investigates aggregate eighth-grade behavior problems. Uniforms have no effect on changes in student behavior in middle school. Factors implicated in positive behavioral climates are higher student socioeconomic status, being in Catholic schools, and student perceptions of the safety of the school. This is intriguing in that, as we saw in chapter 5 (table 5.4), uniform policies actually *decreased* students' perceptions of the behavioral climate. If we combine that analysis with this one reported in table 6.15, we see that uniforms may detrimentally affect aggregate student behavior through lowering student perceptions of the safety climate of their school.

Table 6.15. School-Level Effects of Uniform Policies and Other Variables on Aggregate Eighth-Grade Behavior (OLS Models, Standardized Betas)

Variables	Aggregate Student Behavior Scale
School Characteristics	
Percent Minority	.02
Aggregate SES	−.23***
Catholic	−.11*
Private	.02
Urban	.03
Rural	−.10**
Policy	
Uniform	−.03
School Climate	
Aggregate Student Perc.	−.35***
Constant	6.09***
Adjusted R^2	.27
Standard Error	.63
F-Value	46.83***
Total N	1,013

Note: ***p <.001, **p <.01, *p <.05.

SUMMARY

This chapter has presented empirical analyses intended to test whether uniform policies affect behavioral and social-psychological outcomes in American schools. The results can be quickly summarized. First, uniform policies have no significant impact on measures of self-esteem in middle or high schools. Second, uniform policies have no effect on elementary, middle, or high school students' measures of locus of control and other strategies of psychological coping. Third, switching from schools without policies to schools with policies has no impact on these social-psychological outcomes. Fourth, uniforms simply do not help us understand behavioral problems at school.

7

A SYMBOLIC CRUSADE: THE SCHOOL UNIFORM MOVEMENT AND WHAT IT TELLS US ABOUT AMERICAN EDUCATION

Beware of enterprises that require new clothing.

—Henry David Thoreau, *Walden*

Republicans once made fun of Bill Clinton's proclivity for symbols—remember his call for school uniforms?

—Dionne Jr. (2002)

INTRODUCTION

In just sixteen years (since Cherry Hill), and in some estimations, in just ten years (since Long Beach), the United States went from a handful of public schools using school uniforms as a policy intended to heal all the ills ailing public schools to estimates of fully one-quarter of our public schools having and enforcing mandatory school uniform policies. Contrary to what one reads in the headlines and texts of the nation's most prominent newspapers, contrary to what one hears from the mouths of politicians and educational administrators, and contrary to what one sees on the evening news, there is absolutely nothing simplistic and straightforward about the current crusade to uniform public school students in the United States. The debate over whether or not to uniform the students in our public schools (like public schooling itself) is highly controversial, undeniably complex, and, from the analyses and arguments presented in this book, unquestionably rooted deeply in correspondingly multifaceted social, political, legal, cultural, racial, material, and educational structures. Schools, and the policies they enact, do not exist in vacuums. This has become exceedingly clear as we continue to look at this one particular issue—school uniforms—and what the debate over such a "reform effort" really means, what underlying issues are invoked as this movement continues to move forward, and what school uniforms ultimately teach us about American public education and the direction we might go as a nation that cares deeply about education.[1]

Involvement in the study of the school uniform movement in the United States has provided us with evidence of a long-standing observation made by sociologists, political scientists, educational researchers, as well as parents, community members, and American citizens alike: Schools (and school reform efforts) do not exist in vacuums untouched by the influences of our political, cultural, social, economic, and philosophical structures (see Hallinan 2000 and Hacsi 2003). Indeed, schools, our conceptions of them, of what they should and should not do, of what they should and should not look like, of what they do and do not symbolize, not only do not exist outside of these exceedingly powerful forces but are both the by-products and seeds of such forces—to acknowledge anything different is to seriously misunderstand social, political, economic, cultural, and material experience.

A result of understanding that schools exist within the nexus and matrix of these other structures is to acknowledge that the school uniform movement—and any and all efforts to reform K–12 education in the United States—is a reflection of this precarious position of the institution of education, a mirror (Hughes 1996) of American society.

This chapter summarizes the main findings and points of contention in this book. It assesses where we are in our understanding of the antecedents, processes, and effectiveness of school uniform and dress code policies in the United States. The main goal is to address the very important question, *What is the school uniform issue really about?* Given what we now know, as well as what we have yet to learn, what does the uniform debate really tell us about American education, about school reform, about the role of empirical evidence both in evaluating educational policies, as well as the role of such "evidence" in our courts, about parental and children's rights, about the purposes of education and schooling in the new millennium? These and other questions are addressed critically, with the ultimate goal to create public discussion that focuses on the forest and not simply the trees. Are school uniforms a serious reform or a Band-Aid approach to a complex structure of schooling in America? Is this movement a crusade to change schools and schooling utilizing the *symbol* of school uniforms as its justification? If so, what does this tell us about the reality behind that symbol? What needs to change? How do we go about enacting policies that create the desired change? If not, if uniforms do not, in fact, accomplish these goals, why are we still focused on them as a remedy?

WHAT HAVE WE LEARNED?

We have learned a great deal from this journey through the history, the policies, the contemporary movement, and the empirical analyses of nationally representative data concerning the impact and effectiveness of school uniform policies on a variety of educational and social-psychological outcomes of interest to parents, educators, and Americans in general. Chapter 1 illustrated, through a brief look at the history of uniforming students, that such practices have been around a very long time, steeped in tradition, implemented in a variety of places, for a variety of reasons, with an equally varied number of effects on the outcomes of the children who must wear them. The history is deeply rooted in British social and cultural structures.[2] Symbolically, we have seen that school uniforms have been used to demarcate the classes in two very different senses: 1) to stigmatize lower status, by symbolizing those who are societally disadvantaged; and 2) to distinguish the children of upper-class parents, by symbolizing those who are societally advantaged. We can see this in the contemporary movement to stigmatize minority and poor children through the use of the uniform.

For certain, the school uniform has always been in stark contrast to outside societal trends in fashion. This is an interesting issue, because it bespeaks the classic chicken-and-egg problem: Does the desire to create a distinction between the school and the outside world (e.g., the pursuit of "educational climate") come first, or are the societal trends (Madison Avenue, Land's End, the Gap, etc.) the forces creating this dilemma—forces that *we* have taken part in constructing and reproducing, cohort after cohort. Of course, while Madison Avenue seeks to indoctrinate masses of young children (and their parents) into the culture of consumption and materialism, school uniforms have been used, throughout history, as a method of inculcating the herd instinct, preparing citizens of a certain kind, workers of a certain kind, and individuals of a certain kind. We have seen the notion of "rightful authority" implicit in uniform policies; we have also witnessed rebellion against such assumptions of such authority. In fighting against the doctrine of "separate but equal" and creating an ideal of equality of educational opportunity, as one studies this movement to uniform public school students in the context of hyper-consumption and status distinctions, one wonders if we aren't creating something akin to a context of "equal but separate"—a façade where all *appear* equal, ready to learn, yet with the glaring continuation of segregation, labeling, racism, sexism, patriarchy, classism, and other forms of inequality and hierarchies still intact, still in place. Again, schools do not exist in social vacuums.[3]

We have witnessed students battling these "rightful authorities," questioning and challenging the concept of in loco parentis, demanding freedom of expression and freedom of speech in the halls, across the schoolhouse gate (see Cohen and Zelnik 2002). Shortly afterwards, the conservatism and fear of unseen enemies of the 1980s, the 1990s with its fear of our own children (i.e., via school shootings that have been extremely overrepresented in the media)—fear of the unknown—brought new challenges. With this tide of paranoia and fear, we saw the school uniform movement come to the forefront of potential educational reform efforts aimed at eradicating difference and enhancing educational climates in public schools across our nation.

Using the most recent and comprehensive nationally representative data sets comprising all school levels at which school uniform policies are currently being debated, as well as a comprehensive review of the empirical literature on school uniforms and dress codes' effectiveness, this book has tested the effectiveness of such policies (including dress codes) on a wide variety of outcomes and educational processes. The overwhelming evidence from previous research as well as the analyses in this book is that *uniform policies are not effective.*

The conclusions of this book can be summarized briefly. First, concerning the demography and adoption correlates of uniform policies, it was found that, by the year 2000, a good estimate is that 15.5 percent of our public elementary schools had uniform policies. About half this rate is probably a fair estimate of the degree of implementation in public middle and high schools (about 8 percent). These policies are most prominent in the urban and suburban public school systems, with the fastest growing uniform policy adoptions taking place in small towns and rural areas across America.[4] A majority of adoptions are concentrated in the Southern and Western United States. This more complete picture does indeed contradict portions of the media's claims regarding the location of uniform policies in public schools. Second, our empirical analyses of the correlates to uniform policy adoption showed that uniforms are adopted for both reactionary and demographic reasons, discussed further below. To summarize these results, schools with higher enrollments (and those going through increasing enrollments) as well as poor aggregate school-level academic performance among the student body are more likely to adopt a uniform policy than those with lower enrollments and higher achieving students—all in an effort to increase attendance and achievement. Also, schools with greater levels of poverty, students from families with lower levels of socioeconomic status (a composite of parental education, family income, and occupational status), and higher proportions of minorities are more likely to adopt uniform policies than their more affluent and "whiter" counterparts.

Third, regardless of the key impetus, or sets of impeti, one looks at regarding the reasons that administrators desire to implement school uniforms in their jurisdictions (e.g., increase readiness to learn through enhanced school climate, increase safety at the school proper, decrease competition between students, eradicate differences in the student body, increase attendance, etc.), one can be sure that the ultimate goal of such a policy is to increase academic performance.[5] As we have seen:

1. Uniforms have no significant impact on student perceptions of safety or educational climates in their schools.
2. Uniforms have no significant impact on perceptions of the safety and educational climates of elementary schools—and there is a

wide gulf between student and administrator perceptions of these issues (which is perhaps the more pertinent point).

3. Uniforms have no significant student-level effects on tenth grade-achievement—although they do negatively affect reading scores.
4. Uniforms have no significant student-level effects on eighth-grade achievement.
5. Uniforms have no significant impact on student-level achievement and knowledge in elementary schools (kindergarten or first grade).
6. Uniforms have solidly negative effects on aggregate achievement in high schools.
7. Uniforms have no significant impact on aggregate eighth-grade achievement levels.
8. Uniforms have no significant impact on aggregate elementary academic achievement.
9. Uniforms have no significant impact on academic preparedness, pro-school attitudes, or peer group attitudes toward schooling.
10. One of the most important findings is that there appear to be no benefits secured by students (or schools) that switch from no uniforms to a uniform policy on any of these salient student- or school-level outcomes.

Fourth, uniforms neither directly nor indirectly affect the behavior or social psychologies of American public school students when compared to their nonuniformed, public counterparts. To summarize these results:

1. Uniforms do not significantly affect tenth- or eighth-grade attendance, behavioral problems, or drug use.
2. Uniforms have no significant impact on eighth or tenth graders' self-concepts.
3. Uniforms have no significant impact on eighth or tenth graders' locus of control.
4. Uniforms have no significant impact on kindergartners' self-control or behavioral coping skills.

Fifth, one of the questions that has circulated around the discourse on school uniforms is whether a uniform policy is needed, or whether schools simply need to clarify and enforce the dress code policy they already have in place. The answer to this question, from the analyses presented here, is a loud and clear "clarify and enforce existing dress code policies!" Uniforms offer no significant effects over and above a standard dress code. This may be a finding that schools and administrators may want to seriously consider—simply enforcing the dress code.

The bottom line appears to be this: Despite the media coverage (which has been exceedingly selective and misrepresentative), despite the anecdotal meanderings of politicians, community members, educators, board members, parents, and students, uniforms have not been effective at attacking the very outcomes and issues they were assumed to aid:

1. reduction of violence and behavioral problems;
2. fostering school unity and improving the learning environment;
3. reducing social pressures and leveling status differentials;
4. increasing student self-esteem and motivation;
5. saving parents money on clothing for their children;
6. improving attendance; and, ultimately,
7. improving academic achievement.

These findings exist after controlling for the important variations in schools that affect such outcomes. Despite what many think, these factors do *not* go away with the implementation of a school uniform policy. Most of these control variables are *not* alterable as a result of any school policy. Thus, because uniform policies do not overcome these basic variations in schooling at all levels, educators should focus on processes that are alterable. Not only are school uniforms not an effective policy in public schools, but we have seen throughout this book the many ways in which there have been unintended consequences, unplanned stigmas, unexpected failures, and unintended rifts created between the important actors in the educational process; indeed, we have seen a "bleak" side to school uniforms, or, more accurately, an incompetence that invites strong criticism. All of these consequences raise serious questions regarding this movement and its intended reforms. It is to these that I now turn.

PANACEA OR SERIOUS REFORM? ON THE INCOMPETENCY OF THE SCHOOL UNIFORM MOVEMENT

If one obtains information on the public school uniform movement solely from the news media and fails to read more widely, fails to look at the bigger picture, fails to listen to the constituents of public education, and fails to delve into the court proceedings and board meetings, if one fails to do these and a variety of other critically important endeavors—one will obtain a picture of a movement that has wonderful intentions that *appear* to be working to make a significant mark in the institution of education and the process of public schooling. However, while that may be the cultural "center" of the discourse, it is often only when one looks at the "margins," the powerless, the counterpoint, does one understand the whole picture more effectively.[6] The school uniform movement in the United States has faced wild praise as well as firm criticism. The praise, after years of study and hundreds of empirical analyses, I'm afraid, is untenable. The criticism, on the other hand, is rarely given its "fifteen minutes of fame" (no one likes failure, educational reform "fame" is predicated on *presumed* success) (see Hacsi 2003). However, it is becoming increasingly clear that the criticisms of this movement are well placed; they are often not well-articulated, but they are, despite their seeming vagaries, exceedingly valid.

In 1998, Kerry Ann Rockquemore and I published the following conclusion:

> Requiring students to wear uniforms is a change that affects not only students, but also school faculty and parents. Instituting a mandatory uniform policy is a change that is immediate, highly visible, and shifts the environmental landscape of any particular school. Changing the landscape is a superficial change, but it attracts attention because of its visible nature. Instituting a uniform policy can be viewed as analogous to cleaning and brightly painting a deteriorating building in that on the one hand it grabs our immediate attention; on the other hand, it's only a coat of paint. That type of change attracts attention to schools and implies the presence of serious problems that necessitate drastic change. . . . A policy that is simplistic, readily understandable, cost free (to tax-

payers) and appealing to common sense is one that is politically pleas-
ing and, hence, finds much support. When challenged with broader reforms, those policies with results not immediately identifiable and
those that are costly and demand energy and a willingness to change on
the part of school faculty and parents are unacceptable. (Brunsma and
Rockquemore 1998, 60)

As of this writing, I feel even more confident of that conclusion
now than I did then. In this section, I wish to review the arguments
in this book, to look at the finer points concerning the implementation and protocol of school uniform policies, and to uncover the many
facets of this movement that have had exceedingly detrimental effects
on these schools' ability to school. I will discuss the following broad
contours:

1. the problematic relationship set up between parents and schools
   during the implementation of a school uniform policy,
2. the differential impact of school uniforms on disadvantaged and
   disenfranchised groups in American society,
3. the underlying regression toward racism and classism implied by
   the structure and protocol of school uniform implementation,
4. the reliance on common sense and anecdote in policy formation,
5. the increasing role of corporate control in American public schooling, and
6. the role of fear in dictating educational reform movements and
   policy strategies.

Alienation and Deference: The School Uniform Movement and the Role of Parents

That idea that home–school relationships are crucial to the effective
functioning of schooling processes has deep roots in the sociological
literature on educational process. Parental involvement has been
found to be beneficial not only for individual students but also for the
enhancement of the entirety of a school's educational and safety climate. One cannot say enough about the role of relationships in the
process of schooling.[7] Relationships are key, fundamental, and crucial.

Relationships of all kinds have been found to affect, positively, basic student- and school-level processes:

1. relationships between teachers and teachers (Hoy, Hannum, and Tschannen-Moran 1998; Phillips 1997),
2. relationships between parents and teachers (Bogenschneider 1997; Bryk and Driscoll 1988; Coleman 1988; Hoover-Dempsey, Bassler, and Brissie 1987; Lareau 1987),
3. relationships between students and teachers,
4. relationships between students and students, (i.e., peer networks, see Nichols and White 2001; Pellegrini 1994; Stanton-Salazar and Dornbusch 1995),
5. relationships between the school and its community, and
6. relationships between parents and parents (Bryk, Lee, and Holland 1993; Coleman, Hoffer, and Kilgore 1982).

This body of literature bespeaks the role of social capital in the effective functioning of a community and its schools.

Yet, as we have seen, school uniform policies may be doing more harm to these central relationships than good. Parents often feel completely left out of the decision-making process, and when they are involved, often feel that they do not have enough information, that the policies are not consistently implemented within a given school as well as across other schools in the district. Students, whose voices have been largely ignored in the literature and media coverage of this issue, especially at higher levels of schooling, often instigate rebellion. Via these rebellions and contexts of uncertainty, relationships between students and students suffer, as well as that key component of schooling—the relationship between teachers and students. Teachers are not in absolute agreement[5] regarding the influence of dress policies on their students' achievement and readiness to learn; their jobs are made more difficult, and as a result, relationships may suffer. In the end, what appears to be a policy aimed at invoking community and school sprit, at enhancing climate and other vagaries, may be creating rifts between key groups in schools where there needs to be more consensus. Indeed, this is what has been found to separate effective schools from ineffective ones: social capital (Coleman 1988; Stanton-Salazaar and Dornbusch 1995; Putnam 2000).

The Powerlessness of the Powerless:
The School Uniform Movement and the Assertion
of Administrative Power and Control

Relationships may be suffering as the result of school uniform policies; in addition to the decline of social capital potential, uniforms are
being disproportionately mandated for public school students who represent the disadvantaged of our society. Schools that are predominantly
minority and predominantly lower class, many of whose families fall below the poverty line, are more likely to be faced with a mandatory school
uniform policy. Policies are, by nature, vessels of rules and regulations,
formalized into documents, up for interpretation in the media; for those
who must comply with such policies, school uniform policies are "information rich," but they are implemented in valleys and communities of
social structures that are "information poor." In the end, lacking a voice,
lacking the necessary information, poor and minority parents and their
students are blamed for their status, blamed for their lack of information, blamed for their noncompliance, when they have not truly been
given the necessary tools to work with, and when they almost certainly
have not been given a seat at the decision-making table to level the playing field of schooling to some degree. They are powerless against such
policies (Hirschman 1972).

In this respect, school uniform policies are differentially affecting certain schools and students—and, by default, some families and communities, especially schools with students and families who are already the
most powerless, who are already the most dependent on social safety
nets, who are already trapped in a "welfare to work" climate (that has
been evidenced not to work, see Ehrenreich 2001), who are already ex-
periencing a lack of power and sense of control over their own (and their
children's) lives. The parents of these students have low socioeconomic
status. This means that they did not complete much schooling; they did
not have good experiences with the educational institutions they have
come into contact with; they have very few social and economic resources; and they work at occupations that are not creative, not flexible,
not socially praised, and rarely pay a living wage. Thus, uniform policies,
as they have done throughout history, continue to encourage docility
and obedience toward rightful authority disproportionately among a set
of parents who already defer to educational authority—for structural
and cultural reasons. In fact, Carl Cohn, the superintendent of LBUSD

who began his career as a truant officer (he was head of an anti-gang task force), has said: "School uniforms bespeak authority . . . this is a system where the adults are still in charge" (Sterngold 2000). Which adults is he speaking of?

The Color of Reform: The School Uniform Movement, Racism, and Classism

Coupled with the comments on reproducing the structure of power and powerlessness in our educational institutions, school uniform policies may actually be acting as a marker of lower status—akin to the "charity children" of sixteenth-century England's Christ's Church Hospital school. Though the media have rarely commented on the affinities between compliance with uniforms and the white, dominant class's setting up of suburban enclaves in the 1970s to avoid the poverty and, basically, "black" climate of the inner-city schools, it is clear to me, through the analyses presented in this book, that though the uniform policies themselves are not inherently racist and classist, the manner in which they have been implemented in our nation's schools—in predominantly minority and poor schools—implies that they may be doing more reproduction of the U.S. racist and classist structure than they are attempting to eradicate those differences.[9]

For instance, we know that it is the white parents who opt-out at much higher rates then the minority parents in these predominantly minority, poor, urban schools that have implemented uniform policies. This is strikingly reminiscent of the era of "white flight" in the 1970s (Orfield and Eaton 1996; Steinberg 2001). An impetus behind the school uniform movement is that it was designed (à la Clinton) to solve the problems of "urban education" because "urban education" has failed miserably. *Has* "urban education" failed miserably?[10] And if so, what exactly does this mean? What exactly does a concern with gangs and urban education refer to? I offer an interpretation: As our public schools predominantly are constructed and organized around white, dominant, middle-class ideologies of education and success, these "urban schools" (read "poor and minority," "poor and black") define for the nation models of "failure," "inadequacy," and a culture of mediocrity that is unacceptable in the ideological stream of individualism and racism. My interpretation may be wrong, but if one looks at the structure of funding (through property taxes), of elections, and of gentrification, etc., across this country, one cannot deny that our poor and minority students in these urban areas are being structurally and culturally cheated—not failing of their own accord. Until *we* as a country decide what education is for, until *we* forge relationships and demand change, until *we* demand the kind of education that we desire for our children, until *we* face our fears and our corporate society, reforms such as school uniforms will not be effective.[11]

Anecdotes as Evidence: The School Uniform Movement and the Nation of "Me"

Yet *we* do not act collectively, *we* are privatized, *we* are judgmental; in Jonathan Kozol's words, "we like our own children, but do we like other people's children?" (see Moyers 1993). The "evidence" that has been invoked throughout this uniform movement has been a clear case of "N of 1 thinking"; it has been generalization after generalization from an ever-flowing stream of anecdote, with little to no critical thinking, and certainly no empirical investigation. The movement can be characterized as one of anecdote versus evidence, fear versus rationality, the status quo versus social and educational change. And *we* the people have not truly been at the decision-making table.[12]

The effects on key social relationships in schools has been one of the unintended consequences of the movement. Yet, in this "nation of me" we must understand, again, that schools do not exist in social vacuums. Indeed, social capital has been declining in the United States for decades and not without ramifications and severe implications (Putnam 2000). This societal change, the shift from a focus on public goods to private goods, from accountability to individualism, is an American dilemma. Its roots are both structural and cultural (Bellah et al. 1985). Throughout this ongoing school uniform movement, the media have played a very important role—one that they have misused and misconstrued. One of the ultimate assumptions that has driven the uniform movement from its early years is that school uniforms will prevent distraction in the classroom. The assumption, one that is being watched very closely by the courts (see chapter 3), is that student appearance actually creates a distraction in the classroom. This has not been shown to be the case; there is simply no evidence that it is so.

Student Compliance and Corporate Compliance: The School Uniform Movement's Links with Corporate America

The movement would not have been as successful (in getting schools to agree to implement such policies) if it weren't for the growing climate of corporate influence in our public schools. Tommy Hilfiger, Gap, and other top, trendy clothiers have indeed jumped on the school uniform bandwagon—seeing a market, they smell money. But, please note that it was Gap and Hilfiger and their crusade of consumption, of dividing and conquering a market of youth, that was largely responsible for the original impetus behind the school uniform movement in the first place. It is ironic but also understandable that corporations have joined the hymn of the uniform crusade. There's a buck to be made. But where does the buck stop?

Looking at Land's End for a moment, if one peruses the website for NPD Group, Inc. (www.NPD.com as well as www.landsend.com), it is clear that Land's End created its school uniform division in 1997, at what is probably close to the public school uniform movement's apex. Furthermore, Sears, which owns Land's End, in the year 2003 alone spent approximately $3 million marketing school uniforms to public schools and districts. If one telephones Land's End's corporate offices, one can receive copies of their uniform propaganda. I use the word "propaganda" because the company claims to send you all the studies regarding the effectiveness of uniforms in our schools, and, furthermore, that "all studies show that uniforms help." This is propaganda. If they are utilizing the NPD study (funded by Land's End, and, ultimately, Sears), this study is so wholly flawed as to render itself useless (see chapter 2). In addition, a lobbying group in Alexandria, Virginia, works to get government officials to push school uniforms (lobbying for the clothiers) and, if one asks to look at the members-only part of the website, one is told that only board members from a school listed with them can enter it.[13] As a spokeswoman stated of the process of implementing a uniform policy in a public school and getting everyone on board, "it's all in the wording." That is to say, it's all symbolic.

Fearing Everything: The School Uniform Movement's Capitalization on Fear

One common thread that seems to weave its way through this entire discourse on school uniforms is the movement's capitalization on American's fears. We are an extremely fearful nation (Glassner 2000). Though it is a cliché by now, there remains a good deal of truth in Roosevelt's famous statement: "So, first of all, let me assert my firm belief that *the only thing we have to fear is fear itself*—nameless, unreasoning, unjustified terror which paralyzes needed efforts to convert retreat into advance" (Rosenman 1938, emphasis added). Roosevelt, of course, was speaking to Americans about the Great Depression and how to shake their pessimistic outlook to turn the economic situation around. But in terms of the school uniform movement's capitalization on the fear in Americans, one can see that we do fear that which we do not understand—and understanding takes work and effort.

Such fear about schooling in particular, and society in general, derives from our use of "common sense." Yet common sense is not *common*, and it is dangerous—as Barry Glassner has so effectively documented in *The Culture of Fear* (2000). We do not have common *sense;* in fact it is very difficult for Americans to achieve a sense of common anything. The fear underlying the school uniform movement arises from our collective myths about success, hardship, race, gender, power, class, sexuality, and, ultimately, what education is all about—what is its purpose? It is in schools that we see the struggle over the meaning of our collective myths and their correlate collective fears. What does the uniform movement uncover regarding these fears?

First, it shows that we fear students. Certainly Columbine and the media's coverage of that event reinforced this. But we fear students because of their diversity, because they come from widely varying backgrounds that we fear most because we do not choose to understand that complexity—thus, students embody, for many, the unintelligible diversity of American society. Second, we fear our own children. Not only in the role of student do we fear them, but we fear their unpredictability. Parents and educators alike look upon behavioral problems and, instead of the difficult work of uncovering social and familial and/or school-level patterns and structures that may be part of the problem for individual children, we blame their psychologies and their characters, we attack their childhoods and place them in alternative schooling and/or put them on prescription medications to alleviate the problems. But we still do not understand.

Third, regarding the complex and chaotic structures of public schooling, we uphold the notion of equality of educational opportunity, but we have witnessed its failure. Many have run from the difficulties associated with bringing this ideal into more prominent reality. Regarding schooling and reform efforts like school uniforms, we listen to anecdotes, then we hear a dissenting view, read a dissenting study, and we fear that we will never know the truth, the evidence.

Fourth, the fear is rooted in the desire to control, discipline, and structure an extremely complicated process of schooling children. The uniform seeks to do this through altering appearances, because somehow we believe that appearances matter; superficiality is easier than the truth of hardship, struggle, pain, and worse, hatred. Uniforms have done exactly that, brought home the lesson that appearances matter, the very thing they were supposed to be against (Dowd 1996).

BEHIND THE SYMBOL, BEHIND THE CRUSADE: INTENTIONS AND FEARS

Marshall McLuhan, media critic and social commentator, once wrote an incredibly influential essay, containing the following key phrase, "The medium is the message" (McLuhan 1999 [1964], 7). In terms of school uniforms as a medium, what is their message? What is behind this symbol of the school uniforms? Furthermore, as an educational reform effort utilizing this medium, what message is being sent as numerous students across the country come to school every day wearing this piece of material culture? I want to get even farther behind this symbol and thus behind the movement before leaving the reader. Though discussions of these aspects of this symbol appear throughout the book, I wish to briefly summarize the many arguments regarding what is behind this symbol of the school uniform in several ways: culturally, politically, and socially.

According to sociologist of culture Michael Schudson (1989), in order for a symbol to be effective it must have the following five properties:

1. It must be retrievable (i.e., one must be able to access it—socially and economically).
2. It must have rhetorical force (i.e., it must communicate something effectively).
3. It must have resonance (i.e., it must make sense to the "audience").
4. It must have institutional retention (i.e., it must be fully institutionalized in a particular setting).
5. It must have resolution (i.e., it must enter into one's life at a point where its meaning is relevant).

School uniforms are complicated symbols in Schudson's framework. First, they are assumed to be completely retrievable, yet this is not true across the socioeconomic spectrum, plus there are different types of uniforms that bring different amounts of status. Symbolically, its retrievability is moderate. Second, school uniforms' communicability is suspect. It is assumed that uniforms "bespeak authority" or that they let students know that they are to be in school and ready to learn. On the other hand, the messages that could be construed can and do vary—it's a symbol too of conformity, sameness, stifling, military, groupthink, sexuality, class, distinction, etc. Its rhetorical force is quite weak. Third, school uniforms have resonance only if one assumes a consensus on their usage throughout history. The audience of the public school uniform discourse, with its main symbol of the school uniform itself, is widely varying. I believe that its resonance is extremely low. Fourth, one of the things that the school uniform, as a symbol, has going for it is its retention within the educational sphere, and perhaps nowhere else. That is to say, school uniforms have high institutional retention, in that schooling has a "captive audience" for the reception of the idea of school uniforms—after all, they are *school* uniforms. Finally, a symbol must have relevance to the audience/the wearer. I think that this relevance is quite low. Students know what uniforms are supposed to do, but unfortunately they simply do not do it. As a symbol, uniforms, in Schudson's schema, are relatively weak. In addition to this model, it is clear that uniforms remain highly superficial. Perhaps, in the end, uniform policies reflect the general unease of adults about the state of education, society, and teenagers (Judson 1995).

Politically, we have seen the symbol of school uniforms being utilized in what could be called irresponsible fashions by local, state, and national officials. Are student uniforms really the reform strategy that the American people want? If we look at the structure of our elections in this country, one could question this altogether. We hold elections on working days, which dramatically affects the probability that working-class and poor parents will actually vote (due to lack of job flexibility, child care, mobility, a safe neighborhood, etc.). Voting an official into office is one fundamental way that we enact democratic principles in this republic. However, because of the structure of elections and the contributions of lobbying monies and political action coalitions, poor and working class as well as minority choices and concerns are rarely supported. Yet it is these families whose children's schools are disproportionately faced with mandatory uniform policies. Uniforms have indeed been used as political devices and strategies—but to what end? And to whose benefit?

Finally, socially, the symbol of school uniforms has glossed over important, and much more pressing, concerns for our school-aged children and their families—concerns that exist outside of school and come into the halls of our schools, primarily *because* we have not attended to them in the larger society. I am referring here to racial, class, and gender inequalities. In addition, this symbol glosses over the fact that public schools act as structures that effectively reproduce the class structure generation to generation. They gloss over the important reality that, in many instances, schools are acting as sorting devices and structures that create a docile and subservient workforce (Bowles and Gintis 1976). But perhaps the most violent glossing over of reality that school uniforms as a symbol fail to take into account is the system of school funding in the United States. We can vote in uniforms, but we cannot vote in new taxes or legislate new systems of funding our schools. In going down the symbolic road of school uniforms, we are adopting policies from other industrialized nations (England, France, etc.), but we refuse to follow another common trajectory of these countries—funding schools from our national wealth.

CONCLUSION: WHAT WORKS?

It has been a tall order to achieve a balanced presentation of the school uniform movement in this book. I have tried. The difficulty of achieving balance rests on the fact that there simply is so little of that balance in the information available to scholars.[14] There is a paucity of research that might give a balanced approach to the issue. It is my hope that I have provided that balance in this book to the degree that it is possible. In the end, this movement and my analysis of it have, on the one hand, produced more questions than answers; on the other hand, many of the questions I sought to respond to, to analyze with relevant data, have been largely answered.

It should be clear by now that uniform policies are not effective in our public schools. However, the analysis in this book did uncover several empirical factors that *do* affect the outcomes of interest:

- parental involvement in schooling,
- communications between students and parents about schooling,
- student preparedness for academic work,
- positive approaches to learning,
- pro-school attitudes and peer groups that support these attitudes,
- positive educational climates, and
- safe schools.

These factors do aid in the production of students who feel positively about themselves and their place in the experience of schooling, improve their attitudes toward schooling, and, ultimately, facilitate their academic success. What is clear from these analyses is that school uniforms, as a policy and strategy, do *not* play a role in producing more parental involvement, increased preparedness, positive approaches toward learning, pro-school attitudes, a heightened feeling of school unity and safety, or positive school climates. Therefore, such a policy should not be discussed as increasing the educational atmosphere *at any level of schooling*. It is my hope, again, that these results can direct us away from assumptions, conjecture, and unfounded claims concerning the effectiveness of school uniform policies.

Though many other industrialized nations uniform their students, it is curious that the United States might choose to follow this comparable path while disregarding the other lead taken by other industrialized nations—funding their public schools out of their national wealth instead of the clearly unequal practice of funding schools from local property taxes. Uniforms are a masking of macrolevel problems, a micro- or meso-level masking of more fundamental macrolevel problems and issues facing schools and districts: funding. *If* school uniform policies are implemented in the poorest and minority of schools and systems, what does that acknowledge about declining state and federal funding for schools throughout the 1990s and our overall unequal system of funding schools—the property tax? The larger questions that remain are the following: 1) Which system shall we fix, the schools or the surrounding societal structures that embed these schools? and 2) What is our consensus on the meaning and purpose of education in a postindustrial, postmodern, global society?

APPENDIX A: MEANS, STANDARD DEVIATIONS, RANGES, AND CODING OF VARIABLES

Variables	Mean	S.D.	Range	Coding Description
Tenth Grade:				
Student-Level				
Female	0.50	0.50	0,1	(f1sex) recoded 1 = female, 0 = male
Minority	0.28	0.45	0,1	(f1race) recoded 1 = minority, 0 = male. Some analyses use several dichotomous variables with white as the comparison category.
SES	−0.01	0.77	−3.28 to 2.76	(f1ses) an NCES created composite of socio-economic status that includes parental income and occupational prestige scores.
Parent Education	3.08	1.21	1–6	(f1pared) ranges from (1) "Did not finish high school" to (6) "PhD, M.D., other".
Discuss with Parents	6.08	1.58	3–9	Scale created from summing across f1s105a, f1s105b, f1s105c, which all assess whether or not students discuss school programs, activities, and things studies in class. α = 0.77. High values indicate more discussion.
Parental Involvement	2.83	2.35	0–12	Scale created from summing across f1s106a, f1s106b, f1s106c, f1s106d, which all assess the degree to which parents attend school meetings, contact teachers, attend

Variables	Mean	S.D.	Range	Coding Description
				events, and volunteer. $\alpha = .70$. High values indicate more involvement.
Academic Preparedness	9.71	1.74	3–12	Scale created from summing across fls40a, fls40b, fls40c, which all assess the degree to which the student comes to class with paper/pencil, with books, and with homework. $\alpha = 0.70$. High values indicate more preparedness.
Pro-School Attitudes	64.91	6.60	18–72	Scale created from summing across 18 variables indicating the degree to which the student feels it is not ok to come late to school, use drugs at school, get into fights, etc. $\alpha = 0.88$. High values indicate higher pro-school attitudes.
Peer Pro-School Attitudes	7.22	1.52	3–9	Scale created from summing across fls70a, fls70b, fls70d, which all assess the degree to which the respondent's peers think it is important to attend classes, do homework, and get good grades. $\alpha = 0.81$. High values indicate peers with pro-school attitudes.
Standardized Composite Achievement	50.45	9.92	30.27 to 71.82	An NCES standardized achievement test. See Engels et al. 1994 for more information.
Standardized Reading Achievement	50.34	9.92	30.58 to 68.91	An NCES standardized achievement test. See Engels et al. 1994 for more information.
Standardized Mathematics Achievement	50.50	9.95	31.43 to 71.93	An NCES standardized achievement test. See Engels et al. 1994 for more information.
Standardized Science Achievement	50.44	9.96	31.56 to 2.54	An NCES standardized achievement test. See Engels et al. 1994 for more information.
Standardized History Achievement	50.34	9.96	28.01 to 73.26	An NCES standardized achievement test. See Engels et al. 1994 for more information.
Student Perceived Educational Climate	29.86	4.44	15–52	A scale created from summing across fls7a, b, c, d, f, g, h, l, l, and o, which all assess facets of the educational climate of a school such as: students get along, school spirit, quality of teaching, teacher-student relationships, etc. $\alpha = 0.67$. High values indicate a more positive perception of the school's educational climate.

Variables	Mean	S.D.	Range	Coding Description
Student Behavior	2.86	2.77	0–20	A scale created by summing across fls10a, b, c, d, and e, which all assess the degree to which the respondent was late to classes, skipped classes, got into fights, was suspended, etc. α = .66. High values indicate more respondent behavioral problems.
Self-Concept	−0.001	0.68	−3.58 to 1.35	An NCES standardized self-concept assessment. See Engels et al. 1994 for more information.
Locus of Control	−0.001	0.64	−2.79 to 1.46	An NCES standardized locus of control assessment. See Engels et al. 1994 for more information.
School-Level				
Urban School	0.27	0.45	0,1	(gl0urban) recoded into a dichotomous variable with suburban as the referent category.
Rural School	0.32	0.47	0,1	(gl0urban) recoded into a dichotomous variable with suburban as the referent category.
Catholic School	0.06	0.23	0,1	(gl0ctrl) recoded into a dichotomous variable with public school as the referent category.
Private School	0.03	0.18	0,1	(gl0ctrl) recoded into a dichotomous variable with public school as the referent category.
Uniform Policy	0.05	0.22	0,1	Variable indicating whether school attended by the respondent mandates a school uniform.
Dress Code Policy	0.91	0.28	0,1	Variable indicating whether school attended by the respondent prohibits certain forms of dress.
Attendance Rate	92.70	5.11	40 to 100	(flc26) indicating the average daily attendance rate of the school.
Percent Minority	0.35	0.35	0,1	Aggregation of racial status of respondents from each school.
Percent of Students in College Preparatory Track	50.78	27.57	0–100	(flc11b) percentage of 10th grade students in college preparatory track.
Eighth Grade: *Student-Level*				
Female	0.50	0.50	0,1	(bys12) recoded 1 = female, 0 = male.
Minority	0.31	0.46	0,1	(bys31a) recoded 1 = minority, 0 = male. Some analyses use several dichotomous variables with white as the comparison category.

Variables	Mean	S.D.	Range	Coding Description
SES	−0.12	0.76	−2.97 to 2.30	(byses) an NCES created composite of socio-economic status that includes parental income and occupational prestige scores.
Parent Education	3.01	1.21	1–6	(bypared) ranges from (1) "Did not finish high school" to (6) "PhD, M.D., other."
Discuss with Parents	7.39	2.37	3–24	Scale created from summing across bys36a, b, and c, which all assess whether or not students discuss school programs, activities, and things studies in class. $\alpha = .61$. High values indicate more discussion.
Parental Involvement	2.11	1.22	0–4	Scale created from summing across bys37a, b, c, and d, which all assess the degree to which parents attend school meetings, contact teachers, attend events, and volunteer, etc. $\alpha = 0.76$. High values indicate more involvement.
Academic Preparedness	9.33	1.98	3–12	Scale created from summing across bys78a, b, and c, which all assess the degree to which the student comes to class with paper/pencil, with books, and with homework. $\alpha = 0.70$. High values indicate more preparedness.
Standardized Composite Achievement	50.31	10.00	30.7 to 75.81	An NCES standardized achievement test. See Engels et al. 1994 for more information.
Standardized Reading Achievement	50.03	10.00	31.71 to 70.55	An NCES standardized achievement test. See Engels et al. 1994 for more information.
Standardized Mathematics Achievement	50.03	10.00	33.90 to 77.20	An NCES standardized achievement test. See Engels et al. 1994 for more information.
Standardized Science Achievement	50.03	10.00	32.33 to 77.13	An NCES standardized achievement test. See Engels et al. 1994 for more information.
Standardized History Achievement	50.03	10.00	28.27 to 76.71	An NCES standardized achievement test. See Engels et al. 1994 for more information.
Student Perceived Educational Climate	34.87	4.27	14–55	A scale created from summing across bys59a, b, c, d, e, f, g, h, I, j, k, l, and n, which all assess facets of the educational climate of a school such as: students get along, school spirit, quality of teaching, teacher-student relationships, etc. $\alpha = 0.92$.

Variables	Mean	S.D.	Range	Coding Description
				High values indicate a more positive perception of the school's educational climate.
Student Perceived Safety Climate	33.15	8.44	11–44	A scale created by summing across bys58a, b, c, d, e, f, g, h, I, j, and k, which assess the degree to which students perceive drug use, alcohol use, fighting, disruptions, gangs, etc. a problem at their school. It has been recoded so that high values indicate a safer environment. $\alpha = 0.92$.
Student Behavior	1.67	2.22	0–12	A scale created by summing across bys55a, b, c, d, e, and f, which all assess the degree to which the respondent was late to classes, skipped classes, got into fights, was suspended, etc. $\alpha = 0.76$. High values indicate more respondent behavioral problems.
Self-Concept	−0.001	0.66	−3.61 to 1.25	An NCES standardized self-concept assessment. See Engels et al. 1994 for more information.
Locus of Control	0.001	0.62	−3.01 to 1.52	An NCES standardized locus of control assessment. See Engels et al. 1994 for more information.
Student Perceived Degree of Absenteeism	2.24	0.99	1–4	(bys58b) assessing the degree the respondent feels that absenteeism is a problem at his or her school.
Student Perceptions of Drug Use	1.85	1.09	1–4	(bys58h) assessing the degree the respondent feels that illegal drug use is a problem at his or her school.
School-Level				
Urban School	0.25	0.43	0,1	(g8urban) recoded into a dichotomous variable with suburban schools as the referent category.
Rural School	0.32	0.47	0,1	(g8urban) recoded into a dichotomous variable with suburban schools as the referent category.
Catholic School	0.08	0.27	0,1	(g8ctrl) recoded into a dichotomous variable with public schools as the referent category.
Private School	0.04	0.21	0,1	(g8ctrl) recoded into a dichotomous variable with public schools as the referent category.

Variables	Mean	S.D.	Range	Coding Description
Uniform Policy	0.08	0.21	0,1	(bysc48l) a variable indicating whether or not the school mandates school uniforms to be worn by students.
Dress Code Policy	0.93	0.25	0,1	(bysc48j) a variable indicating whether or not the school prohibits certain forms of dress.
Enrollment	3.43	1.58	1–6	(g8enroll) ordinal variable assessing the enrollment of the school.
Student/Teacher Ratio	17.78	4.54	10–30	(byratio) student/teacher ratio of the school.
Attendance Rate	93.77	3.80	60 to 100	(bysc11) Average daily attendance for the middle school.
Percent Minority	0.34	0.30	0,1	Aggregation of racial status of respondents from each school.
Principal Perceived Degree of Absenteeism	2.85	0.80	1–4	(bysc49b) assessing the degree the principal feels that absenteeism is a problem at his or her school.
Principal Perceptions of Drug Use	3.39	0.67	1–4	(bys49h) assessing the degree the principal feels that illegal drug use is a problem at his or her school.

Kindergarten:
Student-Level

Age (in months)	68.12	6.67		(r1_kage) Child's age in months
Female	0.48	0.50	0,1	(gender) recoded into 1 = female and 0 = male.
Minority	0.43	0.50	0,1	(race) recoded into 1 = minority and 0 = nonminority (white).
Single Parent Household	0.23	0.42	0,1	(P1hfamil) recoded into 1 = single parent household 0 = all other household types.
SES	−0.03	0.79	−4.75 to 2.75	(wksesl) continuous NCES constructed socio-economic status variable comprised of parental income and occupational prestige.
Student Approach to Learning (Fall)	2.95	0.68	1–4	Teacher assessment of whether student has a positive of negative approach to learning—assessed in the Fall.
Student Approach to Learning (Spring)	3.08	0.69	1–4	Teacher assessment of whether student has a positive of negative approach to learning—assessed in the Spring.
Self Control (Fall)	3.07	0.62	1–4	Teacher assessment of whether student has a high or low sense of self-control—assessed in the Fall.
Self Control (Spring)	3.15	0.64	1–4	Teacher assessment of whether student has a high or low sense of self-control—assessed in the Spring.

Variables	Mean	S.D.	Range	Coding Description
Externalization of Problems Behavior (Fall)	1.65	0.65	1–4	Teacher assessment of whether the child externalizes problem behavior (blames others)—assessed in the Fall.
Externalization of Problem Behavior (Spring)	1.69	0.66	1–4	Teacher assessment of whether the child externalizes problem behavior (blames others)—assessed in the Spring.
Internalization of Problem Behavior (Fall)	1.56	0.54	1–4	Teacher assessment of whether the child internalizes problem behavior (blames self)—assessed in the Fall.
Internalization of Problem Behavior (Spring)	1.59	0.53	1–4	Teacher assessment of whether the child internalizes problem behavior (blames self)—assessed in the Spring.
Reading Aptitude (Literacy) (Fall)	2.57	0.79	1–5	Teacher assessment of kindergartner's literacy (Fall).
Reading Aptitude (Literacy) (Spring)	3.34	0.80	1–5	Teacher assessment of kindergartner's literacy (Spring).
Math Aptitude (Fall)	2.55	0.82	1–5	Teacher assessment of kindergartner's math skills (Fall).
Math Aptitude (Spring)	3.51	0.86	1–5	Teacher assessment of kindergartner's math skills (Spring).
General Knowledge (Fall)	2.64	1.01	1–5	Teacher assessment of kindergartner's general knowledge (Fall).
General Knowledge (Spring)	3.57	0.99	1–5	Teacher assessment of kindergartner's general knowledge (Spring).
School-Level				
Private School	0.15	0.35	0,1	(s2kstyp) recoded into dichotomous variable where 1 = private and 0 = public.
Urban School	0.49	0.50	0,1	(kurban) recoded into dichotomous variable with suburban as referent category.
Rural School	0.21	0.40	0,1	(kurban) recoded into dichotomous variable with suburban as referent category.
Total Enrollment	3.06	1.25	1–5	(s2kenrls) ordinal variable assessing the school's enrollment.
Percent Minority	2.56	1.50	1–5	(s2kminor) ordinal variable indicating percent of minority students at the school.
Percent Free Lunch	28.00	27.75	0–93	(s2klnch) percentage of students receiving free lunch.
Uniform Policy	0.18	0.38	0,1	(s2kunifrm) recoded into dichotomous variable where 1 = yes, 0 = no.
Parent Involvement	25.04	4.84	12–35	Scale created from summing across s2rghelp, s2gopcnf, s2openhs,

Variables	Mean	S.D.	Range	Coding Description
				s2artmsc, s2gopta, s2rsfund, and s2plyfai, which all assess the degree to which parents help at the school, attend p/t conferences, attend open houses, PTA, etc. α = 0.80. High values indicate more involvement.
Average Daily Attendance Rate	95.14	2.51	89 to 100	(s2ada) average daily attendance rate for the elementary school.
Principal Perceptions of Safety Climate	16.10	2.58	6–18	Scale created from summing across s2tnsion, s2litter, s2drugs, s2gangs, s2vlence, and s2crime assessing the degree to which principals perceive tension between teachers and administrators, student drug use, gang activity, violence, and crime problems. Recoded so that high values indicate a safer environment. α = .88.
Principal Perceptions of Educational Climate	23.96	3.37	13–30	Scale created from summing across s2absent, s2trnovr, s2chldou, s2cnsnss, s2ordr, and s2ovrcrd assessing the degree to which principals perceive the educational climate, including: teacher absenteeism, teacher turnover, consensus on goals, overcrowding, and classroom order. Recoded so that high values indicate a positive educational environment. α = 0.61.
First Grade: Student-Level				
Age (in months)	86.76	4.42		(r1_kage) Child's age in months.
Female	0.48	0.50	0,1	(gender) recoded into 1 = female and 0 = male.
Minority	0.44	0.50	0,1	(race) recoded into 1 = minority and 0 = nonminority (white).
Single Parent Household	0.20	0.40	0,1	(P1hfamil) recoded into 1 = single parent household 0 = all other household types.
SES	0.005	0.81	−4.75 to 2.75	(wksesl) continuous NCES constructed socio-economic status variable comprised of parental income and occupational prestige.
Student Approach to Learning (Spring)	3.03	0.71	1–4	Teacher assessment of whether student has a positive of negative approach to learning—assessed in the Spring.

Variables	Mean	S.D.	Range	Coding Description
Self Control (Spring)	3.17	0.62	1–4	Teacher assessment of whether student has a high or low sense of self-control—assessed in the Spring.
Externalization of Problem Behavior (Spring)	1.66	0.65	1–4	Teacher assessment of whether the child externalizes problem behavior (blames others)—assessed in the Spring.
Internalization of Problem Behavior (Spring)	1.60	0.52	1–4	Teacher assessment of whether the child internalizes problem behavior (blames self)—assessed in the Spring.
Reading Aptitude (Literacy) (Spring)	3.44	0.91	1–5	Teacher assessment of kindergartner's literacy (Spring).
Math Aptitude (Spring)	3.47	0.89	1–5	Teacher assessment of kindergartner's math skills (Spring).
General Knowledge (Spring)	3.31	0.97	1–5	Teacher assessment of kindergartner's general knowledge (Spring).
School Level:				
Private School	0.15	0.35	0,1	(s2kstyp) recoded into dichotomous variable where 1 = private and 0 = public.
Urban School	0.49	0.50	0,1	(kurban) recoded into dichotomous variable with suburban as referent category.
Rural School	0.21	0.40	0,1	(kurban) recoded into dichotomous variable with suburban as referent category.
Total Enrollment	3.06	1.25	1–5	(s2kenrls) ordinal variable assessing the school's enrollment.
Percent Minority	2.56	1.50	1–5	(s2kminor) ordinal variable indicating percent of minority students at the school.
Percent Free Lunch	28.00	27.75	0–93	(s2klnch) percentage of students receiving free lunch.
Uniform Policy	0.18	0.38	0,1	(s2kunifrm) recoded into dichotomous variable where 1 = yes, 0 = no.
Average Daily Attendance Rate	95.14	2.51	89 to 100	(s2ada) average daily attendance rate for the elementary school.
Principal Perceptions of Safety Climate	16.10	2.58	6–18	Scale created from summing across s2tnsion, s2litter, s2drugs, s2gangs, s2vlence, and s2crime assessing the degree to which principals perceive tension between teachers and administrators, student drug use, gang activity, violence and crime problems. Recoded so that high values indicate a safer environment. $\alpha = 0.88$.

Variables	Mean	S.D.	Range	Coding Description
Principal Perceptions of Educational Climate	23.96	3.37	13–30	Scale created from summing across s2absent, s2trnovr, s2chldou, s2cnsnss, s2ordr, and s2ovrcrd assessing the degree to which principals perceive the educational climate, including: teacher absenteeism, teacher turnover, consensus on goals, overcrowding, and classroom order. Recoded so that high values indicate a positive educational environment. $\alpha = 0.61$.

B

PRESIDENT CLINTON'S STATE OF THE UNION ADDRESS (DELIVERED VERSION)

Mr. Speaker, Mr. Vice President, members of the 104th Congress, distinguished guests, my fellow Americans all across our land:

Let me begin tonight by saying to our men and women in uniform around the world, and especially those helping peace take root in Bosnia and to their families, I thank you. America is very, very proud of you. My duty tonight is to report on the state of the Union—not the state of our government, but of our American community; and to set forth our responsibilities, in the words of our Founders, to form a more perfect union.

The state of the Union is strong. Our economy is the healthiest it has been in three decades. We have the lowest combined rates of unemployment and inflation in 27 years. We have created nearly 8 million new jobs, over a million of them in basic industries, like construction and automobiles. America is selling more cars than Japan for the first time since the 1970s. And for three years in a row, we have had a record number of new businesses started in our country.

Our leadership in the world is also strong, bringing hope for new peace. And perhaps most important, we are gaining ground in restoring our fundamental values. The crime rate, the welfare and food stamp rolls, the poverty rate and the teen pregnancy rate are all down. And as they go down, prospects for America's future go up.

We live in an age of possibility. A hundred years ago we moved from farm to factory. Now we move to an age of technology, information, and global competition. These changes have opened vast new opportunities for our people, but they have also presented them with stiff challenges. While more Americans are living better, too many of our fellow citizens are working harder just to keep up, and they are rightly concerned about the security of their families.

We must answer here three fundamental questions: First, how do we make the American Dream of opportunity for all a reality for all Americans who are willing to work for it? Second, how do we preserve our old and enduring values as we move into the future? And, third, how do we meet these challenges together, as one America?

We know big government does not have all the answers. We know there's not a program for every problem. We have worked to give the American people a smaller, less bureaucratic government in Washington. And we have to give the American people one that lives within its means.

The era of big government is over. But we cannot go back to the time when our citizens were left to fend for themselves. Instead, we must go forward as one America, one nation working together to meet the challenges we face together. Self-reliance and teamwork are not opposing virtues; we must have both.

I believe our new, smaller government must work in an old-fashioned American way, together with all of our citizens through state and local governments, in the workplace, in religious, charitable, and civic associations. Our goal must be to enable all our people to make the most of their own lives—with stronger families, more educational opportunity, economic security, safer streets, a cleaner environment in a safer world.

To improve the state of our Union, we must ask more of ourselves, we must expect more of each other, and we must face our challenges together. Here, in this place, our responsibility begins with balancing the budget in a way that is fair to all Americans. There is now broad bipartisan agreement that permanent deficit spending must come to an end.

I compliment the Republican leadership and the membership for the energy and determination you have brought to this task of balancing the budget. And I thank the Democrats for passing the largest deficit reduction plan in history in 1993, which has already cut the deficit nearly in half in three years.

Since 1993, we have all begun to see the benefits of deficit reduction. Lower interest rates have made it easier for businesses to borrow and to invest and to create new jobs. Lower interest rates have brought down the cost of home mortgages, car payments, and credit card rates to ordinary citizens. Now, it is time to finish the job and balance the budget.

Though differences remain among us which are significant, the combined total of the proposed savings that are common to both plans is more than enough, using the numbers from your Congressional Budget Office to balance the budget in seven years and to provide a modest tax cut. These cuts are real. They will require sacrifice from everyone. But these cuts do not undermine our fundamental obligations to our parents, our children, and our future, by endangering Medicare, or Medicaid, or education, or the environment, or by raising taxes on working families.

I have said before, and let me say again, many good ideas have come out of our negotiations. I have learned a lot about the way both Republicans and Democrats view the debate before us. I have learned a lot about the good ideas that we could all embrace.

We ought to resolve our remaining differences. I am willing to work to resolve them. I am ready to meet tomorrow. But I ask you to consider that we should at least enact these savings that both plans have in common and give the American people their balanced budget, a tax cut, lower interest rates, and a brighter future. We should do that now, and make permanent deficits yesterday's legacy.

Now it is time for us to look also to the challenges of today and tomorrow, beyond the burdens of yesterday. The challenges are significant. But America was built on challenges, not promises. And when we work together to meet them, we never fail. That is the key to a more perfect Union. Our individual dreams must be realized by our common efforts. Tonight I want to speak to you about the challenges we all face as a people.

Our first challenge is to cherish our children and strengthen America's families. Family is the foundation of American life. If we have stronger families, we will have a stronger America.

Before I go on, I would like to take just a moment to thank my own family, and to thank the person who has taught me more than anyone else over 25 years about the importance of families and children—a wonderful wife, a magnificent mother, and a great First Lady. Thank you, Hillary.

All strong families begin with taking more responsibility for our children. I have heard Mrs. Gore say that it's hard to be a parent today, but it's even harder to be a child. So all of us, not just as parents, but all of us in our other roles—our media, our schools, our teachers, our communities, our churches and synagogues, our businesses, our governments—all of us have a responsibility to help our children to make it and to make the most of their lives and their God-given capacities.

To the media, I say you should create movies and CDs and television shows you'd want your own children and grandchildren to enjoy. I call on Congress to pass the requirement for a V-chip in TV sets so that parents can screen out programs they believe are inappropriate for their children. When parents control what their young children see, that is not censorship; that is enabling parents to assume more personal responsibility for their children's upbringing. And I urge them to do it.

The V-chip requirement is part of the important telecommunications bill now pending in this Congress. It has bipartisan support, and I urge you to pass it now. To make the V-chip work, I challenge the broadcast industry to do what movies have done—to identify your programming in ways that help parents to protect their children. And I invite the leaders of major media corporations in the entertainment industry to come to the White House next month to work with us in a positive way on concrete ways to improve what our children see on television. I am ready to work with you.

I say to those who make and market cigarettes: Every year a million children take up smoking, even though it is against the law. Three hundred thousand of them will have their lives shortened as a result. Our administration has taken steps to stop the massive marketing campaigns that appeal to our children. We are simply saying: Market your products to adults, if you wish, but draw the line on children.

I say to those who are on welfare, and especially to those who have been trapped on welfare for a long time: For too long our welfare system has undermined the values of family and work, instead of supporting them. The Congress and I are near agreement on sweeping welfare reform. We agree on time limits, tough work requirements, and the toughest possible child support enforcement. But I believe we must also provide child care so that mothers who are required to go to work can do so without worrying about what is happening to their children.

I challenge this Congress to send me a bipartisan welfare reform bill that will really move people from welfare to work and do the right thing by our children. I will sign it immediately.

Let us be candid about this difficult problem. Passing a law, even the best possible law, is only a first step. The next step is to make it work. I challenge people on welfare to make the most of this opportunity for independence. I challenge American businesses to give people on welfare the chance to move into the work force. I applaud the work of religious groups and others who care for the poor. More than anyone else in our society, they know the true difficulty of the task before us, and they are in a position to help. Every one of us should join them. That is the only way we can make real welfare reform a reality in the lives of the American people.

To strengthen the family we must do everything we can to keep the teen pregnancy rate going down. I am gratified, as I'm sure all Americans are, that it has dropped for two years in a row. But we all know it is still far too high.

Tonight I am pleased to announce that a group of prominent Americans is responding to that challenge by forming an organization that will support grass-roots community efforts all across our country in a national campaign against teen pregnancy. And I challenge all of us and every American to join their efforts.

I call on American men and women in families to give greater respect to one another. We must end the deadly scourge of domestic violence in our country. And I challenge America's families to work harder to stay together. For families who stay together not only do better economically, their children do better as well.

In particular, I challenge the fathers of this country to love and care for their children. If your family has separated, you must pay your child support. We're doing more than ever to make sure you do, and we're going to do more, but let's all admit something about that, too: A check will not substitute for a parent's love and guidance. And only you—only you can make the decision to help raise your children. No matter who you are, how low or high your station in life, it is the most basic human duty of every American to do that job to the best of his or her ability.

Our second challenge is to provide Americans with the educational opportunities we will all need for this new century. In our schools, every classroom in America must be connected to the information superhighway, with computers and good software, and well-trained teachers. We are working with the telecommunications industry, educators, and parents to connect 20 percent of California's classrooms by this spring, and every classroom and every library in the entire United States by the year 2000. I ask Congress to support this education technology initiative so that we can make sure this national partnership succeeds.

Every diploma ought to mean something. I challenge every community, every school, and every state to adopt national standards of excellence; to measure whether schools are meeting those standards; to cut bureaucratic red tape so that schools and teachers have more flexibility for grass-roots reform; and to hold them accountable for results. That's what our Goals 2000 initiative is all about.

I challenge every state to give all parents the right to choose which public school their children will attend; and to let teachers form new schools with a charter they can keep only if they do a good job. I challenge all our schools to teach character education, to teach good values and good citizenship. And if it means that teenagers will stop killing each other over designer jackets, then our public schools should be able to require their students to wear school uniforms.

I challenge our parents to become their children's first teachers. Turn off the TV. See that the homework is done. And visit your children's classroom. No program, no teacher, no one else can do that for you. My fellow Americans, higher education is more important today than ever before. We've created a new student loan program that's made it easier to borrow and repay those loans, and we have dramatically cut the student loan default rate. That's something we should all be proud of, because it was unconscionably high just a few years ago. Through AmeriCorps, our national service program, this year 25,000 young people will earn college money by serving their local communities to improve the lives of their friends and neighbors. These initiatives are right for America and we should keep them going.

And we should also work hard to open the doors of college even wider. I challenge Congress to expand work-study and help one million young Americans work their way through college by the year 2000; to provide a $1,000 merit scholarship for the top 5 percent of graduates in every high school in the United States; to expand Pell Grant scholarships for deserving and needy students; and to make up to $10,000 a year of college tuition tax deductible. It's a good idea for America.

Our third challenge is to help every American who is willing to work for it, achieve economic security in this new age. People who work hard still need support to get ahead in the new economy. They need education and training for a lifetime. They need more support for families raising children. They need retirement security. They need access to health care. More and more Americans are finding that the education of their childhood simply doesn't last a lifetime.

So I challenge Congress to consolidate 70 overlapping, antiquated job-training programs into a simple voucher worth $2,600 for unemployed or underemployed workers to use as they please for community college tuition or other training. This is a G.I. Bill for America's workers we should all be able to agree on.

More and more Americans are working hard without a raise. Congress sets the minimum wage. Within a year, the minimum wage will fall to a 40-year low in purchasing power. Four dollars and 25 cents an hour is no longer a living wage, but millions of Americans and their children are trying to live on it. I challenge you to raise their minimum wage.

In 1993, Congress cut the taxes of 15 million hard-pressed working families to make sure that no parents who work full-time would have to raise their children in poverty, and to encourage people to move from welfare to work. This expanded earned income tax credit is now worth about $1,800 a year to a family of four living on $20,000. The budget bill I vetoed would have reversed this achievement and raised taxes on nearly 8 million of these people. We should not do that.

I also agree that the people who are helped under this initiative are not all those in our country who are working hard to do a good job raising their children and at work. I agree that we need a tax credit for working families with children. That's one of the things most of us in this Chamber, I hope, can agree on. I know it is strongly supported by the Republican majority. And it should be part of any final budget agreement.

I want to challenge every business that can possibly afford it to provide pensions for your employees. And I challenge Congress to pass a proposal recommended by the White House Conference on Small Business that would make it easier for small businesses and farmers to establish their own pension plans. That is something we should all agree on.

We should also protect existing pension plans. Two years ago, with bipartisan support that was almost unanimous on both sides of the aisle, we moved to protect the pensions of 8 million working people and to stabilize the pensions of 32 million more. Congress should not now let companies endanger those workers's pension funds. I know the proposal to liberalize the ability of employers to take money out of pension funds for other purposes would raise money for the treasury. But I believe it is false economy. I vetoed that proposal last year, and I would have to do so again.

Finally, if our working families are going to succeed in the new economy, they must be able to buy health insurance policies that they do not lose when they change jobs or when someone in their family gets sick. Over the past two years, over one million Americans in working families have lost their health insurance. We have to do more to make health care available to every American. And Congress should start by passing the bipartisan bill sponsored by Senator Kennedy and Senator Kassebaum that would require insurance companies to stop dropping people when they switch jobs, and stop denying coverage for preexisting conditions. Let's all do that.

And even as we enact savings in these programs, we must have a common commitment to preserve the basic protections of Medicare and Medicaid— not just to the poor, but to people in working families, including children, people with disabilities, people with AIDS, and senior citizens in nursing homes.

In the past three years, we've saved $15 billion just by fighting health care fraud and abuse. We have all agreed to save much more. We have all agreed to stabilize the Medicare Trust Fund. But we must not abandon our fundamental obligations to the people who need Medicare and Medicaid. America cannot become stronger if they become weaker.

The G.I. Bill for workers, tax relief for education and child rearing, pension availability and protection, access to health care, preservation of Medicare and Medicaid—these things, along with the Family and Medical Leave Act passed in 1993—these things will help responsible, hardworking American families to make the most of their own lives. But employers and employees must do their part, as well, as they are doing in so many of our finest companies—working together, putting the long-term prosperity ahead of the short-term gain. As workers increase their hours and their productivity, employers should make sure they get the skills they need and share the benefits of the good years, as well as the burdens of the bad ones. When companies and workers work as a team they do better, and so does America.

Our fourth great challenge is to take our streets back from crime and gangs and drugs. At last we have begun to find a way to reduce crime, forming community partnerships with local police forces to catch criminals and prevent crime. This strategy, called community policing, is clearly working. Violent crime is coming down all across America. In New York City murders are down 25 percent; in St. Louis, 18 percent; in Seattle, 32 percent. But we still have a long way to go before our streets are safe and our people are free from fear.

The Crime Bill of 1994 is critical to the success of community policing. It provides funds for 100,000 new police in communities of all sizes. We're already a third of the way there. And I challenge the Congress to finish the job. Let us stick with a strategy that's working and keep the crime rate coming down.

Community policing also requires bonds of trust between citizens and police. I ask all Americans to respect and support our law enforcement officers. And to our police, I say, our children need you as role models and heroes. Don't let them down.

The Brady Bill has already stopped 44,000 people with criminal records from buying guns. The assault weapons ban is keeping 19 kinds of assault weapons out of the hands of violent gangs. I challenge the Congress to keep those laws on the books.

Our next step in the fight against crime is to take on gangs the way we once took on the mob. I'm directing the FBI and other investigative agencies to target gangs that involve juveniles in violent crime, and to seek authority to prosecute as adults teenagers who maim and kill like adults.

And I challenge local housing authorities and tenant associations: Criminal gang members and drug dealers are destroying the lives of decent tenants. From now on, the rule for residents who commit crime and peddle drugs should be one strike and you're out.

I challenge every state to match federal policy to assure that serious violent criminals serve at least 85 percent of their sentence. More police and punishment are important, but they're not enough. We have got to keep more of our young people out of trouble, with prevention strategies not dictated by Washington, but developed in communities. I challenge all of our communities, all of our adults, to give our children futures to say yes to. And I challenge Congress not to abandon the Crime Bill's support of these grass-roots prevention efforts.

Finally, to reduce crime and violence we have to reduce the drug problem. The challenge begins in our homes, with parents talking to their children openly and firmly. It embraces our churches and synagogues, our youth groups and our schools.

I challenge Congress not to cut our support for drug-free schools. People like the D.A.R.E. officers are making a real impression on grade schoolchildren that will give them the strength to say no when the time comes.

Meanwhile, we continue our efforts to cut the flow of drugs into America. For the last two years, one man in particular has been on the front lines of that effort. Tonight I am nominating him—a hero of the Persian Gulf War and the Commander in Chief of the United States Military Southern Command—General Barry McCaffrey, as America's new Drug Czar. General McCaffrey has earned three Purple Hearts and two Silver Stars fighting for this country. Tonight I ask that he lead our nation's battle against drugs at home and abroad. To succeed, he needs a force far larger than he has ever commanded before. He needs all of us. Every one of us has a role to play on this team.

Thank you, General McCaffrey, for agreeing to serve your country one more time.

Our fifth challenge: to leave our environment safe and clean for the next generation. Because of a generation of bipartisan effort we do have cleaner water and air, lead levels in children's blood has been cut by 70 percent, toxic emissions from factories cut in half. Lake Erie was dead, and now it's a thriving resource. But 10 million children under 12 still live within four miles of a toxic waste dump. A third of us breathe air that endangers our health. And in too many communities, the water is not safe to drink. We still have much to do.

Yet Congress has voted to cut environmental enforcement by 25 percent. That means more toxic chemicals in our water, more smog in our air, more pesticides in our food. Lobbyists for polluters have been allowed to write their own loopholes into bills to weaken laws that protect the health and safety of our children. Some say that the taxpayer should pick up the tab for toxic waste and let polluters who can afford to fix it off the hook. I challenge Congress to reexamine those policies and to reverse them.

This issue has not been a partisan issue. The most significant environmental gains in the last 30 years were made under a Democratic Congress and President Richard Nixon. We can work together. We have to believe some basic things. Do you believe we can expand the economy without hurting the environment? I do. Do you believe we can create more jobs over the long run by cleaning the environment up? I know we can. That should be our commitment.

We must challenge businesses and communities to take more initiative in protecting the environment, and we have to make it easier for them to do it. To businesses this administration is saying: If you can find a cheaper, more efficient way than government regulations require to meet tough pollution standards, do it—as long as you do it right. To communities we say: We must strengthen community right-to-know laws requiring polluters to disclose their emissions, but you have to use the information to work with business to cut pollution. People do have a right to know that their air and their water are safe.

Our sixth challenge is to maintain America's leadership in the fight for freedom and peace throughout the world. Because of American leadership, more people than ever before live free and at peace. And Americans have known 50 years of prosperity and security.

We owe thanks especially to our veterans of World War II. I would like to say to Senator Bob Dole and to all others in this Chamber who fought in World War II, and to all others on both sides of the aisle who have fought bravely in all our conflicts since: I salute your service, and so do the American people.

All over the world, even after the Cold War, people still look to us and trust us to help them seek the blessings of peace and freedom. But as the Cold War fades into memory, voices of isolation say America should retreat from its responsibilities. I say they are wrong.

The threats we face today as Americans respect no nation's borders. Think of them: terrorism, the spread of weapons of mass destruction, organized crime, drug trafficking, ethnic and religious hatred, aggression by rogue states, environmental degradation. If we fail to address these threats today, we will suffer the consequences in all our tomorrows.

Of course, we can't be everywhere. Of course, we can't do everything. But where our interests and our values are at stake, and where we can make a difference, America must lead. We must not be isolationist.

We must not be the world's policeman. But we can and should be the world's very best peacemaker. By keeping our military strong, by using diplomacy where we can and force where we must, by working with others to share the risk and the cost of our efforts, America is making a difference for people here and around the world. For the first time since the dawn of the nuclear age, there is not a single Russian missile pointed at America's children.

North Korea has now frozen its dangerous nuclear weapons program. In Haiti, the dictators are gone, democracy has a new day, the flow of desperate refugees to our shores has subsided. Through tougher trade deals for America—over 80 of them—we have opened markets abroad, and now exports are at an all-time high, growing faster than imports and creating good American jobs.

We stood with those taking risks for peace: In Northern Ireland, where Catholic and Protestant children now tell their parents, violence must never return. In the Middle East, where Arabs and Jews who once seemed destined to fight forever now share knowledge and resources, and even dreams.

And we stood up for peace in Bosnia. Remember the skeletal prisoners, the mass graves, the campaign to rape and torture, the endless lines of refugees, the threat of a spreading war. All these threats, all these horrors have now begun to give way to the promise of peace. Now, our troops and a strong NATO, together with our new partners from Central Europe and elsewhere, are helping that peace to take hold.

As all of you know, I was just there with a bipartisan congressional group, and I was so proud not only of what our troops were doing, but of the pride they evidenced in what they were doing. They knew what America's mission in this world is, and they were proud to be carrying it out. Through these efforts, we have enhanced the security of the American people. But make no mistake about it: important challenges remain. The START II Treaty with Russia will cut our nuclear stockpiles by another 25 percent. I urge the Senate to ratify it—now. We must end the race to create new nuclear weapons by signing a truly comprehensive nuclear test ban treaty—this year.

As we remember what happened in the Japanese subway, we can outlaw poison gas forever if the Senate ratifies the Chemical Weapons Convention—this year. We can intensify the fight against terrorists and organized criminals at home and abroad if Congress passes the anti-terrorism legislation I proposed after the Oklahoma City bombing— now. We can help more people move from hatred to hope all across the world in our own interest if Congress gives us the means to remain the world's leader for peace.

My fellow Americans, the six challenges I have just discussed are for all of us. Our seventh challenge is really America's challenge to those of us in this hallowed hall tonight: to reinvent our government and make our democracy work for them.

Last year this Congress applied to itself the laws it applies to everyone else. This Congress banned gifts and meals from lobbyists. This Congress forced lobbyists to disclose who pays them and what legislation they are trying to pass or kill. This Congress did that, and I applaud you for it. Now I challenge Congress to go further—to curb special interest influence in politics by passing the first truly bipartisan campaign reform bill in a generation. You, Republicans and Democrats alike, can show the American people that we can limit spending and open the airwaves to all candidates.

I also appeal to Congress to pass the line-item veto you promised the American people.

Our administration is working hard to give the American people a government that works better and costs less. Thanks to the work of Vice President Gore, we are eliminating 16,000 pages of unnecessary rules and regulations, shifting more decision-making out of Washington, back to states and local communities.

As we move into the era of balanced budgets and smaller government, we must work in new ways to enable people to make the most of their own lives. We are helping America's communities, not with more bureaucracy, but with more opportunities. Through our successful Empowerment Zones and Community Development Banks, we are helping people to find jobs, to start businesses. And with tax incentives for companies that clean up abandoned industrial property, we can bring jobs back to places that desperately, desperately need them.

But there are some areas that the federal government should not leave and should address and address strongly. One of these areas is the problem of illegal immigration. After years of neglect, this administration has taken a strong stand to stiffen the protection of our borders. We are increasing border controls by 50 percent. We are increasing inspections to prevent the hiring of illegal immigrants. And tonight, I announce I will sign an executive order to deny federal contracts to businesses that hire illegal immigrants.

Let me be very clear about this: We are still a nation of immigrants; we should be proud of it. We should honor every legal immigrant here, working hard to become a new citizen. But we are also a nation of laws. I want to say a special word now to those who work for our federal government. Today our federal government is 200,000 employees smaller than it was the day I took office as President.

Our federal government today is the smallest it has been in 30 years, and it's getting smaller every day. Most of our fellow Americans probably don't know that. And there is a good reason: The remaining federal work force is composed of Americans who are now working harder and working smarter than ever before, to make sure the quality of our services does not decline.

I'd like to give you one example. His name is Richard Dean. He is a 49-year-old Vietnam veteran who's worked for the Social Security Administration for 22 years now. Last year he was hard at work in the Federal Building in Oklahoma City when the blast killed 169 people and brought the rubble down all around him. He reentered that building four times. He saved the lives of three women. He's here with us this evening, and I want to recognize Richard and applaud both his public service and his extraordinary personal heroism.

But Richard Dean's story doesn't end there. This last November, he was forced out of his office when the government shut down. And the second time the government shut down he continued helping Social Security recipients, but he was working without pay.

On behalf of Richard Dean and his family, and all the other people who are out there working every day doing a good job for the American people, I challenge all of you in this Chamber: Never, ever shut the federal government down again.

On behalf of all Americans, especially those who need their Social Security payments at the beginning of March, I also challenge the Congress to preserve the full faith and credit of the United States—to honor the obligations of this great nation as we have for 220 years; to rise above partisanship and pass a straightforward extension of the debt limit and show people America keeps its word.

I know that this evening I have asked a lot of Congress, and even more from America. But I am confident: When Americans work together in their homes, their schools, their churches, their synagogues, their civic groups, their workplace, they can meet any challenge.

I say again, the era of big government is over. But we can't go back to the era of fending for yourself. We have to go forward to the era of working together as a community, as a team, as one America, with all of us reaching across these lines that divide us—the division, the discrimination, the rancor—we have to reach across it to find common ground. We have got to work together if we want America to work.

I want you to meet two more people tonight who do just that. Lucius Wright is a teacher in the Jackson, Mississippi, public school system. A Vietnam veteran, he has created groups to help inner-city children turn away from gangs and build futures they can believe in. Sergeant Jennifer Rodgers is a police officer in Oklahoma City. Like Richard Dean, she helped to pull her fellow citizens out of the rubble and deal with that awful tragedy. She reminds us that in their response to that atrocity the people of Oklahoma City lifted all of us with their basic sense of decency and community.

Lucius Wright and Jennifer Rodgers are special Americans. And I have the honor to announce tonight that they are the very first of several thousand Americans who will be chosen to carry the Olympic torch on its long journey from Los Angeles to the centennial of the modern Olympics in Atlanta this summer—not because they are star athletes, but because they are star citizens, community heroes meeting America's challenges. They are our real champions.

Now, each of us must hold high the torch of citizenship in our own lives. None of us can finish the race alone. We can only achieve our destiny together—one hand, one generation, one American connecting to another. There have always been things we could do together—dreams we could make real—which we could never have done on our own. We Americans have forged our identity, our very union, from every point of view and every point on the planet, every different opinion. But we must be bound together by a faith more powerful than any doctrine that divides us—by our belief in progress, our love of liberty, and our relentless search for common ground.

America has always sought and always risen to every challenge. Who would say that, having come so far together, we will not go forward from here? Who would say that this age of possibility is not for all Americans? Our country is and always has been a great and good nation. But the best is yet to come, if we all do our part.

Thank you, God bless you and God bless the United States of America. Thank you.

ENDNOTES

INTRODUCTION

1. One of the key studies on the inner workings and effectiveness of Catholic schools in the United States is Anthony Bryk and colleagues' *Catholic Schools and the Common Good* (Bryk, Lee, and Holland 1993). In 381 pages and some 15,000 lines of information and argumentation in that book, which exhaustively covers virtually every aspect of Catholic schools as educational organizations, Bryk et al. mention school uniforms only once (1993, 129).

2. The fact that *students* also sell drugs and construct, as well as live out, their gang pledges/memberships *on campus* is rarely discussed. It appears to always be a vague "them" versus an equally vague "us" in the construction of symbolic boundaries in the discourse of the school uniform movement.

3. It should be noted that the available data at the time, for tenth-grade students, were not actually very useful for testing the growing phenomenon of school uniforms. We have acknowledged this limitation. After all, much of the uniform policy adoption throughout the 1990s took place in K–6 schools. This fact alone is interesting in and of itself since gang colors and gang-related violence are most common in the upper levels of our K–12 system. Limitations notwithstanding, this data set and the subsequent study resulting from it provided the first glimpse into patterns and effects of uniform policies on a variety of outcomes.

4. Though, as of this writing, to my knowledge very few have appeared to utilize that evidence in an attempt to question their potential adoption of a school uniform policy at their schools and/or in their districts.

5. Recently, a critique of the original 1998 piece was accepted for publication in *JER*. The editors allowed us to make a rebuttal; see Bodine and Brunsma and Rockquemore.

6. Recently, a critique of the original 1998 piece was accepted for pc S6. The most active anti-uniform groups are The Parental Action Committee of Polk Country, Florida, headed by Darlene Williams; Parents Against Mandatory Public School Uniforms out of Texas (also called Parental Action Committee); Parents Against Mandatory Uniforms, out of Louisiana; Lowell Freedom, out of Lowell, Massachusetts; and Asserting Parental Rights, It's Our Duty.

7. This is one of the primary design flaws of the published results surrounding the uniform policy of the Long Beach Unified School District (see Stanley 1996).

8. Note that this "reduction in sample size" is only a reduction for calculating the statistics in these analyses. It provides a much more rigorous and conservative estimation procedure for the effects under scrutiny in these reports. It *does not* mean that the sample of students is equal to the "effective N," because we still have, for instance, a sample of 20,000 eighth graders; the effective N reduction is used only to appropriately calculate the regression coefficients. Increased sample size always makes it easier to detect statistically significant findings; this weighting procedure corrects for the design strategies and oversampling strategies of NCES while providing a very rigorous significance test for the betas we are interested in.

CHAPTER I

1. To give an overview of the role of dress in human society is completely outside the scope of this book. However, interested readers should most definitely read the "bible" in this regard, Rubinstein (1995).

2. I would like to note at this point that I am *not* an historian. I do not, in this section, have any outrageous assumptions that what I am providing here is a comprehensive, historically, and methodologically sound chronological and theoretical description of the history of standardized dress in the institution of education. While the research was indeed exciting and the information quite illustrative of various themes and meanings behind the use of such codes in educational organizations, I claim no comprehensiveness to the history provided in this chapter; obviously I am solely responsible for any and all connections and arguments contained within these pages.

3. This is classical sociological material. For more on the authority of society, see Durkheim (1979).

4. Decades of literature have provided evidence that Great Britain and the United States have quite similar degrees of inequality, yet the common notions of the class structure and of the opportunities presented to people by the economy, demography, and institutional structures vary considerably. Britain's class structure is quite overt; that of the United States is exceedingly covert (Kerckhoff 1995; MacLeod 1987; Willis 1977).

5. On preparing workers through the schooling system see primarily Bowles and Gintis (1976).

6. Ronald Reagan, who had been involved in attempting to squash the rebellion and student uprisings at Sproul Hall in Berkeley, was now president of the United States.

7. There is some mention, at times, of a public school uniform policy earlier than 1987. Evidently some schools in Raleigh, North Carolina, experimented with school uniforms in 1972 (for girls only), eventually making them mandatory in their public schools in the 1990s (History 2003). An alternative school in Harlem adopted a uniform policy for its student body in 1984 (Baker and Michael 1987).

CHAPTER 2

1. I have published a heavily edited and modified version of this chapter as *School Uniforms: A Critical Review of the Literature* (Brunsma 2002)—I am much more fond of this version.

2. It is important to note the distinction between a "dress code" and a "uniform" policy. A dress code specifies what *may not be worn*, whereas a uniform policy mandates what *must be worn* (see Paliokas, Futrell, and Rist 1996 for a good discussion of the distinction). Much of the empirical literature does not clearly distinguish between the two forms of policies regarding student dress. In this review, I focus primarily on *uniform policies*.

3. The full bibliography of references I examined in preparation for this literature review is included at the end of this book. In the discussion I have roughly categorized each reference to make them more user-friendly. It should be noted, however, that the categories are not mutually exclusive, and many articles could fall into more than one category.

4. I focus on the empirical research in this review and the findings of said research. I briefly discuss the theoretical underpinnings of this body of work,

though most researchers utilize the anecdotal musings of the pros and cons of school uniforms as their "quasi-theories." There is not enough space here to summarize the legal writings on school uniforms. Interested readers should consult the following for excellent summaries of the legal aspects of school uniform policies (DeMitchell, Fossey, and Cobb 2000; Gilbert 1999; Kuhn 1996; Lane et al. 1994).

5. This line of reasoning resonates closely with the classic research into the "Pygmalion effect" and labeling processes within education. It seems ludicrous to assume that we would want to further strengthen a climate in public schools in which teachers gauge students' potential by what they wear.

6. Another missing element in discussions of school uniform policies is the very fact that gender, as a social and cultural distinction of great import in inequalities of schooling, is exacerbated by the use of school uniforms that themselves are gendered. For some thoughts on this see Prescott (2000).

7. Though Gullatt does not discuss faculty uniforms, this issue is an important parallel to the debate on student uniforms. For some discussion of faculty uniforms see Kirkman (1997).

8. Readers should see a problem with a 33.8 percent return rate. This is quite common among research on school uniform policies. It is even more common in the protocol for adopting a uniform policies—gauging parental support before the implementation of uniforms in public schools. For a more detailed discussion of this problem see chapter 4.

9. Recent data (NPD Group 2001) show that between 1999 and 2001 school uniform sales rose 22 percent, reaching $1.1 billion. This solidly places uniforms in the children's wear apparel market—it now holds 5 percent of this $20.4 billion industry. Several authors have commented on the link between corporations and the school uniform movement (That Uniform Look 1999; Forest 1997; Johnson 2000; Key 2000; Lefevre 1997; Murphy 1998; Speer 1998; Stevenson 1999; White 2000).

10. My assessment of the literature has led me to this conclusion as well: The uniform research (largely anecdotal as it is) speaks more about the deepest fears and anxieties within the American public in general and within our public schools in particular. Other authors have suggested that this movement represents a "diversion" from the real complexities of public schooling and social problems (see Cohn and Siegal 1996 for Siegal's opposing view).

11. In my experience with district-provided data during the course of a school uniform implementation and subsequent study, researchers need to be very cautious of such data. Such data have a tendency to become politicized, hidden, and possibly altered depending on the circumstances and the interests held by constituents. Educators at the school and district levels may wish to put

aside politics and hand over reliable data for researchers to validly assess the school uniform reform. If not, the quest for valid and reliable research on school uniforms' effectiveness may not come to fruition.

CHAPTER 3

1. See Ruggiero (2002); Gilbert (1999); Uniforms Suddenly a Hot Topic (1996); American Civil Liberties Union of Massachusetts (2001); King (1998); and Nelson (1997).

2. See Clinton (1996) and U.S. Department of Education (1996).

3. The Supreme Court has recognized that schools have a "compelling interest in having an undisputed school session conducive to the students' learning" (*Grayned v. City of Rockford*, 408 U.S. 104 (1972), p. 119).

4. The judge in *Pyle v. South Hadley School Committee* (1994) noted that dress codes can protect students from "an environment of unrelenting winks, snickering, and sexual proddings" (170). The expert witness for the plaintiffs agreed that sexual innuendoes in an educational environment can make students uncomfortable and can interfere with their ability to study.

5. Justice Black's dissent in *Tinker* lamented that this "case, . . . wholly without constitutional reasons . . . subjects all the public schools in the country to the whims and caprices of their loudest-mouthed, but maybe not their brightest, students" (1969, 752).

6. Pp. 3164–3165. The Court is referring to a United States Supreme Court decision about the right of Cohen to wear a jacket with the lettering "Fuck the Draft" emblazoned on the back.

7. See *Chandler v. McMinnville School District* (1992), which concluded that any case that does not involve vulgar, lewd, obscene, or plainly offensive speech and is free of the imprimatur of the school falls under the *Tinker* analysis; *Saxe v. State College Area School District* (2001), which ruled that under *Fraser*, a school may categorically prohibit lewd, vulgar, or profane language, and under *Hazelwood*, a school may regulate school-sponsored speech (that is, speech that a reasonable observer would view as the school's own speech) on the basis of any legitimate pedagogical concern. Speech falling outside of these categories is subject to *Tinker*'s general rule: It may be regulated only if it would substantially disrupt school operations or interfere with the rights of others.

8. 10. You've ever been shirtless at a freezing football game.

9. Your carpet used to be part of a football field.

8. Your basketball hoop used to be part of a fishing net.

7. There's a roll of duct tape in your golf bag.

6. You know the Hooter's [sic] menu by heart.

5. Your mamma is banned from the front row at wrestling matches.

4. Your bowling team has it's [sic] own fight song.

3. You think the "Bud Bowl" is real.

2. You wear a baseball cap to bed.

1. You've ever told your bookie "I was just kidding." *Sypniewski* (2002, 249–250)

9. See *Sypniewski* (2002, fn. 6) for the dress code.

10. In the *Manual on School Uniforms*, the U.S. Department of Education advises that "in the absence of a finding that disruption of the learning environment has reached a point that other lesser measures have been or would be ineffective, a mandatory school uniform policy without an opt-out provision could be vulnerable to a legal challenge" (1996). See also Murray (2000), arguing that an opt-out provision in the Lowell (Massachusetts) Public Schools is necessary (640).

11. Pp. 439–440. See fn. 3 for a discussion of *Karr v. Schmidt*. Also, the First Circuit in *Richards v. Thurston* (1970) stated that "a school rule that which forbids [certain articles of clothing] . . . while on school grounds would require less justification than one requiring hair to be cut, which affects the student twenty-four hours a day, seven days a week, nine months a year" (1285). For a similar argument, see *Issacs* (1999), which distinguished hairstyle regulations from dress code regulations: "Headgear, like other clothing and unlike hair, is easily removed and replaced. Shermia is free to wear her headwrap outside of school and, apparently, is even free to wear the headwrap to and from school. The school rules simply require that she leave the headwrap in her locker during the school day" (339).

12. Page 441, fn. 3. "Our analysis simply acknowledges that certain choices of clothing may have sufficient communicative content to qualify as First Amendment activity" (441, fn. 3). However, the court expressly declined to define the contours of the "extent or type of clothing necessary to communicate a discrete message in order to afford First Amendment protection" (441, fn. 3).

13. "Regarding the 'coerced speech' argument, the students argue that mandatory uniforms convey a particularized message that the school district wishes to express, namely that students have respect for the authority of teachers and administrators, have Forney school and civic pride, and support school policies" (fn. 8).

14. The court did not require a demonstration that the goals be met through a demonstration of statistically significant improvement (365).

15. However, see *Castorina* (2001) (Kennedy, concurring), in which the concurring opinion asserted that the *Canady* (2001) evaluation using *United States v. O'Brien* (1968) was appropriate. The case concerned the wearing of T-shirts with the Confederate flag emblem. The ban was found to be unconstitutional.

16. However, the court did not address the threshold question that triggers *Hazelwood School District v. Kuhlmeier* (1988), whether the activity reasonably bears the imprimatur of the school. The court in *Phoenix Elementary v. Green* (1997) bypassed the threshold and turned to the standard of legitimate pedagogical concern.

17. However, see Weisenberger: "As courts further dilute *Tinker*, school administrators will regain control of their schools, at the expense of student expression" (2000, 61).

CHAPTER 4

1. The percentage of public schools that had school uniform policies in 1988, according to NELS data, was approximately 0.6—less than 1 percent. These data, however, were for public middle schools. It is possible that the percentage of elementary schools that had uniform policies in 1988 was somewhere between 1 and 2 percent. Given this tentative estimation, from the beginning of the uniform movement in American public schools (1987–1988) the increase, across the board, but most prominently in elementary schools, was from 1.5 percent in 1988 to 11.5 percent ten years later.

2. A November 2000 study conducted by the NPD Group, which surveyed K–8 schools across the country, found 13.6 percent of these public schools had uniform policies (NPD 2001).

3. This list of common anecdotal themes is drawn largely from the newspaper and other media accounts of public school uniform adoption and usage from 1987 to 2003. I have combined these sixteen years of writing and reporting on uniform usage to gain insight into overarching archetypes of reasons administrators have sought uniform policies. Had we looked at the various themes *year by year* we would see that, over time, some reasons received more emphasis than others, gaining or decreasing in emphasis year by year. In other words, there would be a trend of coverage and emphasis if we looked at the year-to-year coverage.

4. On gangs see Stinchcomb (2002); on social causes of violence see Brownstein (2000); National Research Council (1993); and Sampson et al. (2002). On the sociology of consumption see Gottdiener (2000); Ritzer (2004);

and Zelizer (2002). On the sociology of fashion and clothing see McCracken (1988) and Simmel (1904).

5. These utterly illogical statements sit atop the plethora of arguments about school uniforms' potential effects as among the most superficial and unclear of all. Just one *minute's* more thought brings into clear focus how foolhardy such statements are. The idea that clothing could somehow erase racial and/or gender distinctions is absolutely mindless and, one should add, dangerous, due to the long-standing fact of differential treatment given to students of color and girls in practically every aspect of their educational trajectories.

6. In none of these correlations is there to be read by any means a causal relationship; the data simply do not exist to allow us to test those larger claims at this point. However, some of the associations are quite strong and hopefully will encourage other researchers to investigate them more fully (when the data become available). The last two, gender of principal and schools with foci, deserve a bit more explanation. First, it is quite interesting that schools that already have a focus are less likely to implement a school uniform policy. This is one of the assumptions of the uniform movement—that uniforms will provide that focus for students. It is not clear that this is the case. In fact in later chapters (5 and 6) we will see that they do not. There have also been quite a few innuendos in the media coverage that school uniforms (especially those uniform styles typically worn by girls) represent a particularly sick manifestation of patriarchal hegemony (e.g., jokes about Clinton wanting uniforms so he can peer at school girls in uniform). The finding that female principals are more likely to have school uniform policies for their students than male principals seem to contradict to this idea, but it may not because oppressed groups, like women, often tend to adopt patriarchal ideologies even when they may continue to oppress members of their group.

7. That school uniform policies should be considered *part* of an overall comprehensive strategy of educational reform and school safety was *not* a solid part of the early discourse on school uniform policies. Certainly the media coverage implied that schools adopting uniform policies (as well as the arguments of school officials themselves) saw such policies as *the* strategy to combat the variety of ills facing their particular school and/or American public education in general. Only very recently have uniforms been discussed by those involved in the decision-making processes as one facet of an overall strategy. If uniforms were part of more comprehensive strategies in our public schools, then the need to collect extremely precise data to tease out the effectiveness of such policies would be even greater. Unfortunately, most districts do not collect this kind of data.

8. On social scientific research methodologies and corresponding issues of nonresponse bias and survey item construction, see Frankfort-Nachmias and Guerrero (2002); Schutt 1996; and Neuman (2003).

9. We must also realize that, from the mid-1990s until the present day, school uniforms have been *big business*. I recall walking through one cathedral of consumption (i.e., a mall) late this summer and seeing that the Gap had as its front window display Back to School: school uniforms, left side for girls, right side for boys. It was a *huge* display—reflecting a *huge* market, a growing market, a captive market. This structure of the clothing industry and its marketing campaigns highlighting school uniforms can be seen as a set of parameters that make the implementation of school uniform policies, and the assumed benefits of them, even more difficult to achieve. It is also another way in which commercialism has hit very close to the inner workings of our public schools. For more on this increasing problem of public schooling see Arizona State University's Commercialism in Education Research Unit. CERU, directed by Dr. Alex Molnar, "conducts research, disseminates information, and helps facilitate dialogue between the education community, policy makers, and the public at large about commercial activities in schools. CERU is guided by the belief that mixing commercial activities with public education raises fundamental issues of public policy, curriculum content, the proper relationship of educators to the students entrusted to them, and the values that the schools embody" (http://www.asu.edu/educ/epsl/ceru.htm).

10. One intriguing set of data I have worked with in these regards I received from Mount Carmel Elementary School during the discovery period of that particular case. I received the log for the Mount Carmel Area Elementary School (MCE) Student Support Room from the beginning of the 2000–2001 school year until December 5, 2000. This document kept track of the individual students who were sent to this room for a variety of reasons: misbehavior, make-up tests, general behavioral problems, to finish various work assignments, disobedience, etc. In looking through these logs, a primary reason that students were sent to the Support Room was for not adhering to the dress code. The Support Room did not exist before the implementation of the uniform policy at MCE, and the overwhelming presence of students in the support room who were there because of uniform policy infringements raises several concerns: 1) that the Support Room was a logistical necessity to house all the students who did not comply with the new policy, which 2) seems to indicate that teachers are having to deal with much more individual infractions than previously, and 3) that the policy is responsible for loading teachers with the added role of "fashion police" so often cited in the anecdotal research on the negative impact of uniform policies on teacher workload and disciplinary infractions, thus 4) possibly lending credibility, in this case, to the *creation* of more problems stemming from the uniform policy itself. It is also plausible that students who must report to the Support Room are not defined in ways

that would lead to increases in traditional detention, suspension, and other disciplinary measures about which information is sent to the Pennsylvania Department of Education (PDE), masking the fact that there *are* more policy infractions than may be reflected in the forthcoming 2000–2001 data from PDE as well as the MCE data on detentions and suspensions. In fact, if one uses a method of extrapolation *and* adds those going to the Support Room for uniform policy infringements (about 194), this alone would raise the detention rate for 2000–2001 to around 700! This would indicate an unprecedented increase in detentions for MCE—one directly related to the implementation of a uniform policy and the Support Room.

11. Setting up an antagonistic relationship with parents can be extremely detrimental to the functioning of a school. Given the vast amount of research on the positive benefits of parental involvement in school (Grolnick et al. 1994; Hoover-Dempsey and Sandler 1997; Kerbow and Bernhardt 1994; Lareau and Shumar 1996; Muller and Kerbow 1994), any policy that might disrupt this important relationship could be exceedingly dangerous to the effective operation of the school and the subsequent educational and behavioral outcomes of its students.

12. In some cases funds have been diverted from other school and district coffers to pay for the costs involved in litigation.

13. There also appears to have been a great deal of collaboration between superintendents and other district administrators regarding the variety of maneuverings a system can take to undermine challenges and circumvent dissent among the parents and students regarding the legal issues of uniform policies. If one peruses the Internet for ten minutes, one runs across sites that detail ways in which this can be done.

14. It has been quite frustrating to witness the lack of evaluations and publicly available results of evaluations regarding various district and school forays into school uniform policies.

15. It appears to be the case that schools are using a standard approach that, if compliance dips as low as 70 percent, the school should consider abandoning the uniform policy, for these and other related reasons (Bernet 2003).

CHAPTER 5

1. For an exception, see Murray (1997); however, as discussed in chapter 3, Murray's analysis is full of methodological problems and leaps in logic.

2. It is ironic that given the criticisms of perception studies in chapter 2—that their most inherent flaw is that they attempt to show effectiveness through quantifying anecdotes and opinions to hold a uniform policy in high regard by their constituents, and that, in surveys like the ELCS and/or NELS, measures of safety and educational climates utilize principal/administrator perceptions of their schools' climates—in the analyses presented here these perceptions are *not* affected by uniform policies. Typically it is the effectiveness of the policies that is assumed to be "proven" through administrators' perceptions, yet these very perceptions are not distinguishable between administrators within schools that have such policies and those in schools that do not.

3. In fact, it is simple, uncontrolled bivariate relationships like these that are typically reported in published accounts of the effects of school uniforms on any number of outcomes, including achievement. This is a major flaw in most of the "research" on school uniform effects: the lack of control variables. It is entirely possible that the association between two variables can be explained by any number of omitted and extremely important control variables. In all of the models in this series of reports, the important educational and social controls are put in place to more fully understand the relationship between uniforms and outcomes. Without such controls, researchers and educators often reach faulty conclusions because they have not adequately controlled for other factors influencing the very outcomes of interest. Implementing a policy on such flawed methodologies is dangerous.

4. The eighth-grade data set does not include measures of pro-school attitudes and peer pro-school attitudes; those were added in the next wave (tenth grade) of data collection. Because pro-school attitudes are closely related to the educational climate of a school, I have used the eighth-grade student perceived educational climate scale to control for these factors.

5. To my knowledge there is no data set that collects the vast array of important educational indicators and student-level variables (as ECLS and NELS do) that *also* looks much more closely into the *type* of uniform policy and dress code each school has. These policies do vary quite a bit (especially dress codes); however, the only data available are the set I am utilizing in these analyses. They state whether the school has a uniform and/or a dress code policy but do not go into detail regarding the policies (most likely due to problems of confidentiality and the ability to possibly identify a particular school if researchers were given the specifics of a policy).

6. It should be noted that having more cases in this analysis is more than desirable; often it is imperative. Any effects that are found would most likely only be made stronger and more robust with more cases in the focal category.

CHAPTER 6

1. This approach to modeling is to be understood in the following way: If there is an effect of a particular independent variable (e.g., uniforms) on a particular dependent variable (self-concept), this indicates that some of the variations in self-concept scores are due to whether students wear uniforms or not. Given that effect (if there is any), the addition of other variables to the model gives researchers a chance to see if there is any covariation between the original independent variable of interest (i.e., uniforms) and these new variables. If the effect of the original variable decreases after the addition of these variables, then one can conclude that one of the *mechanisms* through which uniforms affect the outcome of interest is those processes measured by the additional variables. If there is no decrease, then those additional variables, while they may explain more variation in the outcome, are explaining unique variation not already explained by uniforms—therefore, the exact mechanisms of uniforms' effects on an outcome are not determined.

2. Readers may be unfamiliar with the conventions in multiple regression tables presented in this series of reports. I will briefly outline the main components of these tables. The title refers to the dependent variable (or variables) that is under scrutiny. The variables are those used to predict the outcome (dependent variable). For most of the analyses in this report, readers should key themselves into the uniform (or dress code) variable. The numbers presented in the table are standardized beta coefficients that give an indication of the direction, magnitude, and statistical significance of the particular effect. For example, in table 6.1 the effect for being female in the first model (Model 1) is $-.14^{\circ\circ\circ}$. This means that tenth-grade females have, on average, lower self-concept scores than do tenth-grade males. Furthermore, it indicates that they fall, on average, .14 of a standard deviation below males on self-concept. This statistic also indicates a highly significant result (i.e., one that is not caused by chance, sample design, or sampling error). Conventions in scientific research state that a statistic that has a 5 percent margin of error *or less* (i.e., 5 percent of the time samples are drawn we would expect *not* to find this result) is acceptable and is, therefore, called "a statistically significant result." The "$\circ\circ\circ$" refers to a result that could not be a result of sampling error .001 or 1/100 (or less) of a percent of the time. Others include: "$\circ\circ$" = .01 or less and "$\circ$" = .05 or less. The "Adjusted R^2" is a measure of the amount of variation in the dependent variable explained by a variable or set of variables in the model. An R^2 of 1.00 would indicate a model that explained the outcome completely—this is unheard of in all science. In table 6.1, Model 1, the control variables alone explain 3 percent of tenth-grade students'

self-concept scores. The "F-Value" indicates whether the model, as a whole, "fits" or is saturated with redundancies. Finally, the "N" refers to the total number of cases used in the analyses. With weighted analyses there are two relevant Ns, one for the total number of cases used in the analyses and one for the number of cases used to calculate the statistical significance of the coefficients. I hope this guide helps.

3. It is important to keep in mind that high values on the locus of control variable indicate a student with a more developed *internal* locus of control.

CHAPTER 7

1. On the rise of education as the new frontier and the ideological formation of schooling as the new frontier see Bowles and Gintis (1976).

2. Indeed, the vast majority of nations that were once British colonies still utilize the school uniform for their primary and secondary schooling.

3. On continuing segregation see Massey and Anderson (2001) and Orfield and Eaton (1996). On continued labeling in schools see Rosenthal and Jacobson (2003 [1968]). On continuing racism see Bonilla-Silva (2001, 2003) and Feagin and McKinney (2003).

4. Rural schools are an interesting complication to the enigma of school uniform adoption patterns, for they simply do not have the kinds of problems that were associated with early uniform adopters: gangs and endemic violence.

5. Interestingly enough, in a recent conversation between this author and a representative of the Department of Education, I was told, after asking when the *Manual* would be updated, "The Department of Education is not interested in that reform [uniforms] any longer, the Department is interested in academic achievement."

6. On cultural and structural centers and margins ("peripheries") see Shils (1982).

7. The GOALS 2000 legislation included, as its eighth goal, to increase parental involvement in public schools. However, there was a lack of understanding of the complexities of home–school relations and a lack of tools put in place to see an increase in parental involvement in American schools.

8. Though the media often take, for instance, 60 percent to represent 100-percent approval rates.

9. On the reproduction of the racial system see Bonilla-Silva (2001, 2003) and Feagin and VanAusdale (2002).

10. Some argue that this has all been a myth; see Berliner and Biddle (1996).

11. On educational reform in this light see Hacsi (2003) and Giroux (2003).

12. On the various dimensions of power see Lukes (1986), Gaventa (1982), and Clegg (1989).

13. I have even been told by one source (who wishes to remain nameless) that, according to this lobbying group, they are currently sponsoring a bill that would make uniforms mandatory in all public schools.

14. Given the nature of the information I have attempted to obtain to supplement my analyses here, from state departments of education, local school boards, national associations of administrators, legal firms, etc., such information has not been forthcoming. In many cases, there are high fees to be paid for such information.

REFERENCES

Abdullah, Miriam Tan. (2000, September 6). Uniforms Do Not Mean Uniformity. *New Straits Times—Management Times*, Kuala Lumpur, Malaysia.

Alberto, Deborah. (2001, June 6). School Uniform Case May Hit Court in Summer. *Tampa Tribune*, p. A3.

American Civil Liberties Union of Massachusetts. (1997, May 9). News Release, *All This in the Name of Order*, at users.aol.com/mcluf/lawr.htm (accessed February 4, 2004).

Ang, Rebecca P. & Weining, C. (1999). Impact of Domain-Specific Locus of Control on Need for Achievement and Affiliation. *Journal of Social Psychology*, 139(4), 527–529.

Aucoin, Don. (1997, February 12). Weld Pushes for Uniforms in Schools. *The Boston Globe*, p. A1.

Baker, James & Michael, R. (1987, November 30). Dressing to be Successful. *Newsweek*, 110, p. 62.

Baltimore School Rule: Uniforms for Students. (1987, September 20). *New York Times*, p. A75.

Bannister v. Paradis, 316 F. Supp. 185 (D.N.H. 1970).

Bass, S. L. (1988, October 2). A Public School Seeks Equality in Uniformity. *New York Times*, p. 4.

Beale, T. C. (n.d.) "Eat for Success." Unpublished story circulated on listservs.

Bedard, Paul. (1996, March 25). All Uniformly in Agreement. *Insight on the News*, p. 37.

Behling, Dorothy. (1994). School Uniforms and Person Perception. *Perceptual and Motor Skills*, 79(2), 723–729.

Bellah, Robert N., Madsen, R, Sullivan, W. M., Swidler, A. & Tipton, S. M. (1985). *Habits of the Heart: Individualism and Commitment in American Life*. Harper & Row.

Bennet, J. (1998, July 21). Clinton Urges Structure, Rules in School. *New York Times*, p. A12.

Berliner, D. C. & Biddle, B. J. (1996). *The Manufactured Crisis: Myths, Fraud, and the Attack on America's Public Schools*. Boulder, CO: Perseus Publishing.

Bernet, Brenda E. (2003, September 6). Trustees May Change Policy on Uniforms. Fort Worth *Star-Telegram*.

Bernstein, Ruth P. (1995). *Dress Codes: Meanings and Messages in American Culture*. Boulder, CO: Westview.

Bethel School District No. 403 v. Fraser, 478 U.S. 675 (1986).

Bivens v. Albuquerque Public Schools, 899 F. Supp. 556 (D.N.M. 1995).

Black, S. (1998). Forever Plaid? *American School Board Journal*, 185(11), 42–45.

Blackburn, L. (1998, April 24). Light on a Dark Age. *Times Educational Supplement*, p. C39.

Bodine, A. (2003). School Uniforms and Discourses on Childhood. *Childhood; A Global Journal of Child Research*, 10(1), 43–63.

———. (2003). School Uniforms, Academic Achievement, and Uses of Research. *Journal of Educational Research*, 97(2): 67–72.

Bogenschneider, Karen. (1997). Parental Involvement in Adolescent Schooling: A Proximal Process with Transcontextual Validity. *Journal of Marriage and the Family*, 59, 718–733.

Bonilla-Silva, Eduardo. (2001). *White Supremacy and Racism in the Post-Civil Rights Era*. Boulder. CO: Rienner.

———. (2003). *Racism Without Racists: Color-Blind Racism and the Persistence of Racial Inequality in the United States*. Lanham, MD: Rowman & Littlefield.

Bourdieu, Pierre. (1977). *Outline of a Theory of Practice*. New York: Cambridge University Press.

———. (1986). *Distinction: A Social Critique of the Judgment of Taste*. Cambridge, MA: Harvard University Press.

Bowles, Samuel & Gintis, H. (1976). *Schooling in Capitalist America: Educational Reform and the Contradictions of Economic Life*. New York: Basic.

Britt, Jolynn. (2001). *Teachers' Perceptions About the Impact of School Uniforms on the Learning Experience of Students in an Alternative Public School*. Unpublished Dissertation, Colorado State University.

Broussard v. School Board of City of Norfolk, 801 F. Supp. 1526 (E.D. Va. 1992).

Brown v. Board of Education, 347 U.S. 483 (1954).

Brownstein, H. (2000). *The Social Reality of Violence and Violent Crime*. Boston: Allyn & Bacon.

Brunsma, David L. (2002). *School Uniforms: A Critical Review of the Literature*. Bloomington, IN: Phi Delta Kappan International.

Brunsma, David L. & Rockquemore, K. A. (1998). Effects of Student Uniforms on Attendance, Behavior Problems, Substance Use, and Academic Achievement. *Journal of Educational Research*, 92(1), 53–62.

———. (2003). Statistics, Soundbytes, and School Uniforms: A Reply to Bodine. *Journal of Educational Research*, 97(2): 72–77.

Bryk, Anthony & Driscoll M. (1988). *The School as Community: Theoretical Foundations, Contextual Influences, and Consequences for Students and Teachers*. Chicago: University of Chicago Press.

Bryk, Anthony S., Lee, V. E. & Holland, P. B. (1993). *Catholic Schools and the Common Good*. Cambridge, MA: Harvard University Press.

Buckley, William F., Jr. (1996, February 26). School Uniforms?! *National Review*, p. 71.

Byars v. City of Waterbury, 47 Conn. Supp. 342 (Conn. Super. 2001).

California District Will Require Pupils to Wear Uniforms. (1994, March 30). *New York Times*, p. B10.

California Goes Beyond Dress Codes. (1994, August 24). *New York Times*, p. B8.

California Leads Nation in Public School Uniform Use. (1997, March 31). *California School News*, p. 4.

Camden School District Accepts Uniform Option. (1988, May 24). *New York Times*, p. C9.

Canady v. Bossier Parish School District, 240 F.3d 437 (5th Cir. 2001).

Carbonaro, William J. (1998). A Little Help from My Friend's Parents: Intergenerational Closure and Educational Outcomes. *Sociology of Education*, 71(4), 295–315.

Carlson, Margaret. (1996, March 11). No Sleep for the Weary. *Time*, p. 16.

Carnegie, Dale. (1990 [1936]). *How to Win Friends and Influence People*. New York: Pocket Books.

Carro, Geraldine. (1982, September). Dress Codes Make a Comeback. *Ladies' Home Journal*, 99, p. 103.

Caruso, Peter. (1996, September). Individuality vs. Conformity: The Issue Behind School Uniforms. *NASSP Bulletin*, 83–88.

Castorina v. Madison County School Board, 246 F.3d 536 (6th Cir. 2001).

Chaika, Gloria. (1999). School Uniforms: Panacea or Band Aid? *Education World*, at www.education-world.com (accessed February 4, 2004).

Chandler v. McMinnville School District, 978 F.2d 524, 529 (9th Cir. 1992).

Chesler, M., Sanders, J. & Kalmuss, D. (1988). *Social Science in Court: Mobilizing Experts in the School Desegregation Cases.* Madison: University of Wisconsin Press.

Chilling the Fashion Rage. (1990, January 22). *Time,* p. 27.

Clegg, Stewart R. (1989). *Frameworks of Power.* Thousand Oaks, CA: Sage.

Clinton, William Jefferson. (1996, February 24). *Remarks by the President on School Uniform Program. Jackie Robinson Academy, Long Beach California,* at www.ed.gov/pressreleases/02-1996/whpr28 (accessed July 18 1998).

Clinton's Initiatives. (1998, October 8). *CQ Researcher,* p. 894.

CNN Cable Programming. (2001, October 5). *Your Health: Back to School: Dress Codes.* Television broadcast, cnn#15300901.

Cohen, Robert & Zelnik, Reginald E. (eds.) (2002). *The Free Speech Movement: Reflections on Berkeley in the 1960s.* Berkeley: University of California Press.

Cohn, Carl A. (1996). Mandatory School Uniforms. *The School Administrator,* 53(2), 22–25.

Cohn, Carl A. & Siegal, L. (1996). Should Students Wear Uniforms? *Learning,* 25(2), 38–39.

Coleman, James S. (1961). *The Adolescent Society.* New York: Free Press.

———. (1988). Social Capital in the Creation of Human Capital. *American Journal of Sociology,* 94, S95–S120.

———. (1990a). *Equality and Achievement in Education.* Boulder, CO: Westview.

———. (1990b). *Foundations of Social Theory.* Cambridge, MA: Belknap.

Coleman, James S., Hoffer, T., & Kilgore, S. (1982). *High School Achievement: Public, Private, and Catholic Schools Compared.* New York: Basic.

Comer, J. (1988). Educating Poor Minority Children. *Scientific American,* 259(5), 2–8.

Cook, Stephanie. (2000, August 8). Do School Uniforms Stifle Expression or Protect Students? *Christian Science Monitor,* 92(180), 12.

Cornelius v. NAACP Legal Defense and Education Fund, 473 U.S. 788 (1985).

Creel, Jimmy. (2000). *A Study of the Implementation of a Standardized Dress Code and Student Achievement of African American Students in a Suburban High school: A Companion Study.* Unpublished Dissertation, Sam Houston State University.

Curry, Jack. (1988, October 16). Uniforms Earning High Marks at Public Schools. *New York Times,* p. 10.

Daniels, Lee A. (1987, December 6). Uniforms a Hit at Four Public Schools. *New York Times,* p. A32.

Davidson, Alexander & Rae, J. (1990). *Blazers, Badges and Boaters: A Pictorial History of the School Uniform.* Horndean: Scope International.

Davidson-Williams, Carolyn M. (1997). Case Study of the Mandatory Enforcement of a Voluntary Student Uniform Policy. *Dissertation Abstracts*, 57(10–A), 4199.

DeMitchell, Todd A. (2001). School Uniforms and the Constitution: Common Dress in an Uncommon Time. *Education Law Reporter*, 157(1).

DeMitchell, Todd A., Fossey, R. & Cobb, C. (2000). Dress Codes in the Public Schools: Principals, Policies, and Precepts. *Journal of Law and Education*, 29(1), 31–50.

Dennis, Karen E. (1998). *An Examination of Dress Codes and School Uniforms in Schools of the 1990's*. Unpublished Doctoral Dissertation.

Denno v. School Board of Volusia County (1997).

Dionne, E. J., Jr. (2002, August 20). Bush Squawks over Minor Spending. Is Anyone Listening? *Washington Post*, p. A13.

Do Clothes Make the Student? (1995, December 10). *New York Times*, p 33.

Donohue, John W. (1996, July 20). There's Something About a Uniform. *America*, p. 18.

Doulin, Tim & Sternberg, R. E. (1996, March 2). School Uniforms Can Help, Some Officials Say. *Columbus Dispatch*, p. D1.

Dowd, Maureen. (1996, January 28). School Uniform Blues. *New York Times*, p. 13.

Dress Right, Dress. (1987, September 14). *Time*, 76.

Durkheim, Emile. (1979). *Essays on Morals and Education*. New York: Routledge & Kegan Paul.

Dussel, Ines. (2001). *School Uniforms and the Disciplining of Appearances: Towards a Comparative History of the Regulation of Bodies in Early Modern France, Argentina, and the US*. Unpublished Doctoral Dissertation, University of Wisconsin at Madison.

Educational Testing Service. (2000). *The Links among School Discipline, Student Delinquency, and Academic Achievement*, at www.aypf.org/forumbriefs/1999/fb032699.htm (accessed February 4, 2004).

Ehrenreich, Barbara. (2001). *Nickel and Dimed: On (Not) Getting by in America*. New York: Henry Holt.

Ellertson, Roland Vernon. (1969). *A Legal Evaluation of Dress Codes in a Selected Sample of Public School Districts in the Twin Cities Metropolitan Area*. Unpublished Doctoral Dissertation, University of Minnesota.

Essex, N. L. (2001). School Uniforms: Guidelines for Principals As Schools Increasingly Adopt Dress Codes, *Principal*, 80(Part 3), 38–39.

Etonians Shed Top Hat and Tails Outside School. (1972, November 14). *New York Times*, p. A12.

Evans, Dennis L. (1996). School Uniforms: An "Unfashionable" Dissent. *NASSP Bulletin*, 80(582), 115.

Feagin, Joe R. & McKinney, K. D. (2003). *The Many Costs of Racism*. Lanham, MD: Rowman & Littlefield.

Feagin, Joe R. & VanAusdale, D. (2002). *The First R: How Children Learn Race and Racism*. Lanham, MD: Rowman & Littlefield.

Feinberg, Lawrence. (1981, April 17). End of US Regulations on School Attire Urged. *Washington Post*, p. A26.

Forest, Stephanie A. (1997, September 8). Dressed to Drill: School Uniforms Are Hot—Merchants Are Cashing In. *Business Week*, p. 40.

Fosseen, Linda Lee Sbel. (2002). *School Uniforms and Sense of School as Community: Perceptions of Belonging, Safety, and Caring Relationships in Urban Middle School Settings*. Unpublished Doctoral Dissertation, University of Houston.

Fowler v. Williamson, 448 F. Supp. 497 (W.D.N.C. 1978).

Frankfort-Nachmias, Chava & Leon-Guerrero, A. (2002). *Social Statistics for a Diverse Society* (3d ed.). Thousand Oaks, CA: Pine Forge Press.

Frazer-Barnes, Katharine. (1999, November 5). Rules Too Tight for Comfort. *Times Educational Supplement*, p. C24.

Friere, Paolo. (2000[1980]). *Pedagogy of the Oppressed*. New York: Continuum.

Gano v. School District, 674 F. Supp. 796 (D. Idaho 1987).

Gaventa, John. (1982). *Power and Powerlessness: Quiescence and Rebellion in an Appalachian Valley*. Urbana: University of Illinois Press.

Gilbert, Christopher B. (1999). We Are What We Wear: Revisiting Student Dress Codes. *Brigham Young University Education and Law Journal* 1, 3–18.

Giroux, Henry A. (2003). *The Abandoned Generation: Democracy beyond the Culture of Fear*. London: Palgrave Macmillan.

Glassner, Barry. (2000). *The Culture of Fear: Why Americans Are Afraid of the Wrong Things*. New York: Basic.

Goldstein. M. (2003, April 20). Parents to Sort Out School Wardrobe. *Boston Sunday Globe*, p. 6.

Goodnough, Abby. (2001, June 12). Bloomberg Backs School Uniforms and Teacher House Calls. *New York Times*, p. B4.

Gottdiener, Mark (ed.). (2000). *New Forms of Consumption: Consumers, Culture, and Commodification*. Lanham, MD: Rowman & Littlefield.

Grantham, Kimberly. (1994). Restricting Student Dress in Public Schools. *School Law Bulletin*, 25(1), 1–10.

Gray, Valerie Lynn. (1996, September 1). Trend Report: School Uniforms. *Woman's Day*, p. 58.

Greco v. Mount Carmel Area School Board. No. 4, CV-00-1900 (2001).

Gregory, Nancy-Bruggemann. (1998). Effects of School Uniforms on Self-Esteem, Academic Achievement, and Attendance. *Dissertation Abstracts*, 58(8–A), 3035.

Griffith, James. (1999). School Climate as "Social Order" and "Social Action": A Multi-Level Analysis of Public Elementary School Student Perceptions. *Social Psychology of Education*, 2(3–4), 339–369.

Griffiths, Sian. (1994, February 4). Cracking the Right Dress Code. *Times Educational Supplement*, p. A4.

Grolnick, Wendy S. & Slowiaczek, M. L. (1994). Parents' Involvement in Children's Schooling: A Multidimensional Conceptualization and Motivational Model. *Child Development*, 65, 237–252.

Gullatt, David E. (1999). Rationales and Strategies for Amending the School Dress Code to Accommodate Student Uniforms. *American Secondary Education*, 27(4), 39.

Gursky, Daniel. (1996). "Uniform" Improvement. *Education Digest*, 61(7), 46.

Hacsi, Timothy A. (2003). *Children as Pawns: The Politics of Educational Reform*. Cambridge, MA: Harvard University Press.

Hallinan, Maureen T. (1987). *The Social Organization of Schools: New Conceptualizations of the Learning Process*. New York: Plenum.

———. (1995). *Restructuring Schools: Promising Practices and Policies*. New York: Plenum.

Hallinan, Maureen T. (ed.). (2000). *Handbook of the Sociology of Education*. Norwell, MA: Kluwer Academic/Plenum Press.

Hannover, Bettina & Kuehnen, U. (2002). "The Clothing Makes the Self" Via Knowledge Activation. *Journal of Applied Social Psychology*, 32(12), 2513–2525.

Hargreaves-Mawdsley, W. N. (1963). *A History of Academical Dress in Europe Until the End of the Eighteenth Century*. Westport, CT: Greenwood.

Harper v. Edgewood Board of Education, 655 F. Supp. 1353 (S.D. Ohio 1987).

Hazelwood School District v. Kuhlmeier, 484 U.S. (1988).

Hinchion-Mancini, Gail. (1997). School Uniforms: Dress for Success or Conformity? *The Education Digest*, 63(4), 62.

Hines v. Caston Public School Corporation, 651 N.E.2d (Ind. App. 1995).

Hirsch, E. D., Jr. (1987). *Cultural Literacy*. Boston: Houghton Mifflin.

———. (1999). *The Schools We Need and Why We Don't Have Them*. New York: Anchor Press.

Hirschman, Albert O. (1972). *Exit, Voice, and Loyalty: Responses to Decline in Firms, Organizations, and States*. Cambridge, MA: Harvard University Press.

History. (2003). At www.rakeigh-p.schools.nsw.edu.au/history.htm (accessed October 14, 2003).

Holloman, Lillian O. (1995, Winter). Violence and Other Antisocial Behaviors in Public Schools: Can Dress Codes Help Solve the Problem? *Journal of Family and Consumer Behavior*, 33.

Holloway, Lynette. (1999, September 4). Just How Uniform Must Uniforms Be? *New York Times*, p. B1.

Hoover-Dempsey, K. V. & Sandler, H. M. (1997). Why Do Parents Become Involved in Their Children's Education? *Review of Educational Research*, 67(1), 3–42.

Hoover-Dempsey, K. V., Bassler, O. C. & Brissie, J. S. (1987). Parent Involvement Contributions of Teacher Efficacy, School Socioeconomic Status, and Other School Characteristics. *American Educational Research Journal*, 24(3), 417–435.

Hopgood, Mei-Ling. (1996, January 23). Uniformity: With New Dress Program, Elementary School Seeks to Promote Togetherness Among Pupils. *St. Louis Post Dispatch*, p. B1.

Howard, Judith A. (2000). Social Psychology of Identities. *Annual Review of Sociology*, 26, 367–393.

Hoy, W. K., Hannum, J. & Tschannen-Moran, M. (1998). Organizational Climate and Student Achievement: A Parsimonious and Longitudinal View. *Journal of School Leadership*, 8, 336–359.

Hughes, David. W. (1996). *School Uniforms: A Mirror of Society*. Unpublished Doctoral Dissertation, University of Wisconsin—River Falls.

Isaacson, Lynne. (1998). Student Dress Policies. *ERIC Digest*, 117, EDO-EA-98–1.

Issacs v. Board of Education of Howard County, Maryland, 40 F. Supp. 2d 335, 339 (D. Md. 1999).

Jacobs, Margaret A. (1995, December 5). Court Lets Public School Require Uniforms. *Wall Street Journal*, p. B1.

Johnson, Christopher. (2000, August 21). School Shopping List Sheds Light on Economics of School Uniforms. Martins Ferry (Ohio) *The Times Leader.*

Jones, Christopher David. (1997). *Staff Members' Perceptions of Middle School Culture in Middle Schools That Have Implemented School Uniform Policies*. Unpublished Doctoral Dissertation, Pepperdine University.

Judson, George. (1995, October 5). Uncool in School: Dress Code Debate. *New York Times*, p. B7.

Karr v. Schmidt, 460 F.2d 609 (5th Cir. 1972).

Kerbow, D. & Bernhardt, A. (1994). Parental Intervention in the School: The Context of Minority Involvement. In Schneider, B. & Coleman, J. S. (eds.), *Parents, Their Children, and Schools*. Boulder, CO: Westview.

Kerckhoff, Alan C. (1995). Reforming Education: A Critical Overlooked Component. In M. Hallinan (ed.), *Restructuring Schools: Promising Practices and Policies*. New York: Plenum.

Key, Angela. (2000, October 16). Uniforms Are Runway Ready. *Fortune*, 76.

Killen, Rob. (2000). The Achilles' Heel of Dress Codes: The Definition of Proper Attire in Public Schools. *Tulsa Law Journal*, 36, 459.

Kim, Yunhee. (1999). Perception towards Wearing School Uniforms. Unpublished Doctoral *Dissertation Abstracts*, 59(8–A), 2917, Section A: Humanities and Social Sciences.

King, James. (1996). Uniforms As a Safety Measure. *American School & University*, 68(6), 38.

King, Keith. (1998). Should School Uniforms Be Mandated in Elementary Schools? *Journal of School Health*, 68(1), 32.

Kirkman, Susannah. (1997, August 29). Style Counsel: Advice on Teachers' Appearance. *Times Educational Supplement*, p. A20.

Klahr, Gary Peter. (n.d.). "The Dangers of the School Uniform Movement," at www.geocities.com/SunsetStrip/Mezzanine/1105/uniforms.html (accessed October 14, 2003).

Kommer, David. (1999). Beyond Fashion: School Uniforms in the Middle Grades. *Middle School Journal*, 30(5), 23.

Kozol, Jonathan. (1992). *Savage Inequalities: Children in America's Schools.* New York: Perennial.

Kuhn, Mary Julia. (1996). Student Dress Codes in the Public Schools: Multiple Perspectives in the Courts and Schools on the Same Issues. *Journal of Law and Education*, 25(1), 83–106.

Kulas, Henryk. (1996). Locus of Control in Adolescence: A Longitudinal Study. *Adolescence*, 31(123), 721–729.

Lane, Kenneth E., Schwartz, S. L., Richardson, M. L. & VanBerum, D. W. (1994). You Aren't What You Wear. *The American School Board Journal*, 181(3), 64–65.

LaPoint, Velma, Holloman, L. O. & Alleyne, S. I. (1992). The Role of Dress Codes, Uniforms in Urban Schools. *NASSP Bulletin*, 76(546), 20.

———. (1993). Dress Codes and Uniforms in Urban Schools. *The Education Digest*, 58(7), 32.

Lareau, Annette. (1987). Social Class Differences in Family-School Relationships: The Importance of Cultural Capital. *Sociology of Education*, 60, 73–85.

———. (2000). *Home Advantage: Social Class and Parental Intervention in Elementary Education, Updated Edition.* London: Falmer Press.

Lareau, Annette & Shumar, W. (1996). The Problem of Individualism in Family–School Policies. *Sociology of Education*, (Extra Issue), 24–39.

Lefevre, Patricia. (1997). Newark Has "No Sweat" Policy on Uniforms. *National Catholic Inquirer*, 34(2), 8.

Lewin, Tamar. (1997). Dress for Success: Public School Uniforms. *New York Times*, p. A1.

Lewis, Neil A. (1988a, September 8). Public School Students to Receive Uniforms. *New York Times,* p. B1.

———. (1988b, October 8). Uniforms: Schools Like Idea. *New York Times,* p. A31.

Littlefield v. Forney Independent School District, 268 F.3d 275 (5th Cir. 2001).

Loesch, Paul C. (1995). A School Uniform Program That Works. *Principal,* 74(4), 28, 30.

Long v. Board of Education of Jefferson County, 121 F.Supp.2d 621 (W.D. Ky. 2000).

Lukes, Steven (ed.). (1986). *Power.* New York: New York University Press.

Lumsden, Linda & Miller, G. (2002, January 13). Dress Codes and Uniforms. *Research Roundup,* 1894, 1–5, at www.naesp.org/misc/rrsum02.htm (accessed January 13, 2003).

MacLeod, Jay. (1987). *Ain't No Makin' It: Leveled Aspirations in a Low-Income Neighborhood.* Boulder, CO: Westview.

Magers, Phil. (2003, July 31). Analysis: Tax Breaks Offered in Hard Times. *Washington Times.*

Mallios, Harry Carl. (1970). *A Study of Legal Opinion Pertaining to Control of Pupil Dress and Appearance in Public Schools, 1960–1969.* Unpublished Doctoral Dissertation, University of Miami.

Manual on School Uniforms. (1996). Washington, DC: U.S. Department of Education.

Marks, John. (1998, October 26). Uniform Disagreement. *US News & World Report,* 30.

Massey, Douglas & Anderson, E. (eds.) (2001). *Problem of the Century: Racial Stratification in the United States at Century's End.* New York: Russell Sage Foundation.

McCarthy, Coleman. (1996, March 29). Uniforms Not a Cure for Schools' Ills. *National Catholic Reporter,* 22.

McCarthy, Teresa M. (1998). *A Case Study of Self Expression, Self Esteem, and School Uniform Opinions in a New York City Middle School.* Unpublished Doctoral Dissertation.

McCarty, Jacqueline Marie. (2000). *The Effects of School Uniforms on Student Behavior and Perceptions in an Urban Middle School.* Unpublished Dissertation, Old Dominion University.

McCracken, Grant. (1988). *Culture and Consumption: New Approaches to the Symbolic Character of Consumer Goods and Activities.* Bloomington: Indiana University Press.

McDaniel, Jo Beth. (1996, September). Can Uniforms Save Our Schools? *Reader's Digest,* 79.

McDowell, Lena & Sietsema, J. P. (2003). *Directory of Public Elementary and Secondary Education Agencies 2001–02.* Washington, DC: National Center for Education Statistics, U.S. Department of Education. (NCES 2003351).

McNeal, Ralph B., Jr. (1999). Parental Involvement as Social Capital: Differential Effectiveness on Science Achievement. *Social Forces,* 78(1), 117–146.

McNiece, Rosie & Jolliffe, F. (1998). An Investigation Into Regional Differences in Educational Performance in the National Child Development Study. *Educational Research,* 40(1), 17–32.

Meadmore, Daphne & Symes, C. (1996). Of Uniform Appearance: A Symbol of School Discipline and Governmentality. *Discourse,* 17(2), 209–225.

Melvin, Tessa. (1994, August 7). Blackboard: Uniform Diversity in California. *New York Times,* p. A7.

Memorandum on the School Uniform Manual. (1996, March 4). *Weekly Compilation of Presidential Documents,* 368.

Merritt, Ruth. (1996, May 28). School Uniforms Help Prevent Violence. *St. Louis Post Dispatch,* p. B11.

Mitchell, Alison. (1996, February 26). Clinton Will Advise Schools on Uniforms. *New York Times,* 24.

Model Guidelines for the Wearing of Uniforms in Public Schools: A Report of the Department of Education to the Governor and the General Assembly of Virginia. (1992). House Document No. 27. ERIC No. ED348760.

Moyers, Bill. (1993). *Children in America's Schools.* Documentary produced by Jeffrey Hayden.

Muller, Chandra & Kerbow, D. (1994). Parent Involvement in the Home, School and Community. In Schneider, B. & Coleman, J. S. (eds.), *Parents, Their Children, and Schools.* Boulder, CO: Westview.

Murphy, Mary Louise. (1997). Public School Uniforms: A Case Study of One School's Experience. Unpublished Doctoral Dissertation. *Dissertation Abstracts,* 58(12–A),: 4561. Section A: Humanities and Social Sciences.

Murray, Nancy. (2000). Symposium: Creating a Violence Free School for the Twenty-First Century: Panel Three: Striking a Balance: Students, Educators, and the Courts: School Safety: Are We on the Right Track?, *New England Law Review,* 34, 635.

Murray, Richard K. (1997, December). The Impact of School Uniforms on School Climate. *NASSP Bulletin,*106–112.

Myers, Marie S. (1963, November 19). Why Uniforms? *America,* 109, 630–632.

NAESP. (2000). *Backgrounder on Public School Uniforms,* at www.naesp.org/ContentLoad.do?contentId=929 (accessed February 5, 2004).

A Nation at Risk: The Imperative for Educational Reform. (1983). Washington, DC: U.S. Department of Education

National Research Council. (1993). *Understanding and Preventing Violence.* Washington, DC: National Academy Press.

Nelson, Troy Y. (1997). If Clothes Make the Person, Do Uniforms Make the Student?: Constitutional Free Speech Rights and Student Uniform. *Education Law Reporter* 1, 118.

Neuman, W. Lawrence. (2003). *Social Research Methods: Qualitative and Quantitative Approaches (Fifth Edition).* Boston: Allyn & Bacon.

Neumark, Victoria. (1992, September 18). Uniformly Uplifted. *Times Educational Supplement,* p. 12.

New Haven School to Require Uniforms. (1988, September 8). *New York Times,* p. C8.

New Jersey v. T.L.O., 469 U.S. 325 (1985).

Nichols, Joe D. & White, J. (2001). Impact of Peer Networks on Achievement of High School Algebra Students. *Journal of Educational Research,* 94(5), 267+.

Noddings, Nel. (1999). Renewing Democracy in Schools. *Phi Delta Kappan,* 80(8), 579–583.

NPD Group, Inc. (2001). *NPD Reports U.S. School Uniform Sales Soar to $1.1 Billion,* at www.npd.com/corp/content/releases/press_010208.html (accessed on February 5, 2004).

Nygren, Judith. (1996, December 3). Panel Ordered to Discuss School Uniforms in Public Survey Responses. *Omaha World Herald,* SF13.

Offer, D., Ostrov, E. & Howard, K. I. (1981). The Mental Health Professional's Concept of the Normal Adolescent. *Archives of General Psychology,* 38(2), 149–152.

Olesen v. Board of Education of School District No. 228, 676 F. Supp. 820 (N.D. Ill. 1987).

Orfield, Gary & Eaton, S. (1996). *Dismantling Desegregation: The Quiet Reversal of Brown v. Board of Education.* New York: New Press.

Orfield, Gary & Kornhaber, M. (eds.) (2001). *Raising Standards or Raising Barriers? Inequality and High Stakes Testing in Public Education.* New York: Century Foundation Press.

Page, Reba & Valli, L. (eds.) (1990). *Curriculum Differentiation: Interpretive Studies in U.S. Secondary Schools.* Albany: State University of New York Press.

Paliokas, Kathleen L., Futrell, M. H. & Rist, R. (1996). Trying Uniforms on for Size. *The American School Board Journal,* 183(5), 32–35.

Palko v. Connecticut, 302 U.S. 319 (1937).

Parcel, Toby L. & Geschwender, L. E. (1995). Explaining Southern Disadvantage in Verbal Facility Among Young Children. *Social Forces,* 73(3), 841–875.

Pate, Sharon Shamburger. (1998). *The Influence of Mandatory School Uniform Policy in Two Florida School Districts.* Unpublished Doctoral Dissertation, Florida State University.

Pellegrini, A. D. (1994). A Longitudinal Study of School Peer Networks and Adjustment to Middle School. *Educational Psychology*, 14(4), 403–414.

Peterson, Bill. (1979, November 20). HEW Resumes Watch on School Dress Codes. *Washington Post*, p. A2.

Phillips, M. (1997). What Makes Schools Effective? A Comparison of the Relationships of Communitarian Climate and Academic Climate to Mathematics Achievement and Attendance During Middle School. *American Educational Research Journal*, 34, 633–662.

Phoenix Elementary School District No. 1 v. Green, 943 P.2d 836 (1997).

Pickles, P. L. (2000). Mandating School Uniforms at All Grades. *The School Administrator*, 57(Part 11), 51–52.

*Plessy v. Ferguson*163 U.S. 537 (1896).

Portner, Jessica. (1998, January 21). California District Points to Uniforms for Plunging Crime Rate. *Education Week*, 17.

Posner, Marc. (1996). Perception versus Reality: School Uniforms and the "Halo Effect." *The Harvard Education Letter*, 12(3), 1.

Postman, Neil. (1996). *The End of Education: Redefining the Value of Education*. New York: Vintage.

Prescott, Janet. (2000, April 21). The Long and the Skirt of It. *Times Educational Supplement*, 27.

Presidential Radio Address—Clinton's Address. (1996, October 14). *Weekly Compilation of Presidential Documents*, 32(41), 1971.

Presidential Radio Address—Clinton's Memorial Day Address. (1998, June 1). *Weekly Compilation of Presidential Documents*, 34(22), 957.

Pros and Cons of School Uniforms. (1999, September). *USA Today*, p.6.

Putnam, Robert. (1995, Spring). The Prosperous Community—Social Capital and Public Life. *The American Prospect*, 27–40.

———. (2000). *Bowling Alone: The Collapse and Revival of American Community*. New York: Simon & Schuster.

Pyle v. South Hadley School Committee, 861 F.Supp. 157 (D. Mass. 1994).

Reinolds, Chris. (2001, April 12). Cherokee Survey Shows Parents, Teacher Support School Uniforms. *The Atlanta Journal and Constitution*, p. C1.

Remarks Prior to a Roundtable Discussion on School Uniforms in Long Beach, CA. (1996, March 4). *Weekly Compilation of Presidential Documents*, 368.

Reply. (1964, January 11). *America*.

Rex, James H. (1970). *An Assessment and Comparison of Teacher Perceptions of Discipline and Dress Regulations*. Unpublished Doctoral Dissertation, University of Toledo.

Richards v. Thurston, 424 F.2d 1281 (1st Cir. 1970).

Richburg, Keith B. & Cooke, J. (1980, October 17). Barry Favors Uniform School Clothing. *Washington Post*, p. A1.

Ritzer, George. (2000). *The McDonaldization of Society*. Thousand Oaks, CA: Pine Forge Press.

———. (2004). *The Globalization of Nothing*. Thousand Oaks, CA: Pine Forge Press.

Robinson, Sonya D. (1995). *Attitudes of University Administrators Regarding Faculty Dress Code at Virginia State University*. Unpublished Doctoral Dissertation, Virginia State University.

Rosenberger v. Rector & Visitors of University of Virginia, 515 U.S. 819 (1995).

Rosenthal, Robert & Jacobson, L. (2003 [1968]). *Pygmalion in the Classroom: Teacher Expectation and Pupil's Intellectual Development*. Carmarthen, UK: Crown House Publishing.

Rossi, Peter. (1969). No Good Research Goes Unpunished: Moynihan's Misunderstandings and the Proper Role of Social Science in Policy Making. *Social Science Quarterly*, 50(3), 469–479.

Roswell, Charles. (1996, April 12). Time to Slaughter Sacred Cows. *Times Educational Supplement*, p. B6.

Rubinstein, Ruth P. (1995). *Dress Codes: Meanings and Messages in American Culture*. Boulder, CO: Westview.

Rueter, Ted. (1997). The ACLU Blocks Common Sense and Freedom. *The American Enterprise*, 8(4), 35.

Ruggiero, Angela L. (2002). Mandatory Public School Uniforms: Restricting or Protecting Pupils? *Quinnipiac Law Review*, 21, 691.

Ryan, Rosemary & Ryan, T. E. (1998). School Uniforms: Esprit de Corps. *School Community Journal*, 8(2), 81–84.

Sack, Joetta L. (1998, April 8). Budget Plan Approved; Tax Break Debate Set. *Education Week*, p. 30.

Sacks, Peter. (2001). *Standardized Minds: The High Price of America's Testing Culture and What We Can Do About It*, Cambridge, MA:. Perseus Publishing.

Sager, Michele. (1999, May 16). Suits May Become Uniform of the Day. *Tampa Tribune*, p. A1.

Sampson, Robert J., Morenoff, J. D. & Gannon-Rowley, T. (2002). Assessing "Neighborhood Effects": Social Processes and New Directions in Research. *Annual Review of Sociology*, 28, 443–478.

Saslow, Linda. (1998, December 6). Glen Cove Weighs Uniforms for Its Schools. *New York Times*, p. 2.

Savage, Ania. (1973). Private Schools Relaxing Uniform Rules. *New York Times*, p. 92.

Saxe v. State College Area School Dist., 240 F.3d 200, 214 (3d Cir. 2001).

School Dress Code Upheld by Judge Pending Trial. (1999, June 5). *New York Times*, B4.

School Uniforms Growing in Favor in California. (1994, September 3). *New York Times*, p. 8.

Schutt, Russell K. (1996). *Investigating the Social World: The Process and Practice of Research*. Thousand Oaks, CA: Pine Forge Press.

Scriven, Eldon G. & Harrison, A., Jr. (1971, November). Student Dress Codes. *Journal of Secondary Education*, 291–292.

Seeley, D. S. (1989). A New Paradigm for Parent Involvement. *Educational Leadership*, 47(2), 46–48.

Sernau, Scott. (2001). *Worlds Apart: Social Inequalities in a New Century*. Thousand Oaks, CA: Sage.

Sher, Ina-Mae. (1995). *An Analysis of the Impact of School Uniforms on Students' Academic Performance and Disciplinary Behavior*. Unpublished Doctoral Dissertation, University of Alabama.

Shils, Edward. (1982). *The Constitution of Society*. Chicago: University of Chicago Press.

Shimizu, Bruce. (2000). *A Study to Determine What Impact, If Any, the Implementation of a Mandatory Uniform Dress Code Policy Has Had on Improving Student Behavior among Ninth-Grade Students in Three California High Schools*. Unpublished Doctoral Dissertation, University of La Verne.

Simmel, Georg. (1904). Fashion. *International Quarterly*, 10, 130–155.

Smolen, Wendy & Chudnofsky, L. (1999, September 1). School Style. *Parents*, 191.

Snyder, Susan. (2000, September 29). With School Uniforms, Compliance Is In Style. *The Philadelphia Inquirer.*

Speer, Tibbett L. (1998, November). Fashion That Works . . . or Not. *Techniques*, 39.

Stanley, Sue. (1996). School Uniforms and Safety. *Education and Urban Society*, 28(4), 424.

Stanley, T. L. (1999, February 22). Scholastic Enters School Uniform Niche. *Brandweek*, 16.

Stanton-Salazar, Ricardo D. & Dornbusch, S. M. (1995). Social Capital and the Reproduction of Inequality: information Networks Among Mexican-Origin High School Students. *Sociology of Education*, 68(2), 116–137.

State of the Union. (1996). *Washington Post Online*, at www.washingtonpost .com/wp-srv/politics/special/states/docs/sou96.htm (accessed February 4, 2004).

Steinberg, Stephen. (2001). *Turning Back: The Retreat from Racial Justice in American Thought and Policy*. Boston: Beacon.

Steinhauer, Jennifer. (2003, February 11). Bloomberg, With Promises to Keep, Says He Kept Many. *New York Times*, p. B4.

Sterngold, James. (2000, June 28). Taking a New Look at Uniforms and Their Impact on Schools. *New York Times,* p. B11.

Stetzner, Kate. (1999). How Safe Are Your Schools? *School Administrator,* 56(6), 22–24.

Stevenson, Henry L. (1999). *An Analysis of Requiring School Uniforms and its Impact on Student Behavior: Implications for School Reform.* Unpublished Dissertation, Texas Southern University.

Stevenson, Zollie, Jr. & Chun, E. W. (1991). *Uniform Policy/Dress Codes: School Staff and Parent Perceptions of Need and Impact.* ERIC Document Reproduction Number ED331933.

Stewart, Barbara. (1997, September 7). At P.S. 71, Reeboks and Baggies Give Way to Uniformity. *New York Times,* p. 9.

Stinchcomb, Jeanne B. (2002). Promising (and Not-So-Promising) Gang Prevention and Intervention Strategies: A Comprehensive Review of the Literature. *Journal of Gang Research,* 10(1), 27–46.

Stinespring, John A. (1968, February). Let's Stop This Nonsense About Student Dress. *NEA Journal,* 57, 58.

Strauss, Robert. (2003, June 8). A Dress Code with Teeth. *New York Times,* p. 6.

Sykes, Charles J. (1995). *Dumbing Down Our Kids: Why America's Children Feel Good About Themselves But Can't Read, Write, or Add.* New York: St. Martin's Press.

Synott, John & Symes, C. (1995). The Genealogy of the School: An Iconography of Badges and Mottoes. *British Journal of Sociology of Education,* 16(2), 139–152.

Sypniewski v. Warren Hills Regional Board of Education, 307 F.3d 243 (3d Cir. 2002).

Tanioka, Ichiro & Glaser, Daniel. (1991). School Uniforms, Routine Activities, and the Social Control of Delinquency in Japan. *Youth and Society,* 23(1), 50–75.

Teacher Opinion Poll. (1969, May). *Today's Education,* 63.

Terminello v. Chicago, 337 U.S. 1 (1940).

Texas v. Johnson, 491 U.S. 397 (1989).

That Uniform Look. (1999, March). *Forecast,* p. 6.

Thomas, Susan. (1994, October 20). Uniforms in the Schools. *Black Issues in Higher Education,* 44.

Thompson, Mary Holland W. (1999). Issues Forum: Revisiting School Uniforms. *The Educational Forum,* 63(4), 300.

Tillman, Tim. (1999). *Polk County School Uniform Compliance Data,* at www.gate.net/~rwms/UniformComplianceData.html (accessed February 4, 2004).

Tinker v. Des Moines Independent School District, 89 S. Ct. 733 (1969).

Triest, R. K. (1997, January/February). Regional Differences in Family Poverty. *New England Economic Review*, 3–17.

Turner, Ralph. (1960). Sponsored and Contest Mobility and the School System. *American Sociological Review*, 25.

Uniform Improvement. (1999, September). *Psychology Today*, 14.

Uniforms Out of Fashion? (2002). *New York Times*, at www.nea.org/neatoday/0301/trends.html (accessed February 5, 2004).

Uniforms Suddenly a Hot Topic: Can Students Dress for Success? (1996, April). *School Violence Alert*, 2(4)

"Uniforms" That Break the Dress Code. (1991, August). *Seventeen*, 50(8), 21.

United States v. O'Brien, 391 U.S. 367 (1968).

United States v. Schwimmer, 279 U.S. 644 (1929).

U.S. Department of Education. (1996). *Manual on School Uniforms*, at www.ed.gov/updates/uniforms (accessed May 1, 2000).

Utsey, Shawn O., Ponterotto, Joseph G. & Reynolds, Amy L. (2000). Racial Discrimination, Coping, Life Satisfaction, and Self-Esteem Among African Americans. *Journal of Counseling and Development*, 78(1), 72–80.

Volokh, Alexander & Snell, L. (1998). *School Violence Prevention: Strategies to Keep Schools Safe (Unabridged)*. Policy Study No. 234, at www.rppi.org/education/ps234.html (accessed February 4, 2004).

Walters, Pamela Barnhouse. (2000.) The Limits of Growth: School Expansion and School Reform in Historical Perspective. In Hallinan, M. (ed.), *Handbook of Sociology of Education*. New York: Kluwer

Weinberger, Morris J. (1970, April). Dress Codes: We Forget Our Own Advice. *Clearing House*, 44, 471–473.

Weisenberger, Clay. (2000). Constitutionality or Conformity: When the Shirt Hits the Fan in Public Schools. *Journal of Law & Education*, 29, 51.

Wells, Amy Stuart & Crain, R. (1997). *Stepping Over the Color Line: African American Students in White Suburban Schools*. New Haven, CT: Yale University Press.

Welsh, Wayne N. (2000). The Effects of School Climate on School Disorder. *The Annals of the American Academy of Political and Social Science*, 567, 88–107.

West, Charles, Tidwell, D. K., Bomba, A. K. & Elmore, P. A. (1999). Attitudes of Parents about School Uniforms. *Journal of Family and Consumer Sciences*, 91(2), 92.

What's Wrong with Public School Uniforms. (1988, October 24). *New York Times*, p. A16.

White, K. A. (2000). Do School Uniforms Fit? *The School Administrator*, 57(Part 2), 36–41.

Wichelns, Jean Decker. (1968, May). The Great Hatt and Hayre Controversy. *NEA Journal*, 57, 30–31.

Wilkins, Julia. (1999, March). School Uniforms: Not Clear That School Uniforms Will Reduce Violence. *The Humanist*, p. 19.

Will, George F. (1996, January 28). Uniformly Positive: At a Jewel of a Public School in Phoenix, Clothes Make the Gentleman—and the Young Lady. *Pittsburgh Post-Gazette*, p. B3.

Will Uniforms Help Curb Student Violence? (1996, April 1). *Jet*, 12.

Williams-Davidson, Carolyn M. (1996). Case Study of the Mandatory Enforcement of a Voluntary Student Uniform Policy. Unpublished Doctoral Dissertation. *Dissertation Abstracts*, 57(10–A), 4199, Section A: Humanities and Social Sciences.

Willis, Paul E. (1977). *Learning to Labor*. Aldershot, UK: Gower.

Wolf, Janette. (1996, March 1). Style to Set Your Cap At. *Times Educational Supplement*, p. C2.

Woodard, Wiley M. (1989, January). New Rule: Dress Like Me. *Black Enterprise*, 19, 15.

Woods, H. & Ogletree, E. (1992). *Parents' Opinions of the Uniform Student Dress Code*. Washington, DC: U.S Department of Education. (ERIC Document Reproduction No. ED 367 729).

Wragg, Caroline. (2002). Performance-Related Pay and the Teaching Profession: A Review of the Literature. *Research Papers in Education*, 17(1), 31–51.

Wren, David J. (1999). School Culture: Exploring the Hidden Curriculum. *Adolescence*, 34(135), 593–596.

Yonkers Mayor Proposes School Uniform Policy. (1995, October 4). *New York Times*.

Zaff, Jonathan F., Blount, R., & Phillips, L. (2002). The Role of Ethnic Identity and Self-Construal in Coping among African-American and Caucasian American Seventh Graders: An Exploratory Analysis of Within-Group Variance. *Adolescence*, 37(148), 751–773.

Zelizer, Viviana. (2002). Kids and Commerce. *Childhood*, 9(4), 375–396.

Zernike, Kate. (2002, September 13). Plaid's Out, Again, As Schools Give Up Requiring Uniforms. *New York Times*, p. A1.

Zirkel, Perry A. (1998). A Uniform Policy. *Phi Delta Kappan*, 79(7), 550–551.

INDEX

ABOUT THE AUTHOR

David L. Brunsma is an assistant professor of sociology at the University of Missouri—Columbia. He is currently working on two books, one on the interrelations between the macro- and micro-strategies and politics of racial identity for multiracial individuals and the other a reader compiling new research on school uniform policies.

ABOUT THE CONTRIBUTOR

Todd DeMitchell spent eighteen years in the public schools as a teacher, principal, and superintendent before joining the faculty at the University of New Hampshire. He studies the legal mechanisms that have an impact on schools and has authored/co-authored two books, four book chapters, and more than eighty-five articles. He is currently working on a study of professionalism and unionism and is studying the policy response to Supreme Court cases on student drug testing.